TEXAS STYLE JUSTICE

A NOVEL

SUSAN P. BAKER

Refugio Press

TEXAS STYLE JUSTICE
- A Novel -
Copyright © 2018 by Susan P. Baker

ISBN: 978-0-9962021-9-0

This is a work of fiction. Names, places, characters and incidents are either the product of the author's imagination or are used fictitiously, and any resemblance to any actual persons, living or dead, organizations, events or locales is entirely coincidental.

Interior formatting by Laurie Barboza
Cover design by Laurie Barboza

Produced in the United States of America.

For information and/or permission to use excerpts, contact:

Refugio Press
P.O. Box 3937 Galveston, TX 77552.

Books by Susan P. Baker

Novels:

My First Murder
No. 1 in the Mavis Davis murder mystery series

The Sweet Scent of Murder
Mavis Davis No. 2, Mavis's search for a missing teenager turns into
a murder investigation in Houston's Ritzy River Oaks.

Death of a Prince
Mother & daughter criminal defense lawyers defend the alleged
murderer of a millionaire plaintiff's attorney

Ledbetter Street
A mother fights the system for guardianship of her autistic son.

Suggestion of Death
A father who can't pay his child support investigates the mysterious
deaths of other deadbeat dads.

UNAWARE
Attorney Dena Armstrong is about to break out from under
the two controlling men in her life, unaware that a stranger has
other plans for her.

Nonfiction:

Heart of Divorce
Divorce advice especially for those who are considering
representing themselves.

Murdered Judges of the 20th Century
True stories of judges killed in America.

www.susanpbaker.com

Dedication

For my oldest granddaughter, Megan, the most artistic person I know.

CONTENTS

Acknowledgments

A number of people supported the writing and production of this novel. Since I worked on it on and off for several years, and wrote some others in the middle, I'm afraid my memory isn't serving me well so if I've forgotten anyone, I beg your indulgence.

I want to thank early readers Kathryn Lanan and Pat Pore, as well as participants in the Writers Retreat Workshop. Later, the Galveston Novel and Short Story Writers group patiently read every early chapter. I especially want to thank Dan McKeithan for information on *The Judge.*

And Elizabeth Lyons for her encouragement, among other things. Your ability to soldier on set a good example not only for me but for other authors.

Chapter 1

DISTRICT JUDGE VICTORIA VAN FLEET SCOOPED up an immense file and reached for the door to her courtroom, opening it to the tinkling of a tiny bell the court reporter had tied above it so she'd know when the judge was entering.

Since there was no bailiff, Jennifer, the court reporter, announced her, "All rise."

Today was the first day of her new term. Torie wanted to start out on a good note even though the litigants were repeat offenders, divorced parents who insisted on fighting to the death over their children.

"Good morning." She scanned the counsel tables as she took the bench, confirming she had the right case file. The Campbells, as she thought of them even though they were now divorced, each stood with a new attorney. Torie had first heard their interminable case from hell four years earlier, just after she'd begun her first four-year term of office.

"Good morning, Judge," the attorneys and their clients responded in unison, after which the ex-Campbells turned their backs to each other. Mr. Campbell, a thin man with dishwater brown hair and a receding hairline, faced his attorney, a tall, light-haired woman with a horse face. The former Mrs. Campbell, an elegant-looking woman whose French manicure glinted in the fluorescent light, faced her stocky, broad-shouldered, melon-headed lawyer.

Contempt filled Torie like a bad breakfast burrito. Dropping Campbell file number twenty-five on the counter next to her desktop computer, she sat down. Observing the ragged edge of her own closely chewed nails, she thought maybe she'd spring for a set of nails like the ex-Mrs. Campbell's. She'd like to have hands that pretty again. "Be seated."

The lawyers and their clients sat, the lawyers immediately paging through their materials. Both had files several inches thick. Laptops yawned open. Briefcases stood within reach. Pen and paper lay at the ready. Overcoats were draped over the bar separating the lawyer area from the gallery, something attorneys familiar with Torie knew she disliked. She refrained from chastising them since neither of them had ever been to her court. If she'd had a bailiff, the bailiff would have told them or at least moved their coats to a different location, but the county commissioners' court refused to fund bailiffs for the judges.

"Cause number forty-five thousand and twenty-three." Her voice echoed in the large, high-ceilinged courtroom. "In the Interest of the Campbell Children." The clock on the wall to her left clicked to the next minute as she made eye contact with Jennifer, who grimaced. The ancient wall furnace, trying to eke out some heat, knocked like an impatient visitor. Time to get on with it. "What do we have this morning?"

Melon-head scrambled back to his feet. "Richard Garcia from San Antonio for the former Mrs. Campbell, now Mrs. Garcia, Your Honor." He was a Latino male not nearly as handsome and sexy as her own husband, Sergio, but she couldn't let her mind linger on Sergio. At that moment, she wore her judge's hat.

She glanced from Mr. Garcia to his client. Was he the former Mrs. Campbell's new husband, chic as she was? An improbable match.

Horse-face pushed up from her chair. "Laura Blankenship of Austin for Mr. Campbell, Judge. It's our motion."

"Nice to meet both of you." Torie wished she meant it. What she really wanted was for the lawyers to go away and drag the Campbells with them. "So what's the hearing about today, counsel?"

"Several things, Your Honor." Ms. Blankenship took a step toward the bench. "The underlying lawsuit is a modification of child custody. We want to change the joint managing conservatorship to a sole managing conservatorship—"

"Judge," Mr. Garcia interrupted, walking forward as well. "They've filed the motion in less than one year—"

"It *is* a year. Exactly a year." Ms. Blankenship inched nearer. "And there are exigent circumstances, Judge Van Fleet."

Mr. Garcia, not to be outdone, drew even closer. "No way, Your Honor. Campbell's making a mountain out of a—"

"Just a moment—" Torie held up her hand.

Ms. Blankenship pointed to Mr. Campbell's ex-wife. "Mrs. Garcia left Germania County and moved with the children to Bexar County over the Christmas holidays without telling Mr. Campbell—"

Mr. Garcia stepped between Ms. Blankenship's outstretched finger and Mrs. Garcia as if Ms. Blankenship's finger were a gun about to go off. "It's not that far—"

Wham! Torie gaveled the block. "I said, 'Just. A. Moment.'" She pointed the gavel at them. "Back up, both of you, before you're standing on top of the bench."

Ms. Blankenship bit on the corner of her mouth as she crab-stepped a couple of feet toward her table. Mr. Garcia retreated to his client's side and whispered in her ear a little too familiarly. Torie hoped she was correct about their being married, else Mr. Garcia was headed for the ethics committee for messing around with a client.

"All this debating is well and good, but what's *today's* hearing about?" She aimed the gavel at Ms. Blankenship. "You. Speak."

Ms. Blankenship drew herself up as tall as she could and adjusted the lapels of her suit jacket. "Show cause hearing for temporary orders. We want temporary custody pending final trial."

"Because?" Torie ducked her head and made a note on a legal pad.

"Because she—Mrs. Garcia—has done irrevocable damage to the children." Ms. Blankenship ticked off the offenses on her fingers. "By one, moving them in the middle of the school year. Two, away from family and friends. Three, to another county. Four, to a new school. And finally," she turned and gave Mrs. Garcia the fish-eye, "with no notice to their father."

Torie crossed her arms, the gavel dangling from her fingers. "And you believe this has done serious damage to the children?"

"Irrefutably, Your Honor." Ms. Blankenship's haughty tone made it clear she thought a lot of herself and her argument.

Torie's ears burned. She directed the gavel at the woman again. "Watch that attitude. You aren't doing yourself any favors."

She turned the gavel on Mr. Garcia. "How do you respond to this allegation?"

Mr. Garcia performed a little soft shoe. "We don't see it as so serious, Judge. The children are happy as long as they're with their mother."

"Why didn't she notify their father before she moved?"

"Well, ma'am, you being the judge on the original case, I'm sure you understand that Mrs. Garcia was in fear for her safety—"

Ms. Blankenship waved her arms. "Oh, come on. There were never any allegations of family violence."

"Well . . . " Torie remembered the unproven allegations. A bruise. A swearing match. Had Mr. Campbell hit Mrs. Campbell? Not enough evidence.

"Judge, if there had been a finding of family violence, Mr. Campbell never would have gotten joint custody." Ms. Blankenship had drawn dangerously close to the bench again. Torie could just about reach out and whack one of her flapping hands.

Torie controlled the eye roll that was her second nature. Her stare remained steady and straight and would have done a poker player proud. "I'm well aware of the circumstances, Ms. Blankenship." She shot Mr. Garcia a look. "Okay, both of you. I've got to appear at county commissioners' court to speak to the county fathers about courthouse security, so you have thirty minutes to convince me."

"But Judge—" Mr. Garcia raised his hands in an appeal to heaven.

"Thirty minutes. I have a full docket today and a meeting with a large group of folks this evening. I know y'all are from out of town, but in this courthouse, there is no associate judge for either of the district judges. Two of us hear everything, and we each have three other counties in our districts. Our calendars are always over-booked." She positioned herself with a pen and note pad. "Thirty minutes, take it or leave it. Or . . ." she spread her lips in a thin smile, "you may certainly go to mediation for the sole purpose of determining where the children will reside during the pendency of this case."

Mrs. Garcia rose halfway out of her chair and hissed at Mr. Garcia who pushed her back down. "That'll never work." He moved his briefcase to the front of his table and sat down. "We're ready."

Ms. Blankenship muttered under her breath, "You afraid to let your wife be in the same room with my client?" She smirked as she whipped around counsel table and took her seat.

There it was. Mr. Garcia, who jumped up to protest, had married Mrs. Campbell. No wonder he was so quick to rile. Torie waved him down. This was one of those times she wished the law gave her the option to bypass the parents and place the children with the grandparents. If the ex-Campbells kept up their battle, their children could wind up in a mental hospital before they were grown, the stress of the continuous court fights driving them nuts. Torie should know. She and her ex drove their own daughter over the edge.

"Ms. Blankenship, I'm not going to tolerate any of that kind of talk in my courtroom. You, Mrs. Garcia, and you, Mr. Campbell, if you insist on continuing your fight, stand up and raise your right hands."

They stood, and she swore them in. "Be seated. Ms. Blankenship, call your first witness, and just give me the salient points."

Torie hoped the children weren't aware their parents were back in court. This go-round, maybe the parents would keep their fat mouths shut and not put the kids in the middle.

Something about the father's body language as he swaggered to the witness stand reminded Torie of her ex-husband, Bert. His expression. A look in his eye. Whatever it was, memories of their years of battling over their daughter crowded her brain.

When she'd run for election the first time, she'd thought she'd be able to put her own bad experiences in court behind her, that she wouldn't have any difficulty hearing cases similar to her own. She had no difficulty being fair to both sides, she knew that, though on occasion it could be hard. But sometimes, some little thing would trigger a painful memory and remind her of why her daughter, Cassie, had committed suicide.

Chapter 2

JUDGE ADRIAN FROTHINGHAM, ADMINISTRATIVE Judge for the Tenth Judicial Region of Texas, was on the bench, presiding over a recusal hearing when the sound of a klaxon blared behind him in his chambers. *Ah-roo-guh. Ah-roo-guh.* Adrian flinched and ran his palm across his forehead as if to wipe away the sound of a submarine about to dive. The aggravating ringtone was one he'd assigned to his abettor.

Adrian was about to decide whether or not one of the judges in his region should be removed from a lawsuit due to bias toward one side. The cell phone braying in his chambers distracted him, inspired a desire to smash it into bits. He'd assigned the aggravating ringtone to a man who'd begun their relationship in the guise of a friend with the simple act of treating Adrian to a few meals. Ultimately, the man revealed himself as a shape shifter, a corrupter.

Ah-roo-guh. Ahh-roo-guh. Even though the noise sounded in the distance, the attorneys responded to the sound of the cell phone with fear, the scent of which pervaded the courtroom. They checked to be sure they'd switched off their own. The last thing any attorney worth a plug nickel wanted was to offend the judge. Next, each nudged his client, wanting to be sure the client's phone was off. Then, glancing at the opposing attorney and the opposing attorney's client, and at the bailiff and the court reporter, they waited to see what the judge would do since all of them knew the noise came from his chambers.

Adrian knuckled his silver mustache. He picked at his well-trimmed brows. With each ring, his breath became shallower and shallower. Finally, the noise ceased. He let his head fall back onto the headrest of his executive chair, drawing a deep breath—a drowning man reaching the surface—straightened up, and turned his attention back to his courtroom.

Before testimony could resume, the klaxon sounded again. Anger burning in his stomach, Adrian said through clenched teeth, "Counsel, we'll take a ten minute recess." He'd learned long ago that if the man he knew was on the other end of the line, the man he'd assigned that ring to, that he thought of as Karl-the-Corrupter, wanted to talk to him badly enough, Adrian might as well take the call. Karl wouldn't quit until he made contact. The judge unfolded his long legs and left the bench, striding into chambers, letting the door latch behind him before snatching the phone off his desk. "Yes, what is it?" He booted the other door, the one to his outer office, closed, so his assistant, Viola, couldn't overhear the conversation.

"Judge, how're you this fine day?" Loud, cheerful bravado blared into Adrian's ear.

Their relationship was like a little Texas two-step. Karl had invited him to dance. Adrian had accepted. Now he had to dance to Karl's tune.

"I'm fine, just fine, Karl. Thanks for asking. How was your holiday?"

"Wonderful. Enjoyed that bit of snow on Christmas Eve. You?"

"Yes, the grandchildren built a snowman, a rather scrawny one, but they had fun. So what can I do for you?" Adrian walked to the window and stared out between the blinds at the cars in the small parking lot. Thin ice covered the windshields. He'd need to get his scraper out before he left for home.

Being the presiding judge, he could office wherever he wanted. He'd chosen and had remodeled an old house in a Hill Country town pretty close to the center of his region. None of the judges in his region could say he'd chosen a particular location because of favoritism.

"Did I interrupt anything?" Karl chuckled.

"Time for a break anyway." Adrian tried to keep the edge out of his voice. "I've only got a few minutes. What do you want?"

"That's what I like about you, Judge. A man who's a straight shooter, who gets right to the point, who knows what he wants."

"Yes, well—" Adrian glanced over his shoulder at his office furnishings, the books lining the bookcases, the state-of-the-art computer on the corner of his desk, the custom-framed documents hanging on the walls. He liked his job, enjoying the power to decide not one or two cases each day but to act on so many different issues facing the courts in his region and in the state. He enjoyed meeting with the other administrative judges, the Supremes, the governor and his staff.

"Actually, I was calling to ask you to lunch."

Adrian's stomach churned. "'Fraid I can't today. Got recusal motions lined up until four-thirty."

"No, no, Judge. You know me-e-e-e. I'm much more considerate than that. How does Thursday sound? Think you can have your calendar under control by then? I was thinking Ralph's on the River, perhaps a little filet mignon?"

Resigned to the impossibility of brushing Karl off, Adrian cleared his throat. "Thursday at twelve-fifteen? I'll meet you there."

"Don't you even want to know what I want to talk about?"

Adrian stared at the sleet filtering through the oak trees. Such a serene setting for such a malevolent business. His real desire would be not only to put off discussing anything other than the weather with Karl for as long as they both should live, but that Karl would forget he ever knew him. "If it can't wait."

"I guess you haven't heard then."

"Heard what?"

"Justice McWilliams passed."

"Of course I've heard." Karl was the last person with whom Adrian wanted to discuss the death of a colleague. And anyway, what difference did it make to Karl? It wasn't any of Karl's business that later that day Adrian would tweet the sad news to every judge in his region who used Twitter and e-mail the rest of them.

"You knew him, right?"

Certainly he'd known McWilliams. It was hard to be one of ten administrative judges in the state and not know the nine Supremes. He'd seen McWilliams at educational conferences several times a year. They weren't friends, but he'd known and respected the man.

Karl breathed heavily into the phone. "You don't have anything to say?"

"What do you want me to say?" Adrian glanced at his watch. He hated to be late from breaks. If he demanded punctuality from the attorneys and other court participants—which he did—the least he could do was give them the same respect.

"Okay, we can discuss McWilliams later. But here's what I want you to think about between now and Thursday, *Judge*." Karl snickered, sounding every bit the imbecilic, bullying teenager Adrian thought he'd probably been. "By lunchtime Thursday, you need to give us—me—the name of someone we can recommend to the governor for nomination to that bench."

Adrian felt like he'd inhaled sewer gas and coughed. "You all aren't asking me to put myself up?"

"No, no, certainly not. We like you just where you are. You're doing a fine job. A fine, fine job."

Adrian didn't know whether to be relieved or not. But to be placed in the position of tapping someone for a life under the thumb of Karl and his ilk, a life of hell? If there was any way he could avoid doing that, he would. "Well, I don't know—"

"Sure you do, *Judge*. Give it some thought between now and Thursday. I'm sure you can come up with someone who we can help secure that bench and who would be a grateful *friend* to us in exchange."

Something akin to heartburn leaked into Adrian's chest. "It's a big state, Karl. A lot of judges will be vying for that job."

"I happen to know the governor feels the rural counties should have more of a voice on the court. That's where you come in."

If it wasn't bad enough that Karl and his cronies at Lawyers for Lawsuit Equity had a death grip on him, now they wanted a man on the Texas Supreme Court.

"You do see that, don't you, *Judge*?"

Adrian was in league with Lucifer and his cronies, had been for a good long while, but to put another person in the same position would be a new low, even for him.

"Hello? *Judge*? You there?"

He clenched his teeth and swallowed the sour slime in his throat. "Yes, Karl. I'm here. I really need to get back to court. We'll talk more about this on Thursday." He switched off his phone and threw it on his desk. Swinging the door wide, he hoped his self-loathing wasn't flashing across his face like the flickering of a neon sign about to burn out.

Chapter 3

TORIE STEPPED INSIDE THE COMMISSIONERS' courtroom just thirty-five minutes after the Campbell hearing had begun and wrinkled her nose at a disgusting smell.

People of all different colors, sexes, sizes, and ages attended the meeting to have their issues decided by the four elected county commissioners and the county judge, who was really an administrator. Torie recognized several people.

"Hey, Don," she said, greeting one man. "You on the agenda?"

He nodded. "Still working on that bridge issue. You?"

Torie nodded back. "Still working on that security issue."

"Too bad you have to go through all this to be safe in your own courtroom."

She shrugged, not wanting to continue the conversation. She still had a hard time dealing with people's sympathy. Everyone in the county knew what had happened, knew a raving lunatic had beaten her in her own courtroom. Talking about it wouldn't make her feel any better. She continued working her way to the front, shaking hands with friends and supporters and county employees.

She didn't see the district attorney. She didn't see the justice of the peace. She didn't even see Judge Beth McGruter, her dear friend, whose court was across the hall from hers. Once again she alone championed the cause of courthouse security.

After the Campbell hearing, she'd hung up her robe and pulled on her navy woolen jacket over a long-sleeved blouse, matching pants, and navy stilettos. She always wore stilettos so she wouldn't be so short. She'd been picked on when she was young because she was short and blonde, people constantly making blonde jokes, and even some of her teachers assuming she didn't have a brain. She did everything she could so that wouldn't happen in adulthood.

As she edged through the crowd, the unusual odor hung in the air so overwhelmingly that her eyes watered. The wall furnace spewed dry heat. The commissioners' courtroom, consisting of ten rows of wide wooden benches, was overcrowded with people from all walks of life—farmers, ranchers, bankers—squeezing in next to each other. Before long, body odor would be as overwhelming as whatever offended her now. Luckily, she had only one item on the court's agenda.

As she drew closer to the platform where the commissioners sat, the smell grew stronger. When she spotted a vacant seat on the front row, she realized the reason why. Commissioner Jones was eating sausages again at his seat on the commissioners' dais in spite of the other commissioners having complained about it.

She didn't want to imagine what made the sausages reek worse than a laborer's unwashed armpit. Commissioner Jones, the pig farmer—a boor of a man—was oblivious to his audience, all of whom kept their distance. Torie swallowed the revulsion she felt when she spotted the Styrofoam plate piled high with the odoriferous tubes, like large links of dog poop. He stuffed his mouth with three fingers of one hand and gripped a wad of white paper napkins with the other.

Voices came from the open doorway to the commissioner's left. Loud voices. She recognized Judge Johnson's as well as that of her only ally on the court, Harold Holtzbrink. With people talking behind her she couldn't make out more than two words—*metal detector.*

She hadn't quite warmed the bench when the county clerk handed her the day's agenda. Not surprisingly, her item was almost at the end. The county judge and she had been butting heads for almost a year. He knew if he placed her item close to the end she couldn't wait for them to reach it. She'd have to return to court. And if she weren't there to speak to her issue, they'd skip it. She pursed her lips.

The debate in the office next door ceased, and one-by-one the county commissioners entered the room. Each took his assigned seat designated by his name imprinted in white on a black plastic placard glued to the front of the long oaken dais.

When he spotted her, Harold shook his head. He mouthed, "*Sorry.*"

Her chest tightened. She should leave, but anger at the commissioners' apathy made her stay and fight. With Harold as her only ally, it was four against two as it had been from the beginning. Months had passed, and they kept putting obstacles in her path. Though she knew she might be wasting her time, she would never give up until there was some semblance of security in their courthouse.

Before he sat down, the county judge, who reigned from the center chair, rapped Commissioner Jones on the shoulder. "Get that nauseating mess out of here. And don't just dump it in the trash either."

Jones, his chin dripping with grease, shrugged and carried the plate and his girth into the next room.

"Good morning good people, good Texans, of Germania County. Welcome to the first County Commissioners' Court meeting of the New Year. Please stand for this morning's invocation to be given by—" he glanced at the pages in his hand— "the Reverend Felix Osterman, followed by the Pledge of Allegiance to these United States and the Pledge of Allegiance to the great State of Texas."

Knowing the ceremonious nature of the commissioners' court meetings, Torie practiced patience. She stood. She bowed her head. She recited the pledges. She sat. Afterward, the county judge ran through his weekly spiel, briefly explaining how things worked and thanking everyone for being there—so much political play-acting to Torie's way of thinking. Commissioner Jones, wiping his face, joined them just as the judge began with the agenda.

Torie slid to the center of the front row, directly opposite the county judge, and tried to get his attention without being obtrusive. He was going to pull a power play. He was going to make her sit through forty some-odd items before he reached hers. Though she tried to catch his eye, he was experienced at avoiding conflict. He'd been elected ten times.

Her fingers drummed on her legs. Her eyes roved from one end of the dais to the other. Harold was the only man willing to connect. Lunkheads. They took up one agenda item after another, approving bills that needed to be paid, ratifying grants, approving resolutions, until she felt like jumping up on the platform and cramming the multi-page agenda down their throats.

Frustration burned her eyes. Memories of the man who had assaulted her came rushing back. He'd come to her attention because he'd been dressed in frayed, dirty jeans and a black T-shirt—inappropriate garb for a court hearing. When she'd looked at him, the man had leapt like a circus acrobat from where he stood next to his ex-wife in the front of the courtroom, to the top of the bench, one foot landing on Torie's hand, pinning her in place, preventing her escape. The other foot landed with a splat on his case file. His black high-top tennis shoes, almost even with her face, had white laces sticking up like stray hairs.

Fear had forced a scream out of her. Seated in her chair, she could do no more than push him off her hand and try to back away from the bench, stopping when she hit the wall behind her. She didn't have a moment's warning, no time to flee down the steps and into chambers. He grabbed her arms, squeezing and shaking her. He ranted and raved and boxed her with his fists. She screamed again, wondering if anyone would respond. She had no bailiff. No protection. Squatting on her desk mat, he hovered over her, pummeling her head and shoulders. Shocked at the force of his slaps and slugs, she tried to cover her face, block his fists, push him away, the court commotion a dull roar like morbid background music.

His rants grew louder, drowning out everything else. "Fucking bitch! I'm going to kill you! Goddamn fucking bitch! You ruined my life!" His breath foul, his spittle spotted her face as he continued his diatribe. Each time she tried to break free, he forced her back; his fists—his body—like a battering ram.

A long few minutes later, he cried out like a wounded animal. He was being pulled off her, his blows finally intermittent. He entwined his fingers in her hair and held on, pulling and twisting, his rage continuing. Someone untangled his fingers and dragged him away.

When she peered through bruised eyes and wet eyelashes, a slew of deputies surrounded Carr, towered above him, shoved him to the floor. One kneed his back, cuffing his hands. A deputy on each side took an arm and dragged the man, his body a dead weight, his feet splayed behind him.

Now, her attention returned to the matters at hand as her cell phone vibrated. A text had come from her court coordinator. "Attys for 10 a m hearing sent away for coffee. Back at 1030+. Nettie."

Torie refocused, realizing she'd had a flashback. Her therapist had warned that with PTSD a flashback could happen at any time. Her heart beat like a snare drum. She'd had flashbacks only two other times but never in a public place, never where people could see her. She looked up to find Harold watching her. She mouthed, "*Help*."

Harold gave her an I-got-this nod. When the county judge paused, Harold cleared his throat and stuck out his hand, waving from his end of the row. "Um, Judge Johnson, I see one of our district judges in the audience. I imagine she's got cases to hear upstairs. Couldn't we take her agenda item next?"

The county judge cut his eyes at Harold in a look that said he'd as soon swallow Drano. With a roomful of onlookers, he could do nothing more than nod politely and acknowledge Torie.

"Why Judge Van Fleet, good morning. I didn't see you there."

The jerk's faux friendly tone made her want to take his gavel and shove it up his nose, the long way.

"Good morning, gentlemen." She stood. "Bless your

hearts for taking my agenda item out of order. I sure appreciate your indulgence."

"Yes, well I see you're number—" Johnson thumbed through the docket "—forty-five." He showed his Joker smile and feigned surprise. "We can't have you sitting down here all morning when you have important work to do upstairs. Can we, Commissioners?"

Harold was the only one with an audible response. The others mumbled and stared past her. "Okay, well, what do you have for us today, Judge Van Fleet?" He peered over his black-framed reading glasses, his speckled eyebrow hairs curling upward like fringe.

She waved her copy of the marshal's report. "Each of you has been presented with a copy of the security survey conducted by the U.S. Marshal."

"That we have, young lady, that we have." Commissioner Vacek, white-haired and wrinkled, liked to pass himself off as wise and wizardly, but Torie knew him as a cunning curmudgeon. Every time she'd appeared before them, he'd gutted her request like he would a deer.

"I'm sure y'all have had a chance to read it and know his recommendations." She sought each man's eyes, but they were all selectively blind.

"Just what are you getting at?" Commissioner Pig Farmer's chin still glistened from his snack.

"Well, as you can see, Commissioner, the marshal is recommending a bailiff for each court, including this one, metal detectors at every entrance, secure parking for the judges and each of you, and two deputies to accompany prisoners to court." She wanted to add that the marshal's recommendations were the same ones she'd made six months earlier, but they already knew that.

"Your point being?" Commissioner Pig Farmer cupped his hands behind his head, elbows wide, and leaned back in his chair.

"What I'm asking for, gentlemen, is a budget amendment for these four items—four things that could save your lives."

"Do you have any idea what the cost would be to the county?" Commissioner Schaper tapped his forefinger on the counter and leaned toward her, his face flushed.

The county judge, glancing at the audience to be sure they were paying attention, said, "I don't see why we should spend all those taxpayers' dollars on metal detectors and deputy salaries to man it when no one has been killed here."

"Yet," Torie said from between her teeth. She ordinarily had the patience of a cat herder, but the burn in her stomach moved up her esophagus and into her throat. What would it take to convince them? How many more times would she have to come begging? Would someone really have to die?

Harold caught her eye and shook his head. Torie swallowed the words that threatened to spew forth and wished she had three more gavels.

Harold leaned on his elbow and looked down the row. "Are you forgetting, gentlemen, that last year Judge Van Fleet was the victim of a brutal beating in her very own courtroom? That Wesley Carr jumped up on her bench and throttled her?"

"A metal detector wouldn't have stopped that." Commissioner Pig Farmer licked his lips like he was about to sit down to another meal.

Harold slapped his pen on the counter. "But a bailiff could have."

"I'm not supporting a budget amendment." The county judge's tone said the discussion was over.

"I say we put it on the workshop agenda sometime in the next few months." Schaper pulled out his cell phone and began tapping it.

Torie wanted to pull a Wesley Carr and jump up on the dais and throttle each of them. She gripped the rolled up marshal's report behind her back. "May I remind you, gentlemen, that my assailant is scheduled to be released in the next few months?"

"Well, I can't help that." The county judge opened his laptop, which obscured his face. "But we can workshop the security issue if you like."

"Move to table," Commissioner Jones, the pig farmer, said.

"Second," Commissioner Vasek said.

"All in favor?" Judge Johnson asked, swooshing his head right to left.

Torie spun about and stalked to the back of the room, eyes on the door, stiletto heels rap, rap, rapping on the granite floor, in a hurry to get away before she exploded. When she reached the back of the room, she exited into the hall with the satisfaction of knowing she hadn't even given them a backward glance.

Chapter 4

TORIE RAN UP THE CONCRETE STAIRS WITH HER stilettos in one hand and jacket in the other, breathing hard, furious with the commissioners and the county judge. She couldn't wait to tell Beth the commissioners said they'd rather someone die than spend money on security.

She swept past Beth's court coordinator, Charlotte, who had a gooey pineapple kolache in her hand and a guilty look on her face, and entered through the door marked PRIVATE. Beth hovered over a thick red file, her desk covered with neat one-inch stacks of printed pages layered like a line of fallen dominos.

When Beth saw Torie, she frowned.

"I only have a minute." Torie dropped her shoes and threw herself into one of the wingback chairs that faced Beth's desk. "Those blockheads. They tabled it."

"I'd ask you to sit, but you already have." Beth laid down her pen and ran her fingers through her curly black hair. "What do you expect from a bunch of farmers and ranchers? They simply don't understand how dangerous these times are."

"Don't forget we have one lawyer on commissioners' court. Harold. He and I have been trying to educate the rest of them, but either they're a bunch of morons, or they have the world fooled. When I speak with them, maybe I should couch courthouse security in terms of cows and cow pies and chickens and coyotes."

Beth forced a laugh. "Don't be so hard on them. They live in a different world." She sipped from a coffee mug and wrinkled her nose. "You've done all you can."

Torie noted Beth's forced laugh but ignored it. She needed to vent. "No, I haven't. Not yet. You should have heard Johnson and I quote, 'Why should we spend all that money on metal detectors and deputy salaries to man it when no one has been killed here.'"

"'Bout what I would expect from him." Beth picked up her pen.

Clearly, Beth was in the middle of something. Torie wriggled in the wing-backed chair and fidgeted with a baseball-sized clear glass orb she'd picked up from a bowl. She needed to get back to her own courtroom but wanted Beth to give the security issue the attention Torie thought it deserved. "Don't they realize they're in as much danger these days as we are? People don't have boundaries anymore, much less respect for the courts and elected officials."

Sighing, Beth laid down her pen again and began drumming her fingers on top of the open file. "You've got to quit ranting, Torie. They're never going to listen to you."

"I didn't rant. I was so polite you wouldn't have known it was me—like a belle of the old south. I sat quietly, most of the time, with my hands folded like the *little lady* they'd like me to be." Anger burned her throat as she forced back the words she'd like to have said when she'd been downstairs. She tossed the orb from hand-to-hand. "They have the stats. I've shown them it's just a matter of time."

"Honey, we'll have to make do with what we have." Beth stood and stretched. "If you break my crystal ball, I'm going to be so peeved." She rubbed her lower back, her gray sweater rising up, the matching skirt riding loosely on shapeless hips. "God, I'm tired, and it's not even lunch time yet." She patted her stomach. "I could eat though."

"You look like you should eat. Are you losing weight? Hard to believe with all the kolaches and other junk food Charlotte and the sycophants bring in every day. How do you do it? I have to fight to keep every pound off."

"I don't eat that junk, the lawyers do."

"You know, even the U.S. Marshal's office noted what we don't have." Torie counted off each item. "No bailiffs. No panic buttons. No metal detector except on trial days staffed by one deputy sheriff. What a joke. What good would one deputy be in the event someone went off his nut?" She blew out a deep breath. "If they'd just give us *one* of those things it would be a start."

"Torie—honey—I do know."

"Commissioner Pig Farmer said, without showing an ounce of compassion, a metal detector wouldn't have stopped Carr since he used his fists on me." Torie ran the tips of her fingers across the glass ball, feeling its smooth, cold surface. Remembering Wesley Carr's assault twice in one day was almost too much. She still saw his face every night, especially when Sergio worked late at the resort, and she was alone. Fear filled her stomach as Carr's breath and body odor revisited her, his vile words replaying in her ears.

"Torie, I see that glazed look in your eyes again. Quit thinking about Carr," Beth said, pulling a soda out of her small refrigerator and offering it to Torie. "You've got to let it go."

Torie shook her head and stared as Beth opened the can and sat back down. Even Beth, the only other female judge in the region, the only other person who understood the seriousness of the situation, didn't comprehend the enormity of the damage Carr had done. And Torie couldn't explain it. PTSD was so much more than anyone could know unless they'd suffered a shocking event themselves. "I can't let it go, Beth. As long as I'm alive, that man will be after me. You know he gets released soon." She put the ball down and stepped closer to Beth's desk.

"Everyone knows he'll be released soon. Our little Bremerhaven Press has been keeping tabs. August Sykes was up here the other day interviewing everyone but you about it."

"Why doesn't the public put pressure on commissioners' court about security?" Torie fingered a stack of papers at the edge of the desk. "Sykes at least gives it lip service, bringing it up every once in a while in his paper, but the rest of the folks around here don't seem to care."

Beth slapped her hand down on the papers. "Sykes is a Democrat. The commissioners are Republicans. They don't give a rat's ass about what he prints as long as all the other farmers and ranchers keep voting for them. Will you please stop?"

Torie's stomach churned. "The almighty vote. Makes me sick. Aren't we all on the same side? Don't we all want to be safe?"

"Torie, you've got to quit it. Listen, I have work to do. I promised a ruling on this case by the end of today, and you know I like to keep my promises." Beth smiled a gentle smile, her creamy cheeks and twinkling eyes making her very huggable. "Honey, you know I love you like a sister, but could you continue your tirade another time?"

"Okay, Judge. Just thought you'd want to know how it went... I'll just take myself across the hall where they care what I think." Torie flipped her hair.

Beth walked her to the door. "Okay, Judge, you do that. You know I care, so stop trying to make me feel guilty. Save the theatrics for the commissioners."

"I'll be seeing you then." Torie turned the knob and stopped. "Lunch soon, okay? I could go Thursday."

"Sure. I'll buy, and I'm thinking my fav—Ralph's on the River. A little of their famous filet mignon?"

Chapter 5

TORIE CROSSED TO HER OWN CHAMBERS AND flung open the thick, dark oak door with a nameplate that read *Judge Victoria Rawlings Van Fleet*. A burned coffee odor offended her nose when she cleared the doorway.

Nettie, her court coordinator, arms in constant motion, looked up from the computer and waved a stack of pink messages in the air with her left hand while speaking into her headset. Her other hand set down a coffee mug and moved to the mouse next to it. Her long brown hair, woven into a single braid that normally trailed down her back, was draped over one shoulder. Covering the headset's mouthpiece, her eyes dancing, she said, "Commissioner Holtzbrink is waiting for you in chambers, and at least one of the lawyers is back from coffee."

A sweet and competent woman, Nettie relished all the drama and politics and gossip that occurred regularly in the courthouse. If she could, she'd eavesdrop on every meeting.

Torie took the messages. She could imagine the thrill Nettie experienced when Harold popped into the office unexpectedly. Nettie knew about the commissioners' court meeting and would be dying to hear what was said. She also had a minor crush on the commissioner.

Torie copped an attitude of annoyance. "Some ally Harold was," she said, noting the gleam Nettie's eye. "I'll fill you in later."

She entered her chambers through the door marked PRIVATE. "I can't believe you're here. Where was my support, Harold? You said you'd back me up." She pulled off her jacket as she headed for the tiny closet that held her judicial robe.

Harold jumped up from the sofa where he'd been poised over his cell phone. "Today wasn't the day, Judge. I apologize." He scooted from between the coffee table and the sofa. "When I approached the county judge before the meeting, he said wait until budget hearings in the summer—that he wasn't going to entertain a budget amendment—that once carved he wasn't going to alter the stone."

"What a chiseler."

He snorted at her joke. "Yeah, but none of the others wanted to hear it either."

Torie's stomach cried out for an anti-acid. She hung up her jacket and took out her robe. "Carr gets out of the county jail way before budget hearings next summer. What am I supposed to do? Our security is worse than any other rural community in the whole State of Texas."

He stood next to one of the chairs facing her desk. At her nod, he sat down. "Now you know that's not true. Many little counties have less than we do. I bet the three other counties in your district don't have it any better."

"That doesn't make it right. We have nothing here at all. At least in the others a deputy sheriff hangs out in the courtroom when we're there." Though Harold was her friend, the topic raised so much anxiety in her that she had trouble keeping the sarcasm out of her voice. She didn't want to alienate him. She just had trouble controlling herself when they got into those discussions. Everyone wanted her to forget about the assault.

A nerve twitched in his cheek. "We have the metal detector for trial days."

"Which is as good as nothing. Carr can waltz up here any time of the day or night, and no one will be around to stop him. He could plant a bomb. He could rig some elaborate device to take all of us out." She threw the pen she had picked up against the wall and hit the photograph of the governor square in the eye.

"Whoa. What did the governor ever do to you?"

She scrunched up her nose. "I'm pretending that's the county judge." She wished she could poke the county judge in the eye. Maybe he'd be more receptive if he were assaulted.

"We have a night watchman, so Carr couldn't do anything when the courthouse isn't open."

"Hank's like a lump of clay, eighty-five if he's a day, mostly deaf, and sleeps on the job. He reminds me of my lovable, and long dead, grandfather who I wouldn't want for security either."

"Judge, you've got to stop acting so hysterical. The other commissioners don't even like to see your name on the agenda. They're talking about you behind your back, calling you a histrionic female."

Her blood pressure rose about ten points. "As if they even know what that word means, Harold. I'd like to see one of them get their rear-end kicked, then we'd see how fast security zoomed to the top of the agenda." She eyeballed her cell to see if she had any e-mail.

"That may be true, but it wasn't *them*. They don't feel your pain. I'll work for you and security behind the scenes all the way until budget hearings. I promise. Just don't ask to be placed on the agenda again until then, okay?" He stood and glanced at the door. "We'll discuss it some more. Workshop it. I'll make them give it the time the subject is due. I'll make them read your documentation. Show them the incidents that have taken place in Texas and elsewhere."

Torie rummaged in a desk drawer for a bottle of anti-acids. "You know the sheriff is on my side. I told him it's his job to protect us—it says so right in the statute books—but he said how can he do that if y'all won't give him the money for the deputies he needs to do his job."

"I know that. We'll cover that in budget hearings as well. Oh, hey, I did get them to make one concession for you."

"What's that, Harold? A flyswatter?"

"Torie—Judge. I'm trying to help you here."

"I'm sorry. I'm just so damn angry I could choke. What's the concession?" She popped open the anti-acid bottle and put two in her mouth, chewing rapidly. The chalky stuff coated her tongue.

"Two, actually. First, they agreed that anytime you feel the need for added security in your courtroom or in the courthouse, you can call the sheriff's office and ask for a deputy to act as bailiff, hand-screen court participants, walk you to your car, etcetera. And if the sheriff doesn't have enough staff to handle that request, they'll pay overtime for one of the off-duty deputies."

"Well, heck, Harold. That's every day. Why don't they just give me a deputy for a bailiff like I asked them to?"

"Because if they give you one, everyone will want one."

"Oh, please, would it be asking too much for the court officers to feel safe and actually *be* safe?"

"You've gotta stop with the sarcasm. It comes across like acid rain."

"Well, I'm sorry. It's just so ridiculous. If they'd follow the federal marshal's recommendations, do all the security measures outlined in the report—"

"You know they're not going to do that. We've got to approach this thing in baby steps. So call the S. O. if you feel the need and only if you really feel threatened, or they'll change their minds."

"You know, Harold, I've actually been thinking about bringing my own gun."

He shook his head. "Don't do that."

"I'd feel a lot safer if I had a pistol under my robe—or had two, actually—one in some kind of clip under the bench where I could reach it handily and one on the underside of this desk." She reached under the desk as though she had something under it to pull out, and Harold leaned forward like he thought she would come up with something.

"Torie—no . . . "

She slapped her hand on the top of the desk. "Almost had you there. But seriously, my husband bought me a gun. Bet you didn't know that, did you? It's a handgun called *The Judge*. It's really pretty."

Harold cringed, his shoulders rising almost to his ears. "How can you be so flippant about a gun after what happened to you? Someone could take it away from you and shoot you."

She pointed her finger at him. "If y'all aren't going to protect me, I have to take care of myself."

"I still think that's a bad idea, and you can tell Sergio I said that."

"No, listen. *The Judge* is ideal for someone like me. It has a long cylinder and takes either forty-five long Colt shells or four-ten shotgun shells. So you can shoot a bullet if the perp is far away, and you don't want to spray the people around him, but if he gets too close, a shotgun shell. Isn't that cool?"

"What are you talking about? Bringing a weapon to the courthouse?" Harold rose halfway out of his chair and then sat again. "Don't do that. You're so tiny. Do you know how easy it would be for someone to overpower you and take it? Let the sheriff handle this."

Torie put her face in her hands in an attempt to hide the aggravation that was bursting out of her at the seams. "You just don't know how it feels!" She didn't really want a gun, at least not for the office. She did for the house—for when Sergio worked so late that he ended up spending the night at the Lost Oaks Resort where he worked. But threatening to get a gun for the office might alarm *them* enough they'd take action. Oh, who knew what would make them get off their duffs and do something?

"Look, I've already called the sheriff. He agrees. He's going to inform his crew, so they'll know why they're being called in on their days off."

She lifted her head. "Okay. For now, I'll take whatever I can get. But you don't know how creepy it can be to walk into that courtroom where the court reporter—another female, I might add—and I are the only officials, see an ocean of faces, and wonder which one of them hates me enough to blow me away."

"Yeah, I do. It can be the same at commissioners' court meetings, especially at budget time when folks don't want us raising taxes."

She looked at him sideways and squinted. "It's not the same, but okay, maybe you can empathize with me a little bit. What's the second concession, pray tell?"

"Bench armor."

"*Bench armor*. A big bulletproof screen in front of the bench? I heard they had one of those in Beaumont, once. Don't know if it's still there."

"Uh, no. A metal shield. They'll take off the wood paneling, put in a thick metal shield, some kind of bullet proof metal, and replace the paneling, so people won't even know it's there."

"Oh, the wood paneling on the front of the bench? So I'm protected from my knees down, but if the shooter aims at my head—"

"The idea is that you throw yourself onto the floor behind the armor."

Torie laughed. "I'm Supergirl. Faster than a speeding bullet. What a bad joke. That's the dumbest idea on the planet. Don't they know Carr jumped up onto the bench to attack me?"

"Yes, they know."

"That he came over it and backed me up to the wall?"

Harold nodded.

"And didn't I tell them in my letter about that judge in Pennsylvania? He was shot to death by a man who came around the side of the bench when the judge jumped to the floor and pumped bullets into him as he tried to crawl into his chambers?"

Harold started to reply.

"That's why we need a metal detector at every courthouse door. The idea is to keep guns and knives out of the courthouse." Her vision blurred red as she boiled over. "If weapons aren't allowed into the courthouse, at least we'll only be beaten, like I was, and not shot or stabbed to death."

She pulled a tissue from the box on her credenza and dabbed at her eyes. She guessed she *was* a hysterical female, because the whole issue and the commissioners' court attitude toward it struck her as not only ridiculous but reckless.

Harold cleared his throat. "You don't have to take the bench armor if you don't want it. I thought I was doing you a favor." He stood again and pulled his jacket down and straightened his cuffs. "I need to get back. We took a short break."

She hadn't meant to offend her only ally. She blew her nose. "I apologize. I know you're doing your best. I'll take the bench armor. I'll take the deputy. I'll take whatever I can get."

"Okay." He held out his hand, and she took it. "We're supposed to be friends." His tone softened. "Let's not snipe at each other. I'll tell the maintenance supervisor to get with the sheriff. The sheriff can call the marshal's office, and see if he knows someone who will know how to install the armor. I'm trying to help you, Judge. I really am."

Drawing a hesitant breath, she said, "I know. I do appreciate it. You just don't know how scared I am."

"I do. My wife harps on me constantly to make sure you're protected, though she doesn't need to do that. I'm concerned about the safety of all our judges—all our employees for that matter. I just haven't been able to bring the others into the twenty-first century. Did you know they still list their home addresses in the phone book?"

Torie snorted. "I considered some of them backward crackers, but I didn't know they were *that* naive. Why do they even have home phones these days?"

"All right now, Judge." He shook his head. "Just between you and me, try working with them every day."

"Listen, I'm late for my hearing. Appreciate what you're doing." They shook hands again before he left, and she straightened her robe before opening her courtroom door.

Chapter 6

WHEN TORIE ENTERED THE COURTROOM, two lawyers were arguing at one of the counsel tables. No one else was there except the court reporter.

"All rise," Jennifer said.

"We have the file?" Torie asked as she sailed up the steps.

"On the bench, Judge." Jennifer sat down at her chair in front of the bench and pulled her machine between her legs. She popped a scrunchie around her shoulder length, tawny hair and nodded at Torie.

Torie said, "Are y'all here on the Watkins matter?" She read from the file. "Motion for Continuance."

"Judge, I just got a copy of this a few minutes ago," Boyd Charles said, waving the document in the air. Boyd, in his seventies, could be affable, but he was a chronic complainer. "They could have gotten the motion to me earlier if they'd wanted to."

"Couldn't be helped, Your Honor," a young fellow named Steve

Merritt said, smiling with artificially white teeth. Steve was the new darling of his firm. He'd become wealthy in another county and moved his family to the Texas Hill Country where the air was cleaner, there were fewer people, and supposedly a better lifestyle.

"So what is this about?" Torie put on her impartial judge mask and looked from one to the other.

"Your Honor," Boyd said, "Merritt here didn't give me three days notice of this hearing. He faxed something over yesterday afternoon telling me to be here this morning and handed me the motion when I got here."

"Why'd you show up then?" She pressed her lips together, hiding a smile.

"Judge—"

Torie put up her hand. "Hang on a second." She read through the motion. "Okay, Mr. Merritt, you want to say something on the record?"

"Yes, Your Honor. If it pleases the court, this is my first Motion for Continuance in this matter. I know the local rules say that each attorney shall file a vacation letter with the clerk specifying up to five weeks vacation time each year, but I forgot to designate one of my weeks as next week." He paused to draw a deep breath. "I have a prepaid vacation with my family in Colorado. We're going to the lodge we go to every year to ski. I have nonrefundable airline tickets for my wife, my two kids, and myself, and a friend of one of the kids is going. Judge, it would cause extreme hardship on me and my family if we couldn't go on this trip."

"Now see—see—Judge, that's not right. He knows the rules. And we've had the Watkins case on your jury docket for nine months. It needs to go to trial," Charles said.

"Well, Mr. Charles, it's not like you haven't committed this sin yourself, is it?" She cupped her chin in her hand. "Don't I remember the year before last you wanted to go hunting, and you forgot to file your vacation letter? And didn't I let you go?"

"Yes, Your Honor, but that case hadn't been on the jury docket for nine months."

"What's so important about the Watkins case that it can't wait another month? I happen to know another case settled, and I can let you have their slot."

Mr. Charles clenched his jaw, his anger apparent as the muscles flexed in his cheeks. "I've already spent most of this week preparing for trial. If I have to wait a month, I'm going to have to prepare all over again."

Torie stroked her chin like she had a beard. And he'd bill his client all over again. But she said nothing.

"Judge," Merritt said, "the Watkins' will be no worse off in a month than they are today. I promise I'll be ready, and we'll get the case tried."

Torie glanced back at Charles. "Mr. Charles, I don't see why I should penalize Mr. Merritt if it won't do egregious harm to your client to wait another month. Absent that—" she waited for Mr. Charles to whine a reply, and when she didn't hear one, she said, "you have an order, Mr. Merritt?"

"Yes, Judge." He stepped up to the bench and handed her a prepared order that needed only the date of the hearing and her signature.

While she was filling in the blanks, Mr. Merritt said, "I sure do appreciate it, Judge, and so will my family. My kids have been looking forward to this trip for a while now."

"Well, it's not like we don't have anything else on the court's calendar. I have several family law matters for sure, the attorneys complaining they can't get to court soon enough. So no problem." She signed the order and popped it into the file. "If you want a copy, ask the clerk to come and get the file since I have no bailiff—court officer—or anyone else—to take the file back—hint, hint."

Mr. Merritt said, "My firm's contacted the commissioners for you, Judge. Lobbied them several times to get you a bailiff and anything else you need."

"Well, I'm fixing to," Mr. Charles said. "I've been meaning to."

"I appreciate it, gentlemen. Courthouse security is something that should be important to all of us. Good day." She stepped off the bench.

Ping. Her cell. She paused in the doorway to read a message from Adrian, the regional presiding judge, with whom she had an ancient history.

It is with deep sorrow and regret that I inform each of you that Texas Supreme Court Justice Earl McWilliams has met an untimely death.

Torie's heart hopped into her throat. She hated to hear of anyone dying, much less a judge she'd seen a number of times over the four years of her first term. She didn't really know Justice McWilliams though she'd heard him speak at a judicial conference. He'd seemed like a nice man.

She rounded her desk and plopped down, her heart beating out a rock and roll rhythm. Though she felt sorrow and regret for the dead man's family, shamefully her mind raced with other thoughts. Someone would have to fill Justice McWilliams' seat on the Texas Supreme Court.

The possibilities ran through her mind. She was young, yes. She'd just started her second term on the district court bench, yes. She wasn't as experienced as a lot of other judges, yes. But, other than that, why shouldn't she fill the vacancy? She was a good judge, smart, responsible, and, as far as she knew, well thought of.

She needed to speak to Adrian as soon as possible. In spite of their history, he'd advise her. She knew he would. He was still her mentor, if no longer her lover.

How wild would it be if she could skip the normal progression of things—the court of appeals—and jump right to the Supremes? If she could secure the appointment from the governor to the Texas Supreme Court, she'd be that much closer to the U. S. Supreme Court.

A zing of excitement flooded her. She'd need to get busy right away, garner support before everyone she knew committed to someone else. She reached for her laptop to make a list.

First off, call Adrian for lunch. He would help her. She just knew it.

Second, talk to her dad. He would be so proud of her if she were elevated to the highest court in Texas. He would help her. Because of his work over the years in the party, he had a lot of connections.

Third, talk to Sergio. Her heart fell. Sergio had been lobbying her lately to have a baby. He didn't seem to care that she'd told him before they were married she didn't want another child. He didn't care that he'd agreed to that. Now, he'd decided he did want a child and wanted her to acquiesce.

Her stomach rumbled. Lunch time. She'd think about Sergio later. Right now she needed a break and to figure out how she was going to get that appointment.

Chapter 7

WHEN SHE ARRIVED HOME MONDAY NIGHT, Torie followed the aroma of roasting pork from the garage into the back of the house through the mudroom and into the kitchen. A rendition of "Libertango," one of Sergio's favorite songs, flowed from the sound system.

Shedding her coat and jacket and leaving them with her purse on the buffet, she opened the oven door and was met by an invisible cloud from a roasting pork loin. Before she could turn around, arms—strong arms—wrapped themselves around her from the back and lips met the curve of her neck. She tensed and then forced herself to relax. "This better be my husband or I'm calling the law," she said, her voice husky. She released the oven door and backed into the familiar embrace, a sense of safety enveloping her like a warm coat.

Sergio nibbled her neck and spun her around, planting an

intimate kiss on her mouth. From the taste of vodka and vermouth on his tongue, he had a head start on her.

"Yummy," she said when he relaxed his grip.

"How are you, *mi amante*?" The light yellow long-sleeved shirt he wore open at the neck paled next to his dark coloring but brought out the highlights in his hazel eyes. Soft age lines were beginning to frame his mouth.

She traced his lips with her forefinger. God he was sexy. As soon as they had dinner, she hoped they'd make love. "Got a martini for me?"

"Don't worry, you beautiful thing. Yours is on ice." He kissed her again. "And your favorite entree."

"I saw that." But her mind was still on the possibility of some bedroom action. Too many days had passed since the last time they'd been to bed. A spat they'd had about a baby had driven a wedge between them. Maybe he'd given up on it by now.

Torie pushed him away and whirled around in search of her drink. Life couldn't get any better than coming home to such a hunky man, but she wanted to change into something more comfortable. Her stilettos pinched by late in the day, and something softer and less scratchy than wool would be nice. She spotted the martini pitcher resting in an ice bucket and made a break for it. "I can tell you've been bored today."

"I have to be bored to want my wife? My sexy blonde bombshell *esposa*?" He gently elbowed her out of the way and poured her drink.

She liked it when he called her a blonde bombshell. "Goodness, sweetie. It's not hard to tell what's on your mind." He knew her well enough to know sex was frequently on hers, too. Looked like their argument hadn't driven too large a wedge between them. "Come with me while I change." She picked up her glass by the stem, grabbed her jacket from the buffet, and skirted around him, heading to their bedroom, a master suite on the far side of the living area.

Sergio poured a quick refill into his own oversized martini glass and caught up to her, encircling her waist with one arm, his obvious delight at the promise of more intimacy dancing on his face.

"So what have you been doing all day?" She peeled off her clothing, hanging it in her walk-in closet.

Sergio lay back on the bed crosswise, propping himself up on one elbow. His eyes lingered on her body. "Hmm, workout at the club—" He sipped his martini as he watched her remove her clothing. "Paid some bills and looked at some horses."

"You still considering buying a horse? I know you miss riding." His eyes followed her movements, traced her curves. He often watched her like that.

Being six years older than he, she wondered what he saw, whether he thought her body looked as old as her forty-five years. She tried to keep in shape, working out most mornings before she went to the courthouse. Was he comparing her to the girls he saw exercising and swimming at the resort he managed? She didn't have any pounds to spare. Her workouts were not to lose weight but to stay toned. She didn't want her flesh swinging in the wind.

"Oh, I don't know. Even boarding it, a horse would need a lot of attention." He smacked his lips. "I would rather spend time with you."

Clothed in a thigh-length, purple silk wrapper over her bra and panties, she clipped up her white-blonde hair and lay down on the bed next to him, resting her head on his arm. "I would rather you did, too, but I'd understand if you bought one. Really." Maybe he'd stop talking about a baby if he had more than his career and her to keep him occupied. Caring for a horse would take a lot of time.

He kissed her forehead. "We'll see. So how was your day at the office, *mi querido?*"

She smothered a laugh. His voice sounded funny when he called her "my dear" with his bit of accent. "I had a meeting late this afternoon with those folks who started the Family Assistance Center last year. The ones who worked so hard on my campaign."

"Oh yes? How did that go?" He traced her ear with his forefinger.

She sat up and reached for her martini, sipping and watching him over the rim. "Mmm, don't know what I did to deserve you." She kissed him on the cheek. "We brainstormed about starting services and programs in Germania County like they have in large counties."

"For example . . ."

A feeling of pleasure, like a small taste of sugar, stirred her when he asked about her work. She was still not used to a husband who took an interest, still a bit amazed that he would take the time to hear what was going on with her.

"National Adoption Day, for one. It would be an easy program to start, because we could use the model from the big counties." She checked, and he was still listening. "That's when everyone with a pending adoption comes to court on the same day. We could host it on the courthouse lawn, have circus-like tents and pony rides and clowns and those inflatable things the kids jump in—"

"Moonwalks," Sergio said, "or bounce houses some people call them."

"Look at you—a Moonwalk expert."

"A few times we allowed them at the resort for big parties for children—but only in the back of the hotel where no one could see them from the road."

"Oh, neat. Well, that's one idea. Another would be a lot more work but worth it. A possession exchange and visitation center where people could pay a fee to visit with their children or to pick up and drop off their children under supervision. That would be in cases where there are allegations of abuse, stuff like that."

"Maybe do both? Sounds like you had a good meeting." He drained his glass and sat up. "Want a refill?"

"I shouldn't, especially with these jumbo glasses, but just one more." She held hers out. "You make such good raspberry martinis."

They slid off the bed and walked back to the kitchen to the wet bar. His-and-her martini shakers, his, a plain stainless steel, hers, a hot pink, waited for them.

"These people have been really good to me, Sergio." While he mixed their drinks, she tried to judge from his demeanor whether he was angry with her for being late. There was something going on with him, she just wasn't sure what. "I know it was your day off, and I should have come straight home, but I promised I'd work with them, help get needed programs off the ground this term if they'd help me get re-elected."

"I know that. No *problemo*. Why? Do you think I'm mad or something?" He lifted his chin in fake defiance and made goo-goo eyes at her.

She looked sideways at him. "You were watching for me in the window when I drove in."

He shook his head and handed her the refill. "It's fine. Really. I was hoping you'd come home soon, that's all. Is there something wrong with wanting to spend time with my wife?"

"You are without doubt the sweetest man." She took her glass and pushed herself up onto one of the leather-covered cast-iron barstools at the counter, her feet dangling off the floor.

Sergio refilled his own glass and perched on the stool next to her. "What happened with the commissioners?"

"Those numbskulls. It went about as well as you would think. They approved next to nothing." She told him about the meeting and her conversation with Harold Holtzbrink.

"He's a good man," Sergio said. "Always been a friend to you." He sipped from his glass, his eyes roving over her face and then down her body.

His looking tickled her. She struggled not to laugh, to finish what she was saying. "I confess that sometimes I don't treat him like a friend. It's not his fault the other commissioners are so stubborn."

Sergio stroked her arm. "I'm sure he understands that the memory of what that maniac did to you is still fresh in your mind."

She nodded, her whole body shivering with the force of the memories. "He does. The others don't. But I'm not giving up."

"No one thinks you will give up. I just wish I could help you in some way. Want me to kill the maniac for you? Then you won't have to worry. I should have killed him a long time ago."

She flashed her dimples. "That's really sweet, but no. They'd know who did it." She fondled his collar and ran her fingers down his sleeve. "Oh, and get this, the case from hell came back today."

"I thought you finished with that." He took another sip of his drink.

"I thought so, too, but I think it's going to be one of those cases where the parents file a modification suit every year." Thinking about dealing with the Campbell case and their lawyers made her wish even harder that she could get on the Texas Supreme Court. She'd be hearing appeals but would only have to hear argument, not testimony. Which brought her to thinking about when to tell Sergio she was going to vie for the Supremes. Not now. She didn't want to ruin the evening.

"I'm so sorry, *mi amante*," Sergio said. "I know how it affects you."

Shrugging, not wanting to take that line of conversation any further, Torie drained her glass and set it down on the counter. "Let's not talk about work. I'm feeling woozy. I'd better eat something."

"I would like you to sit in the dining room."

"Whatever you want." Her legs felt wobbly as she slid down from the barstool. "I'll get our place settings." The room glowed. Objects wore auras. Definitely too many martinis.

"No, no. Go into the dining room. Save your energy for later." He nuzzled her neck and ran his hand down her hip as she moseyed past.

"Okay, lover boy." Torie half-stumbled into the dining room where he'd set the table with a white linen tablecloth and their best china. A bottle of champagne rested in an ice bucket with a pair of flutes next to it. A crystal vase of several dozen yellow roses, her favorite, adorned the table, causing her knees to weaken.

Definitely he was up to something, but she had no idea what. He couldn't know about the Supreme Court. He wouldn't be celebrating her decision to go for that, no matter what he might say. So were the roses an apology for the tiff they'd had about the baby? Or was he just horny? How funny he could be sometimes.

She poured herself a glass of ice water and sat down. Except for right after their marriage, there had been no similar evenings with Bert, her ex. Just acrimonious evenings. What had made her think of him? The whole relationship had been a mistake, everything except their daughter. She banished thoughts of him.

She rested her forehead on her arm as visions of Cassie haunted her. She was in the middle of a romantic evening with her present husband, a man most women only dreamed about. She needed to put the tragedy of Cassie out of her mind, too.

"Torie, you all right?"

She lifted her head and stared into her husband's endearing face. "*Si, mi esposa guapo.*"

He held a plate in each hand, a white chef's apron tied around his waist. He looked every bit the professional waiter he had been as a boy, before college and training in the hotel business. "*Esposo, mi amante. Esposa* is the female spouse. We need to work on your Spanish, but that is for another day." Placing the plates on the table, he unwrapped the apron and tossed it aside. He opened the champagne and poured them each a glass, handing her one.

"Let's toast," he said.

Torie lifted her glass. "What are we toasting?"

"To us. Happy Anniversary, *mi querido.*"

A shock rocketed through her. "Oh my God!" The champagne glass almost fell from her hand, spilling onto her lap. "I can't believe I forgot. I'm so, so sorry, Sergio."

Sergio kneeled by her side. "It's all right, *mi amante*. I don't mind." He slipped his arms around her, pulling her close.

Torie put her napkin over her head, covering her face. "Don't look at me. I'm a terrible wife. I'm so sorry. I've been obsessed with work."

Sergio laughed and removed the napkin, putting a finger under her chin. "Hey, *mi esposa,* it's *el hombre* who is supposed to remember the anniversary, not *la mujer*." He caressed her cheek, his hand cool from the champagne glass.

She couldn't look at him. She wanted to crawl under the table as he cuddled her. "I feel awful. What's wrong with me?"

"You have a lot on your mind, my dear one. Now take your glass of champagne, what's left of it, and let's drink. To us." He stood and held out his glass until she touched it with her own.

Torie choked down the champagne, managing to get it past the lump of shame in her throat. "How can I make it up to you?"

"Eat your dinner, Victoria." He tapped her on the nose. "It's fine." He went back to his own chair and shook his napkin onto his lap. "Go on, eat."

Torie put a bite of pork tenderloin into her mouth. It could easily have been his best ever, but all she could taste was embarrassment. She chewed and smiled at her husband, the handsome, passionate, but kind and gentle, man who'd persuaded her to marry him a few years ago. His eyes sparkled as he chewed and watched her face.

He patted his mouth and sipped from his glass, his eyes flitting from her eyes to her lips.

Torie bit into the vegetables, tender shoots of broccolini sautéed in some kind of savory sauce. A drop landed on her chin, and Sergio swiped it with his forefinger, his finger then going into his mouth. Again she wondered how she had gotten so lucky the second time around. He was so kind and so calm and so gentle and so very different from her first husband. After she swallowed and before she took another bite, she said, "Honestly, Sergio. Let me make it up to you."

Sergio sipped from his flute. "Yes, *mi amante*. You will. Just finish your meal." His smile was full of meaning.

"Oh. *Okay.*" Though she'd lost her appetite, she knew she needed to eat something to offset all the alcohol. She cut into the pork loin again and put a piece into her mouth. Neither of them spoke until they were through eating, their eyes sending messages to each other.

When she laid her napkin next to her plate, Sergio ushered her into the bedroom, saying they could clean up the kitchen later. Torie didn't object. He brought the remaining champagne, and she carried the flutes. The light jazz from the living room came through speakers in the bedroom's corners. Sergio dialed the lights down. As they peeled each other's clothing away, Torie found herself wanting Sergio more than ever.

He picked her up and put her on the bed. When they were both more than ready, he whispered, "You did go to the doctor for that new pill you wanted to try, did you not, *mi ángel.*"

An adrenaline spike forced her to sit up. "Oh for goodness sake! I can't believe I forgot that, too. I was going to see if they'd fit me in the other day, then something came up." She brushed her hair back. He was going to think she was an idiot. A careless, unthinking idiot.

Sergio, who had been leaning over her, rolled onto his back and stared at the ceiling.

She was pretty sure she knew what he was feeling, and it wasn't good. "But you've still got some condoms, right?"

He reached over and opened his bedside table drawer, making a show of groping around in it. He shook his head. "Empty. I didn't buy any since you were going to the doctor."

She'd just killed their romantic evening with her negligence. How could she have been so forgetful? Sergio shifted onto his side, away from her. She reached for him, pulling on his arm. She scooted over close to him and leaned down, teasing him on the neck with her tongue.

He shrugged her off. "I need a moment."

His tone startled her. He had every reason to be angry. Her carelessness was unforgivable. "It's all right, honey."

"Give me a minute." His voice was gravelly.

"No, it's okay, really." She kissed his neck and tugged on his shoulder until he faced her. "Let's not stop. It's just this one time. I'm sure it'll be all right."

He slid his arms around her. "I want you so much, but are you sure you want to take the chance?"

His warm skin next to hers, his musky scent filling the air around them, the knowledge that he wanted her with all of his being, made her forget all caution. She wanted him just as terribly. She had to have him. "I'm positive," she murmured. "The chances are miniscule for a woman of my age, and it'll only be this one time. I'll call the doctor for an appointment first thing tomorrow." She tickled his lips with her tongue and blew a lock of hair from his forehead. "And you get some condoms in the meantime. Come on, love me."

He pulled her to him, and they made love fiercely, passionately, and deeply, pushing everything out of Torie's mind except for her husband and how dear he was to her. And later, the second time, their lovemaking was more tender, slower, but every bit as delicious.

Chapter 8

TUESDAY NIGHT, A HAILSTORM THREATENED the Hill Country like an approaching marine brigade, marching toward them, locked and loaded, ready to rain down. Torie and Sergio drove across town to her parents' home. Once a week, Sergio brought a meal for four from the resort, and they took it to her parents. That evening, as they approached the front door, the racket coming from inside the house sounded worse than the thunder outside. She and Sergio shed their coats, Sergio hanging them in the hall closet while she took the takeout boxes to the kitchen.

"Hi Daddy," Torie said from the den doorway. When her father didn't respond, she leaned over him and yelled, "I said, 'Hi, Daddy.'"

Her father, a balding man whose remaining hair had gone to white and who was almost as large as his recliner, lay back with the remote control in his lap. As usual, his eyes were stuck to the television, the volume so loud it sounded like the basketball game was in the next room instead of on the TV. "Hey, honey child," her father said and kissed her cheek.

She smiled at the endearment. He'd called her that for as long as she could remember.

Wincing at the raucous noise blaring from the TV, Torie crouched down beside his recliner, like a little dog on her hind legs, and stroked his arm. The lines in his face looked more chiseled than usual.

"Guess what Sergio brought from the restaurant tonight."

"Smells like roast beef and gravy." He shifted his eyes from the game to her face. "That's one young man who knows what I like."

Torie flinched. Did her father mean something by that *young* comment or was she being too sensitive? He could be making no reference at all to Sergio's being younger than her. He could merely see Sergio as young compared to himself whom he considered old.

"Yep, Dad, with all the trimmings. And pecan pie for desert."

"Sounds like just what the doctor ordered."

Torie's breath caught. "Doctor? Have you been to see the doctor?"

"It's an expression, honey child, just an expression. Is something wrong?" He tore his eyes away from the television and patted her cheek.

"Oh, okay. So you haven't been to the doctor?"

He shook his head. "You're impossible sometimes." His attention went back to the TV.

"Good evening, Matthew. What's the score?" Sergio walked around the recliner to shake Torie's father's hand.

"Thirty-three to thirty-one."

"Whoa, what a monster," Sergio said. A huge, new, flat screen television graced the opposite wall. "That thing must be fifty inches."

"*Heh, heh, heh.* An 80-inch ultra HD 3-D," her dad said, as proud as a teenager with his first car. "Of course basketball isn't in 3-D, but sit down. I'll show you what it can do."

Sergio made for the couch, which was adjacent to the recliner. "When'd you get it?"

"Howie and I picked it out last weekend. They delivered it and set it up this morning. Sit down, Torie. You have to put the glasses on, and I can show you what it can do in 3-D."

Torie hadn't even noticed the new television. "No, that's okay. Y'all go ahead." She might have known her brother Howard had a hand in choosing it. Seemed like her father didn't make a decision without Howie's input. "I'll make the salad and see what Mom's up to."

"Your mother's in the guest room. She's thinking of changing the curtains out." He started flipping channels. "I don't know why. We never get any guests, but I guess sewing keeps her busy."

Torie went into the kitchen and tossed the salad. She put the rest of the food in the oven and turned it on the lowest temperature to keep it warm. Her mother, the unequaled queen of etiquette, had already set the table with the silver service and cloth napkins she'd made to match the tablecloth.

Munching on a bit of carrot, she found her mother in the guest room, sitting on the double bed, measuring tape in one hand, a pad and pen in the other. Except for being shorter than her mother, Torie had been made in her image. For just a moment, she paused, looking at her mother, realizing what she'd look like at that age.

"Oh, honey, I didn't hear y'all come in." They hugged and kissed each other on the cheek.

"I don't know how you can hear anything with the TV as loud as

Dad keeps it. I wish you'd talk him into getting hearing aids." Torie glanced at the windows. "He says you're making new curtains."

"Your father. Shows how much he listens. I'm redecorating the entire room. Going to combine my sewing room with this room, so I can put my art supplies in the sewing room."

"You're taking art?" Torie sat on the edge of the bed and stroked the quilt her mother had pieced together from Torie's and Howie's baby clothes.

"This spring at the community college. Mary and I are taking a class together one morning a week while the children are in school." Her mother put the pen down. "We could take the night class instead, if you want to join us."

Torie stomach tightened. She didn't want to hurt her mother's feelings, but take an art class? No way. "That's really sweet, Mom. Thanks for the offer, but I don't have time. You and Mary did the right thing, signing up for a morning class so she wouldn't have to worry about Howie and the kids." Her finger traced a quilt square, pink flowered flannel from a pair of pajamas she had worn when she was a toddler.

Her mother looked like an indulgent teacher, kind eyes, kind smile. "Just thought I'd offer. We didn't think you'd want to, what with judging and politics and that young husband."

Torie wandered around the room, her fingers trailing across the surfaces of the furniture. "Mom, I wish you and Dad would stop saying that. Sergio's not that young and not that new. It's been three years now."

"Well, you know what I mean. A younger man. I'm sure he has plans for you whenever the two of you are home at the same time." Her eyes danced.

"Mom, really. I hope you're not referencing our sex life." Torie's neck grew warm at the memory of the night before. "That's enough of that."

Her mother patted a place on the bed beside her. "Sit down, and tell me what's been going on in your life."

Torie sat and let her mother squeeze her shoulders. "Nothing much. Still trying to get more security at the courthouse. Sergio's thinking of buying a horse."

"What would he want with a horse?" She picked up Torie's hand and held it in both of hers.

"He used to ride a lot when he was younger. Says he misses it, and it's something he can do by himself on his days off." Her mother's fingers were cool. "You know sometimes he works all weekend. He's off during the week, and, of course, I'm at the courthouse."

"You and Sergio talk any more about having a baby?" Her mother's brows drew together.

The warmth Torie had felt in her neck began to feel like flames licking at her face. "You know I'll never have another child after Cassie. Did Sergio say something to you?" She rose, but her mother pulled her back down.

"Don't get upset. You know he thinks of me as his mother since he doesn't have one anymore."

"He did, didn't he?" Her voice rose an octave.

"He may have mentioned he wouldn't mind having a baby."

"Oh, right. He wouldn't mind having a baby. When is he planning on getting pregnant?" How dare Sergio discuss such a sensitive issue with her mother? It didn't matter that his own parents were dead, and he didn't have them to talk to. He had no right to put her in such a spot.

"Very funny, Victoria."

Torie struggled to breathe evenly. Her mother wasn't at fault. The baby thing was an issue she and Sergio were going to have to settle once and for all. "Mom, I've told Sergio I don't want another child. I told him when we started dating seriously, and I told him again before we got married."

"Torie, he's your husband. Don't you want to make him happy?"

"Him? What about me? What about my plans?" No matter how hard she tried not to, she grew angry at any discussion of children.

"You were a good mother, Torie. You know you were."

"If I'd been a good mother, Cassie would still be alive."

"It wasn't your fault. Bert had so many problems."

"I'm not rehashing my life with Bert." Torie studied the older face that so resembled her own. Her mother had been almost as devastated about Cassie as Torie. She knew that. But it didn't make any difference. Besides, her mother had two other grandchildren. She should dote on them.

"Oh, honey . . ."

"No, Mom. I'm not having another baby. End of discussion. And if Sergio brings it up with you, tell him to talk to me." She'd never tell her mother there were times she had a yearning. She'd never admit she knew her biological clock had just about ticked its last. She'd never acknowledge that nowadays women chanced having babies at much older ages than they had twenty years earlier. But another pregnancy wasn't for her.

"Of course, that's between you and your husband. None of my business. I'm just the grandmother." She dropped Torie's hand and straightened her clothing. "But you can see how happy the kids have made your brother. He's such a good father, coaching Stevie's Little League team and helping Lily Ann with soccer."

"Really? Like I don't know that?" She started to say that she had always known how wonderful Howie was, that all her life she'd heard about her big brother, Howie. Howie who was good in math and science while no one expected her to be. Just be sure to excel in English and do passing fair in the boys' subjects. Howie, who played basketball in the winter and baseball in the spring. Howie, who got scholarships to college. And now Howie, the perfect father. Torie stood and brushed at the wrinkles in her pants. "Maybe Howie could have a baby for Sergio."

Her mother's lips stretched thin. "Torie, that's not fair. It's not his fault he was born first and a boy."

"Don't you think I know that? But would you please quit comparing me to him? Anyway, what's he done that's so great? I'm a district court judge. Hello, has anyone noticed that?"

"We're very proud of you. You know that. I just think having another child would complete you."

"Don't you know women don't need children to complete them?"

Her mother looked at her like she wasn't so sure.

"I wish you could understand how much my career means to me. I have ambitions. Someday I may even be on the highest court of the land."

Her mother reached for her hand again and squeezed it. "Of course, if that's what you want. I certainly don't see why you can't be on the Supreme Court if other women are. But how does Sergio feel about that? Wouldn't you have to move to Washington, D.C.?"

At least her mother acknowledged the possibility of Torie realizing her ambitions. "Humph." Torie shook her head. "Sergio.

Howie. You know, our generations think differently. Women have options now, and the best husbands support them in their choices. Come on, let's eat. I'm hungry." She took the pad and paper and the measuring tape and left them on the bed.

As the two women went out into the hall, Sergio disappeared into the kitchen. How much of the conversation with her mother had he overheard?

Chapter 9

AT THE SUB-REGIONAL JUDGES' LUNCHEON ON Wednesday, before Torie and Beth could even hang up their coats, Jack Dobbs hailed them from across the private dining room. "I say there, girls," he said, pushing his chair back and standing like the cartoon rooster Foghorn J. Leghorn ready to give a long-winded speech. "We're taking bets on which of us guys is gonna be the next supreme."

As she draped her coat on the rack, under her breath Torie said to Beth, "Just for fun, let's pretend we don't know what he's referring to." She called to Dobbs on the other side of the room. "Is something going on I don't know about?"

Beth stuffed her gloves in the pocket of her coat and let out a soft snicker that only Torie could hear. "They've got to know we all received the same message from Adrian."

"Yeah, but most of them have their heads up their—"

"Don't say it." Beth took her arm as they walked to the table. "Let's just see where this goes."

"Ha. Ha. Ha. Can't believe I heard it before you did," Dobbs said. The most senior judge in the region, Dobbs liked to play native Texan, always wearing a white felt Stetson, custom leather boots, well-starched jeans and long-sleeved snap-down western shirts. That day, in addition, he wore a new buff-colored leather sports coat.

Torie secretly thought Dobbs was gay but kept her opinion to herself. She didn't need him for an enemy. It could easily be true, but in most of the Texas Hill Country, if one was in politics, sexual orientation became a matter for public discourse.

"Really, what did you hear?" Beth asked, elbowing past him to get to a vacant chair.

"You don't always know everything, Dobbs." Torie took the chair next to Beth. Her mind raced like her Mercedes going ninety-five miles an hour around a curve. Did those guys really think they could be contenders? They all had issues—something embarrassing they'd done that could be used against them in a statewide election. Or personal reasons for wanting to keep their benches as long as they could—for the money or the insurance. Or they just plain weren't ready to retire.

"About Judge McWilliams passing away," Dobbs said.

"Oh, that," Beth said. "You mean the opening on the Supreme Court."

Torie kicked Beth under the table and succeeded in hiding her smile. Dobbs was such a—a character was the most generous thing she could think of at that moment. The other men in the room weren't as bad, though for Torie's taste they all had their moments.

Bo Calhoun actually did own a ranch, in contrast to Jack

Dobbs' acting like he did. Bo spent all his spare time on his ranch. He wasn't one to hang out at his court if there was nothing on his calendar. If someone needed an emergency order signed, they literally had to track him down at his home on the range. One time, she'd been assigned to switch benches with Bo for a few days because of a Motion to Recuse filed against him that the regional presiding judge couldn't hear. The clerks, the coordinator, and the lawyers had been astonished when she stayed until five even though she had to drive over two hours to get home. Each day, they urged her to leave as soon as the last case was heard, but Torie never would.

Bo was an okay guy. He'd been able to persuade his own county commissioners' court to get him a metal detector, a deputy, and even a court bailiff. He'd coached Torie on what to say to her commissioners' court, but it hadn't helped.

Randolph Stewart was an old, bald, fat, short, white guy who didn't perceive his own repulsiveness. Each time she saw him, Torie thought his face couldn't get any redder and his girth couldn't get any broader, but both did. He drove a classic Corvette she couldn't believe he fit inside of. He weighed three hundred, if a pound. She'd seen him on occasion, particularly when he'd been ten years younger, with a young, stylish woman on his arm. She'd always figured the women were gold diggers. As for his abilities as a judge, he was lazy, did as little continuing judicial education as possible, and was frequently reversed on appeal.

Torie and Beth were the only female judges in the area. Some people still considered them a novelty. Some counties had few female lawyers and still no female judges. Of course, to be elected you had to run. And in the Hill Country, fewer women ran than men.

When she and Beth were settled at the round table, Dobbs asked,

"Judge Frothingham coming, Torie?" He sat in the chair closest to the wall. If there had been a head of the table, Dobbs would have taken that seat if Adrian didn't show up. Dobbs always thought he should be in charge.

Why had Dobbs asked her? Beth was hosting, picking up the tab. Did he know about their past relationship? Or did he just think he knew and wanted to give her a hard time? Even if he knew something, what had gone on between her and Adrian was ancient history, predating Sergio by a number of years. Not that she wanted people to know her business. She'd been around long enough to learn that whatever they knew they'd twist to their advantage if they thought it would help their careers. "I haven't heard from him today, have you, Beth?"

Beth shook her head. "I don't know whether he'll be here or not. What about the rest of y'all?"

The others shook their heads.

"We'll give him another few minutes," Dobbs said. "You girls want a drink?"

Torie gave Dobbs a sidelong glance. He was goading her though she didn't know why. "Iced tea," she told the waitress.

"Coffee," Beth said. "I don't see how you can stand drinking iced tea when there's ice on the ground."

"I don't like coffee with a meal." She didn't comment on Jack's rum and Coke, Bo's beer, or Randolph's gin and tonic. What they did was their own business. Typically, though, none of the judges had any cases set for after the lunches in case the discussion ran long. And some of them fancied going home early on any account.

"So if you girls had to choose one of us to be on the Supreme

Court, which one likely would it be?" Dobbs asked, stroking his chin as though he were a wise old man with a beard.

Beth said, "Judge, I don't know why, but it seems today you're hell-bent on aggravating either me or my friend here." She indicated Torie with her thumb. "I wish you'd cease and desist."

"What are you talking about?" Dobbs asked.

"You know good and well," Beth said. "Now behave yourself, and we'll all get along fine."

Dobbs shrugged. "Yes, Your Honor, ma'am. So answer my question. Which one of the three of us?"

"Why would it be one of you?" Torie asked, feeling a slow burn building in spite of herself.

"Aw, come on, it has to be one of us," Randolph said with a grunt. He got up and staggered to the window, moving the drapes to the side as if looking for something.

"Who says?" Beth asked. Her foot struck Torie's calf.

"Rumor. Rumors are flying like they have wings, all over Texas. I've gotten a couple of calls this morning from judges in other parts of the state." Dobbs clapped his hands once making a sound not unlike a muted gunshot. "Everyone says the same thing. It's our turn. The governor has often spoken of wanting more Hill Country representation on that bench."

Torie studied the men. She was more intelligent and more organized than all three of them put together. She worked harder. Heard more cases. Started more programs to help people, especially families and kids but also programs for all types of cases. Mediation and other forms of alternate dispute resolution had been an interest of hers for many years. However, she was not opening her mouth, not yet. She was still getting her support lined up.

"So all three of you are vying for the position?" Beth asked, leaning on her elbows and tenting her fingers. Torie banged her knee against Beth's. Beth knew her ambitions. Their turn to goad the men.

Randolph watched them from where he stood. His face—no, his entire head—was as red as the tablecloth.

"You okay, Judge Stewart?" Torie got up and went to the window. "Want me to open the window and let in some fresh air?"

"Just my blood pressure . . ." Sweat covered his forehead. He wiped his head with his napkin. "I forgot to take my pills. I'll be all right. Go sit down with the others." The bouquet of gin on his breath accosted her.

He probably shouldn't be drinking, but it wasn't her place to say anything. "If you're sure . . . I could drag a chair over here for you." His coloring was way too red. His ruddy complexion explained part of it but not all. She hoped he wasn't fixing to have a heart attack in the middle of lunch.

"Go on. Just give me a minute." His eyebrows drew together until he looked like a fat Mr. Grinch.

Torie lingered a moment longer before returning to her chair and the bantering between Beth and Jack. She longed for a moment to think—a few seconds of quiet to clear her head. If she went for the job, she'd be spending a lot of time in Austin. Austin wasn't that far from Bremerhaven. She'd come home on the nights Sergio was off and on weekends.

"Don't you think so, Torie?" Beth asked, elbowing her.

"Whatever." Torie glanced at the others. They watched her. She squeezed lemon and sweetener into her tea and didn't take part in the conversation, refusing to be drawn in. Her mind racing in several directions at once, she couldn't focus.

If she didn't throw her hat in the ring, no telling when another bench would open up. She sure wouldn't run against an incumbent from her own party. Someone might decide not to run again, but then she'd have the primary and general elections to face, huge amounts of money to raise, an untold number of obstacles, and no leg up. If she could snare McWilliams' job, she'd stand in the stead of an incumbent. Be way ahead of the game. The others were probably thinking the exact same thing.

The decision wasn't difficult. She was going for it, though she wanted to talk to her father about it and get his blessing, and Adrian. But she also wanted to hear what the rest of them had to say.

"I'm not sure," Bo said. "I like my job. I don't want to spend half my life in Austin. And I don't want to run from a gazillion counties."

"Two hundred and fifty-four counties," Dobbs said, his hands flailing in the air. "The whole, entire state, and you're just afraid Constance wouldn't put up with it."

"They don't make that much more money," Bo said. He pulled apart a slice of French bread and tore it into small pieces, dropping them on his plate. "And a real pain in the ass unless you're trying to prove something." He gave Beth and Torie a look as if implying that one or both had something to prove. "Or advance yourself. I'm not sure I want to be any higher up. I feel pretty secure in my district. I haven't had an opponent in the last two elections."

"I might have an opponent next time," Randolph said, trudging back from the windows, breathing a little easier than he had a few minutes earlier. "There's this little lady lawyer who has a bone to pick with me apparently."

Torie cringed. She hadn't heard the "little lady" remark in, oh, maybe a couple of days. When she'd first started practicing law an attorney in another county had called her that. She'd bristled like one of the wild boars she's seen on the backcountry roads. She wondered whether Randolph had phrased his remarks just to annoy her and Beth. "What'd you do to her?" Torie asked.

He eased himself into his chair. "Well—nothing." He glanced from side-to-side. All eyes were on him. He looked mighty uncomfortable, as though he'd said too much already, and patted his face with his napkin before dropping it on his placemat. "Nothing. She just took issue with a ruling."

Dobbs snorted. "You know it wouldn't hurt you to read the law occasionally."

"Shut up, Dobbs," Randolph said. "You don't know what it was about."

"Well, I can imagine it. You don't think the lawyers carry tales about each of us all over the Hill Country? You don't think I've heard about some of the stuff you pull?"

Beth said, "We're not talking about that. We probably all have something we'd rather not be brought up with the electorate."

"He opened the door to it," Dobbs said.

"Christ, man," Bo said. "Stewart is not on trial, and you aren't a prosecuting attorney. Lay off him."

"What are you, his mother?" Dobbs asked.

"No, his father," Bo said.

Torie sat back, watching and listening. She wondered whether something was going on between the three of them that she and Beth weren't privy to. Whatever it was, this was unusual behavior for them. The meetings were usually conducted with more decorum.

"Yeah, yeah, yeah," Dobbs said and tossed the rest of his rum and Coke down his throat.

Beth had told her how it was when she first took the bench, how awkward the meetings had been. The male judges were clearly uncomfortable with a female judge in the same room. They'd gotten over it after about a year, she'd said. By the time Torie came around, it was business as usual. At least as far as she knew. She and Beth didn't see the other judges very often, being from different counties. That's one of the reasons they had the lunches. They exchanged ideas and discussed problems relevant to all of them.

"Well," Dobbs said, "back to my original query, which of us guys do y'all think should, could, or would get the nod?" He glanced from Beth to Torie.

Beth slapped the table. "What makes you think the three of you are the only judges in the Hill Country to be considered?" Plainly, Beth was annoyed that he'd not responded the first time.

"You don't mean you?" Dobbs said, laughing.

Beth's lips pressed together. She clenched her teeth, the muscle in her jaw flexing.

Torie glanced from Beth to Dobbs. The way he talked to her must take her back to her first years on the bench, being taunted by a jerk like Dobbs.

"Well, Austin is technically the Hill Country," Beth answered. "So I'm sure there are others thinking about the appointment. And I'm sure if we got out a map, I could find some other counties that the five of us don't cover that could be construed to be the Hill Country."

"Rumor says there are too many appeals judges and Supremes already from big cities," Randolph said. "The governor wants someone from a smaller county, from multiple counties, from rural counties, farm and ranch-type counties."

"That's us," Dobbs said.

"And Torie and I wouldn't qualify why?" Beth asked.

"Torie, you're unusually quiet today," Dobbs said. "You got something on your sweet little mind?"

Torie shook her head, trying to hide her disgust. "I always have something on my mind. Do you have a particular question you'd like to ask? A point of law you'd like explained?"

Dobbs laughed again. "I know you know better than to think another family law judge could be appointed to the Supremes."

Torie focused on a spot on the wall behind him. She wouldn't let him see she was reining herself in, that she'd like nothing more than to pick up the flower centerpiece and chuck it at him. "I'm not a family law judge. I'm a district court judge same as all of you here. You can read my court's enabling statute. And even if my court were a dedicated family law court, that wouldn't mean I shouldn't vie for the seat just because there are already some on the court."

"Might as well be," Randolph said, his face as red as it had been when he stood at the window.

Torie glared at him. Did he really want to get into the fray?

He eyeballed her, his mouth in a crooked smile. "You do all the family law for Beth in the county y'all share, and you were board certified in family law. Seems to me that makes you a family law judge."

Torie wanted to say, *That no more makes me a family law judge than being fat makes you a hog*, but she didn't. Instead, she said, "Judge, are you trying to get my goat?"

Dobbs guffawed. "You're asking for it, Randolph."

Beads of sweat had broken out on Randolph's forehead. He swallowed the rest of his gin and tonic, and said, "I guess not."

Bo frowned. She'd seen that frown a lot when she'd been on the other side of the bench. If he had something to say, he kept it to himself.

"What's wrong with everyone here today?" Torie's head spun from one judge to the next. "Why is everyone biting at everyone else? Is it that we might all be competing against one another?"

"Ah ha!" Dobbs said. "You *are* considering trying for the appointment."

"I didn't say that," Torie said. "But is it true that all three of you are? Really?" She glanced from man-to-man. "Seriously?"

"Yep," Dobbs said. "Certainly I am. I'm ready to move on to something else."

Bo shook his head. "I already said I don't know."

Randolph cut his eyes at her. "Why do you want to know?"

"Those of us who are not vying for it could support those of us who are," Beth said. "I mean if you think you can. Anyway, I say let's not wait for Adrian any longer. I'm hungry, and it's my turn to buy, so I'm ordering." She flashed them a look, her forehead blanched with impatience. "You guys want another drink? Remember I'm not buying drinks, just food."

"You're no fun," Bo said. He picked up his menu.

Beth signaled the waitress. "We're ready to order."

When the waitress was gone, Torie said, "Hypothetically speaking, why don't you think another family court judge, and I'm not conceding that I am one, could be on the Texas Supreme Court?"

"We already have some. There's no need for another one.

Anyway, it's only logical," Dobbs said. "There are so many big business cases."

"Med mal," Randolph said, still eyeing Torie, his expression like that of a chastised little boy. "Big tort claims like chemical plant explosions, and the issues that arise from them."

Torie's blood rushed in her ears. "Like I couldn't do those? Like I'm too much of a *little lady* to understand civil litigation? You may not know I graduated at the top of my class in law school." What a jerk. He'd better quit while he was ahead. "That include Beth as well?"

"Well—" Randolph began.

"Don't answer that," Beth said. "Or I'll be all over you like a mud-pack. You fellas are a bunch of Neanderthals."

"Hey," Bo said, "don't include me with these two knuckleheads."

"I'm not saying there's no room for another female on the Supreme Court," Dobbs said, "but a female district judge from a big city would stand a better chance because of her experience and her connections, quite frankly. I don't know about Stewart, but I have my share of connections with the governor." He stroked his lapels like an old time politician. "And I did a lot of civil litigation in Austin and San Antonio and Midland/Odessa before getting this bench. I'm probably the most qualified person in the room."

"Bull hockey," Beth said. "You're nothing but a counterfeit cowboy with a big ego. You'd better start checking out your opposition."

Torie laughed so hard that even to herself she sounded like a cackling witch. When she gathered her wits about her she said, "If you guys would think about it, you'd realize you're not any more qualified than we are. And maybe less."

"Ha! You're going for it. Admit it." Dobbs wore a taunting smile.

"I didn't say that. But I won't rule it out either." Torie cut her eyes at him.

"Me either, or me too, I'm not sure where we are in this conversation," Beth said, chuckling. "We're every bit as qualified as any of you."

The waitress entered with more drinks followed by another waitress with their food.

"Well, let the best man win," Dobbs said.

Torie and Beth exchanged glances and shook their heads.

"Wo—man," Beth said.

Torie could hate Dobbs if she really tried. He was obnoxious and an idiot. Let him think she didn't stand a chance while she took all the meetings, did all the necessary things, lined up her supporters. She'd make him eat his words.

As for Beth, Torie thought she had a better chance though she wouldn't tell Beth that. Someone must have been mentoring Beth over the years as Adrian had been mentoring Torie. She had no way of knowing whether Beth had enough connections to help her get the nod. Now that she sized up the situation, could Beth be her worst competition? But Beth hadn't committed yet and might not.

Chapter 10

THURSDAY, ADRIAN FOUND KARL HAWKINS lounging at a balcony table overlooking the river. Adrian admired the view of the wintery green Guadalupe gushing past, though he'd seen it many times. If even a slight breeze had been blowing, he would have insisted on sitting inside. Karl could use his paunch for extra insulation, but Adrian's thin build caused him to get chilled easily.

When Karl waved him over, the muscles in the back of Adrian's neck tightened like twisted ropes. They shook hands, Adrian doing well to hide his revulsion at having to touch the man who he'd let ruin his life. He found contact with any of the attorneys from Lawyers for Lawsuit Equity degrading.

"Sit down, Judge." Karl's mud brown eyes flickered like the LED votive candle in the center of the table. The cold air had turned his cheeks and chin pink. "I had them bring cushions out so our rear ends don't have to rest on these chilly wrought-iron chairs. Don't you just love the fresh air and sunshine in the winter?" He wore a wool overcoat. A hat covered his balding head and calfskin gloves rested next to his plate.

Adrian shivered. "Hope I haven't kept you waiting." Sitting down, he tucked his own gloves into his pocket. He wore an overcoat as well, one with a fox collar, but no hat. He had thick, full, silver hair.

"You got you a Gucci coat, I see," Karl said, a smirk on his face. "Seen it on a lawyer friend in San Antonio." He glanced at his watch and frowned at Adrian.

Adrian let the comment about his coat go by, not wanting to reveal that his wife had made the purchase, but he had to address his tardiness. "I let the witness finish his testimony before breaking. I thought it would be only ten minutes."

"Well, no problem. I just got here a few minutes ago and talked them into letting us have this table and bringing out this heater. We can speak freely out here."

Adrian was glad of the heater though it was just like Karl to bully the wait staff to open the outdoor area and bring not only the heater but cushions for the chairs. Adrian raised his hand to signal the waitress for a menu.

"Don't bother," Karl said. "I already ordered filets for us. I remembered you like yours medium."

Adrian flexed the muscle in his jaw and glanced down at the river running steadily past, occasional debris in frothy foam sweeping by in a dull rushing noise, *swish, swish*. He would try to emulate the river, at least in his steadiness, not let Karl see how he felt. He didn't know what to do about the debris of his life. "I'll have a cup of coffee with it then." He shivered.

Karl waved his fingers at a waitress who stood watching from inside the door. She came out and took their drink orders. When they were alone again, Karl gripped the edge of the table and said, "Well, it's official now. McWilliams had issued a press release stating he was resigning due to *health* reasons, and then he was involved in that accident. Some think it was suicide." He winked at Adrian.

Adrian stroked his mustache with a knuckle. Was there something he was supposed to read between the lines, from the wink or otherwise? If so, he didn't know what. He let it go. "And you're positive the governor will appoint someone from Region Ten?"

"Absolutely. He's said for the last couple of years the next time an opening came up he was appointing someone from the Hill Country. A 'rural' judge as he put it. To achieve more balance on the court." Karl slapped the table. "As if that makes any difference about anything." He snickered.

"You've confirmed it though?"

"Don't worry. We've practically got it engraved in limestone."

The ropes in Adrian's neck twisted tighter. "The governor is a good, well-intentioned man," he said, wanting to add, *Not like you guys*. But he didn't have the gumption.

Karl's eyes darted over Adrian's face. "*If* that's true, and I'm not saying it's not, mind you, we can work around that. So, you have somebody in mind?"

Adrian waited to respond while the waitress set down his coffee. He sipped and savored the delicious dark roast and the warmth of the cup in his hands before answering, wishing he could have his coffee in better company. Placing another judge in the same position as himself repulsed him, but it looked like Lawyers for Lawsuit Equity demanded it. If he didn't cooperate, he'd suffer the consequences, and he couldn't afford to find out what those consequences would be. Had they kept a record of all the things he'd done for them over the years? All the *perks* he taken? If LLE caused him to lose his position and his law license, how would he survive?

Adrian choked back the reply he wanted to say to Karl. Instead, he said, "No, no one yet, but I will have by the time it's necessary. I have several people in mind." Truth be told, he wasn't quite there yet, not quite through considering his options. "Since I put the word out, though, my assistant has been fielding calls all week from judges in the region who would like to be considered."

"So there are a lot of possibilities?" Karl rubbed his hands together.

"They've all heard the rumor that it's to be a judge from a rural county. Any chance the governor will choose from the court of appeals? There's bound to be someone on one of the courts who fits the bill." Adrian could only hope. It'd be one way to get himself off the hook.

Karl hovered over the faux candle centerpiece, his girth not allowing him to get very close to Adrian. "It's our job to convince him that elevating a district court judge is in everyone's best interest."

"Don't know how you do that—what your argument will be." Adrian cupped his coffee in both hands, wishing the solution to his problems would appear on its surface. "Seldom do they have the necessary experience."

"You let us worry about that, Judge." Karl's smile would freeze water. "We've got the governor's ear right now since we helped get him re-elected. It's important we use this impetus. He knows he owes us, but we've got to make it easy for him to choose our candidate." He straightened in his chair. "Say, isn't that Judge McGruter and

Judge Van Fleet being seated at that table inside—on the other side of that picture window behind you?"

Adrian shifted around in his chair. Indeed it was Elizabeth and Victoria. He hoped they wouldn't see him. He especially hoped they wouldn't see him with Karl Hawkins. Though there was nothing wrong with his having an occasional lunch with an attorney so long as he paid his own way, which he had every intention of doing, just being observed could cause talk.

"Yes," Adrian said, hoping Karl wouldn't do anything to draw the women's attention.

Karl prodded Adrian's forearm. "Got either of them in mind? The community thinks a lot of them—they're both brilliant women."

Elizabeth, whom Adrian had known for several decades, was honest and decent. They'd started practicing law around the same time. He would never even consider her, though she'd make a fine justice. Victoria, well, though they'd been lovers in the past, he knew her to be incorruptible as well. He still cared very deeply for her and would never serve her up to the likes of LLE. Her father had been his friend in college, too. No, he'd never give them Victoria.

"You think I would do that to either one of them?" Adrian moved his chair so it faced the river and again focused on the water flow. A thick tree trunk, with roots raised in the air like clawing fingers, floated by. The precipitation from farther north, the snow and the brief ice storm, had ravished the river banks

If only he could travel back in time. If only he'd known earlier what he knew now. If only he'd married a woman who would be happy raising their children in the country and sending them to state-supported schools. Even now his wife still engaged in social nonsense that cost them as much as his take-home pay and made ridiculous purchases, like his coat, for instance.

The waitress serving their steaks interrupted Adrian's reverie. Moments later, Elizabeth and Victoria appeared at his elbow.

"Judge Frothingham, hello," Elizabeth said, holding out her hand. "And Karl Hawkins. What brings you to our little old county on this cold winter day?"

Karl said, "Just breaking bread with my friend here. How are you ladies?"

Victoria reached her hand toward Adrian. "Hi, Judge. Long time no talk to." She shook Hawkins' hand as well. "Nice to see you, Mr. Hawkins. I guess it's been since election night last November."

"Yes—at the courthouse. Congratulations on your second term, by the way."

"Thanks," Victoria said. "Had one of your associates in my court earlier this week. Wanted to go on a ski trip with his family but had forgotten to put his vacation letter on file."

Karl nodded. "I heard about that. Thanks for letting him go."

"No problem. No harm done by continuing the case for another month."

"Well, we'd better let you gentlemen eat your meal before it gets cold," Elizabeth said. "Y'all didn't come all the way out here to visit with us. *Brrr.* I don't know how you stand it out here."

"Coats, ladies," Adrian said. "You left yours inside. Nice to see both of you." He met Elizabeth's eyes momentarily and rested on Victoria's.

"Take care," Karl said.

The two women hurried back inside, Elizabeth tugging the door closed with a bang behind them.

"There go two strong possibilities, Judge. We'd be happy with either of them. The governor would make his female constituents happy by having another female on the court. Some people think since the population is half women, half the courts ought to be women."

Anger rushed through Adrian. "Actually the population is more than half women," he said and popped a bite of steak into his mouth. He didn't want to discuss Elizabeth or Victoria. He couldn't ask it of either of them. Not only that, he wouldn't. They were both fine judges and a credit to the region.

"I think you should reconsider one of them."

Adrian clenched his jaw. "I understand what you're saying, Karl, but both of those women are beyond reproach." He poked his steak knife in the direction of Karl's eyes. "And unapproachable, their reputations impeccable."

"That's not what I hear." Karl leered as he stuffed a buttery lump of potato into his mouth.

What did Karl know? Anger blistered Adrian's insides. He stared Karl down. Good God, he needed to find a way out. "Listen to what I'm saying. It's out of the question. Totally out of the question. I'll find you someone, but it's not going to be either of them."

Adrian ate quickly, not engaging when Karl attempted chitchat. When Adrian finally excused himself, he insisted on paying his own tab, almost having to arm-wrestle Karl for it. He'd taken enough from Karl and his cronies. If nothing else, that was going to stop. Finally, he left, taking the outside stairs to the parking lot so he wouldn't have to walk past Victoria and Elizabeth.

His Blue Tooth system rang with an incoming call as he slung himself into his vehicle. He punched the button and heard Victoria's sultry voice.

"Calling to confirm our lunch tomorrow, Judge," Victoria said. "Westover Inn? I'll meet you at what time?"

"Where're you? Where's Elizabeth?" He cast about but saw no one in the parking lot.

"Beth's still at the table. I'm in the ladies' room. I checked all the stalls. Besides, we're not doing anything clandestine. We're just planning lunch."

"Then why are you checking the stalls?"

"Old habits, I guess. Besides, I don't want Beth to know about our lunch plans. She might be curious about it."

Seeing Karl exit the restaurant's front door, Adrian started his Land Rover and backed out of his parking space, wanting to put distance between them. "Okay, twelve-fifteen, Victoria, if your docket will allow. Mine's clear." He eased over the gravel driveway, avoiding the potholes. "How'd it go at commissioners' court?"

"Horrible. They're a bunch of jerks. I wish you'd tell me how you got your commissioners' court to install security. Mine are a bunch of idiots."

Adrian shook his head. She had never been one to mince words. "Lobbying, my dear."

"Lobbying, my foot. Are you sure money didn't change hands somewhere?" Her laugh was like a songbird's twitter. "Just kidding."

If she knew where money *did* change hands . . . Well, it wouldn't do for her to ever find out. "Some of the plaintiffs' bar made hefty contributions to the county judge's re-election campaign and a couple of well-placed donations to two commissioners' campaigns. All above board, I assure you, my dear."

"Humph," she said. "The Germania County Bar Association is too small, and the lawyers don't care enough to do that. They'll take their chances. I wouldn't be surprised if half of them weren't carrying or at least have some kind of weapon in their briefcases. And me stuck up there, a poor defenseless woman. Maybe I should start bringing my gun to the courthouse. After all, this is Texas. A girl's got to defend herself."

Surprised to hear her being so flippant about security after the beating she'd taken, he played along. Better than getting her back to the subject of Carr, one that oft reared its head. "You would carry a gun? What would it be, a long rifle? A derringer?"

"No, Sergio bought me *The Judge*. I didn't tell you that?"

Concern about her carrying around that pistol niggled at him. "I've heard of it, but no, I don't think it's advisable for you to have a gun. You keep working on your commissioners' court, Victoria. They'll see the merit of it soon enough." In his rearview mirror, Adrian saw Karl drive in the opposite direction. He breathed a sigh of relief. Just heading away from the man eased the tension in his shoulders.

"Sure, they'll see the merit as soon as one of us gets shot and our heirs file whatever they can to get past those stupid laws that limit plaintiffs. By the way, I've instructed Sergio to hire the best attorney he can find, figure out a way to get around that law. I want him to sue the pants off the county if I get killed in the line of duty."

A small shiver tickled his neck. "Don't talk like that." He wished he could say more, but long gone were the days when he could tell her how he felt. He would never get over her, but he had to keep his feelings to himself. She had Sergio now. Much as Adrian loved her, he was glad she had a man like Sergio who revered the ground she walked on but could handle her as well.

Her voice dropped low. "Security is just on my mind right now. Even though Carr has a while to do on his time, he'll still get out of jail someday—probably before summer."

Adrian stopped at the traffic light before taking the highway back to his county. "He'd be a fool to come around the courthouse again, my dear. Your sheriff will have his deputies looking out for you. He promised me."

"Oh, that's sweet, but Jim Bob is not, and has never been, my problem. It's the commissioners and apathy on the part of the other department heads and attorneys. Anyway, I'm trying not to dwell on the subject of Carr. Just wanted to check and make sure our lunch is still on."

"No problem, call me any time, dear girl, you know that."

"Good, because, Adrian, I have something very, very important to discuss with you. Something you can help me with. Something I'm sure you'll agree will make me a lot safer in the future. And it has nothing to do with courthouse security."

Chapter 11

THE NEXT MORNING, THOUGH SHE KNEW SHE had a particularly heavy docket to call, Torie wanted nothing more than to hunker down under the bedcovers. A winter storm had blasted through the night before, wind whipping through the trees, rain becoming hail, striking their metal roof, sounding like a young child set loose with sticks and a set of drums and cymbals. She snuggled in Sergio's arms until they both had to rush or be late for work.

Entering the courtroom later, docket clutched in one hand, Torie gave a passing thought to how cozy the early morning had been, especially in stark contrast to the bright lights and formalities of the courtroom only a short time later. As much as she loved being a judge, could any day at work be as good as a morning at home with Sergio?

Suits filled the courtroom. What seemed like hundreds of cheap suits, expensive suits, silk suits, and polyester suits filled with members of the bar overflowing counsel tables and the jury box and the front row of the spectators' section. All stood when she came in. All sat after she did. The already warm room would grow warmer before docket call ended and not just from the creaking, antiquated furnace boxes clinging to the wall under the windows. One glance at the lengthy docket told her it would be a long, hot, winter morning.

Her practice was to arrange the month's docket so it was a mixture of civil and criminal cases in no predictable order, requiring everyone to be ready on every case. She had learned to do that from a more experienced jurist who instructed new judges in "baby" judges' school. Not knowing where their case fell on the docket caused attorneys to be prepared for trial. When they were prepared for trial, they were more likely to settle civil cases. Defendants in criminal cases, more often than not, would plead guilty on the brink of trial.

She first called a burglary and set it for a plea. The second was an accident outside of town where a driver had swerved to miss a deer and careened into a grape orchard, damaging a fence and several rows of vines. She sent the attorneys out to continue their negotiations. The third was a divorce with a ranch to divide but no children. The fourth was a property boundary dispute. She continued down the docket, calling cases, conversing with lawyers, and making notations on docket sheets. After docket call, when every case that was going to trial was set down for jury selection on Friday afternoon, Torie took up the cases that needed a few additional minutes of her time.

Eventually she came to the final case and the last two lawyers in the courtroom. Standing up at one counsel table, a young male attorney said, "Good morning, Judge Van Fleet. David Souther, of Rogers, Hart, Paltry, and Godwin for the Movant."

"Good morning, Mr. Souther. You're new to this court and

perhaps to the bar, but it's customary when one enters a courtroom for the first time to extend the courtesy of approaching the bench, introducing oneself, and shaking the judge's hand."

"Oh, yes, ma'am," Souther said. He walked stiff-legged from his table to the bench, one of his shoes *thapping, thapping, thapping*, as he approached, and held up a trembling hand.

"It's okay. I'm not going to bite." She clasped his damp, cold hand. Chris Webster, the attorney at the other table, wore a smirk. "You can wipe that expression off your face, Mr. Webster. I remember what happened the first time you came into court to do a plea."

Souther glanced at Webster.

"You can explain how you fainted dead away to Mr. Souther later. Are you ready?"

"Yes, ma'am." Webster shifted from foot-to-foot. "Good morning."

"Good morning to both of you. You can go back to your table, Mr. Souther." She flicked her fingers at him. "You have a summary judgment?"

"Yes, ma'am," Souther said, paging through his file.

"But first, Your Honor," Webster said, "it's not on your docket because I just filed it, but I'd like you to hear another motion."

"You want me to hear a motion that's not on my docket? Which means the other side hasn't had three days' notice?" She glanced at the other attorney. "Is it some kind of emergency, Mr. Webster?"

A dark-headed Texas Ranger, dressed in his full uniform down to the Stetson in his hand, came through the door in the back of the courtroom and sat down on the back row, setting his briefcase on the floor in front of him. Ranger Richard Perez. Ranger Rick, she called him privately to her court reporter. Torie and he exchanged nods. He'd testified the year before about the theft of several large pieces of building equipment. Did he need something or did he just have a few minutes to kill and want to rest his feet?

Webster cleared his throat. "Judge, it's a Motion to Recuse."

Adrenaline swept through Torie. "Motion to Recuse? Me?" Heat rushed into her cheeks. No judge liked to be accused of having a conflict. "You've moved to recuse me?" She snatched the docket sheet out of the file, glancing at the parties' names. "I don't know these people—these litigants—Mr. Webster."

"If you'll read my motion, Judge…" Webster's face had grown blotchy. "It should be in the file. I asked the clerk to bring it over." He straightened his tie and cleared his throat again.

Mr. Souther clasped his hands before him and raised his eyes to the ceiling, like a penitent walking down the aisle after taking communion.

Torie fumbled with the loose paperwork inside the file. "Mr. Webster, did you give a copy to Mr. Souther?"

"Yes, Judge. He has a copy." Webster backed up until he'd put counsel table between himself and the bench. His face looked like he suffered from a bad sunburn.

"I've not read it either, Your Honor," Souther said.

"May we sit down while you peruse my motion, Judge?" Webster asked.

"Yes, of course. Be seated." Just what knowledge could she have that would prohibit her from hearing the case? She ran her finger down the narrative, searching for the conflict until she came to words that caused her to swallow a gasp of surprise. The words were so insulting, she felt like she'd been hit by a one-two punch.

"Movants in the Motion to Recuse allege that Respondent, The Honorable Victoria Rawlings Van Fleet, cannot be impartial in this matter as she received the maximum campaign contributions allowed by law from the Plaintiffs' law firm, that being $1,000.00 per individual attorney, in the last election which took place on November 4th of the year just past."

The words blazed on the page—burning into her like a brand. Torie slammed the motion back into the file as though touching the paper could make its contents true. The scorching implication flared through her body. She'd always been fair to everyone—whether solo practitioner or member of a firm, whether plaintiff or defendant, whether petitioner or respondent—and prided herself on her reputation for never showing favoritism. How dare Mr. Webster and his firm make such an allegation and, worse, put it in writing for the world to see. Staring down at the file, her eyes blurred in undeserved shame. What on earth could have possessed Mr. Webster's firm to file such a document?

The great deal of money from Mr. Souther's firm—though true it fell within the limits of the law—now appeared to have been taken as influence, at least by some. That firm hadn't been the only one to contribute thusly. She wet her lips, her mouth dry, and contemplated her response. Though such large contributions had been unusual in the past in rural judicial districts such as hers, change had come to Texas over a number of election cycles. Those changes had infected even the small counties in the Texas Hill Country. While money hadn't played a major part of campaigns just a few years earlier, now everything was about the money.

Could they really believe it of her, or was something funny going on? The only other explanation she could think of was judge shopping. The motion could be a ploy to get rid of her and get another judge assigned. Lawyers often came up with a variety of strategies to position their cases in a more favorable venue or stall for time. But why now, and why this case? Torie didn't have time to speculate. She had to deal with the motion at face value, whether or not the insult was intended.

"Sir," she said, her words almost too quiet to be heard, because she knew if she didn't speak softly she might let go and yell at the man. She flexed her fists and then her jaw, took a deep breath and let it out. She met Webster's eyes. "Mr. Webster, I don't see a proper ground for recusal stated in this motion."

Webster stood and stroked his nose, followed by his chin. "Judge, you should refer it to the regional presiding judge to decide. You shouldn't hear the motion."

Torie clenched her jaw. "What do you say, Mr. Souther?"

Souther dropped his hands and glanced from Torie to Webster. "I don't know, Judge. This is the first time I've come across anything like this."

"Well, I *do* know," Torie said. "I know the Code of Judicial Conduct as well as the next person, Mr. Webster. And the rules say if a *valid* motion is presented before any matter on the case is heard by the judge, and the judge declines to recuse herself, *then* the judge shall refer the motion to the administrative judge for a hearing." She clasped her dry, cold hands together. "But, here's the rub, Mr. Webster. Your motion states no *valid* objection. Show me in the rules where it says accepting campaign contributions from Mr. Souther's firm is grounds for recusal."

Webster shook his head. "I can't do that, Judge. The rules don't say that."

She slammed her palm onto the counter. "Well, what the heck then, Mr. Webster?"

"Judge Van Fleet, I don't know you very well, but what I've heard about you has always been good. You have a fine reputation among the bar and bench. I just thought you'd see the merit of my motion without it having to strictly conform to the rules. You have to admit, such a large sum of money could influence anyone."

Alarm rang in her ears. To grant such a motion would give credence to the allegations. "Not me, Mr. Webster."

"Well, you should at least refer it to Judge Frothingham for a hearing. You said so yourself." He had moved closer to the bench, but when he finished speaking he stepped back as if he thought she'd throw something at him.

"Maybe I should, sir, in your eyes, but not only is your motion without merit, it doesn't conform to the rules. It's not verified, so I'm not required to rule on it."

She snapped the file closed. "You get all this down, Jennifer?" she asked the court reporter. "Mr. Webster is saying I can be influenced by large campaign contributions." Pain throbbed in her temples. Her vision blurred. "That I can be bought."

"Yes, Your Honor," Jennifer said, glancing over her shoulder. "I wrote it all down." Her cheeks were flushed, too.

"Your Motion to Recuse is overruled, Mr. Webster. Now," she said, casting her eyes in the direction Souther, "do you want to argue your Motion for Summary Judgment or shall I just read the materials in the file and make a ruling?"

Souther and Webster exchanged glances.

Souther said, "Everything on our side of the case is in order, Judge. It's fine with me if you want to take your time and review our documents and make a ruling. No hurry from here."

Webster, whose face was such a dark red it was almost purple, stood at counsel table and twisted a ballpoint pen in his fingers.

"And you, Mr. Webster?" Her forehead drew together.

"Judge, I didn't mean to get you angry." His chin quivered.

"Well, you did, Mr. Webster. I saw from the pleadings that you're not lead counsel on this case. It's not even your signature on the Motion to Recuse." She jabbed her pen in his direction. "You go back to your bosses—the partners—whoever sent you over here and tell them I don't appreciate being insulted."

"Yes, ma'am, Your Honor. No problem. I'll go right back to the office. May I be excused?" His hands shook, and he fumbled with the latches on his briefcase, taking forever to slip his papers inside.

"I need a reply for the record on whether you want to argue your side of the Motion for Summary Judgment or whether I can take it under advisement."

"It's okay with me if you take it under advisement, Judge. I have no problem with that at all." Webster finished putting his things away and snapped his briefcase shut.

"I didn't think that would be a problem, Mr. Webster," she said. "You're both excused." Torie stood and glanced toward the back of the courtroom at the Ranger. "Can I help you, Ranger Perez?"

"No, ma'am. Just happened to be in the county and stopped by to say hello. Maybe some other time we can go to coffee."

"Another time, and I'll take you up on that offer, sir." She found it hard to smile and be friendly, the anger she'd felt a few moments earlier only just starting to drain away. "I hope you don't mind."

"Sure, Judge. I'm here every once in a while. I'll stop by again."

"You do that, Ranger. Thanks for understanding." She picked up the remaining files and strode off the bench.

Chapter 12

TORIE SCANNED THE HORIZON AS SHE DROVE to meet Adrian for lunch. Leafless oaks framed the roadway, their black and gray branches like withering fairy-tale crones reaching for the sky. Evergreen cedar and bent scrub oak filled in the landscape on dusky green ground, coarse clumps of rustic furniture for the birds that remained in the area for the winter. Bits of blue sky broke through the hazy mist as the day grew longer and warmer. The Texas Hill Country was at its most beautiful after a winter storm, wild and stark, tree branches blanketed with fingers of icicles.

She had calmed down since the court hearing, the accusatory court hearing, but driving through the countryside gave her time to think, made her realize how angry and, yes, hurt she'd been less than an hour earlier. Was that attorney really questioning her integrity? Unbelievable. She admired the stark scenery and calmed herself. Forced her thoughts to something else. Something equally provoking. The baby issue.

As she sped up, down, and around the hills to Adrian's home

county, her concerns and questions galloped right beside her. If she had a baby as Sergio wanted, Sergio would be pleased, and that would be a good thing. But what about her constituents? She'd just been re-elected, just started her new term, and within the year she'd be taking maternity leave. Aside from that, how would having a baby affect her chances for the appointment to the Supremes? Would the governor appoint a pregnant woman?

If she gave in and bore a child for Sergio, she could recover quickly and get back to work, taking off no more than a few weeks sick leave and the thirty days vacation to which she was entitled. She'd like to make her husband happy, though having a child was such a big responsibility and would change their way of life.

If she didn't have a baby, would Sergio leave her and find a wife who would? Had Sergio always wanted a child? Had he thought all along he could persuade her after their marriage, or had he changed his mind once they'd settled into married life, fully committed to each other, the relationship cemented?

Parking behind the restaurant, an old two-story clapboard house that had been reincarnated as an eatery, Torie picked her way across the mostly melted ice puddles and entered through the back door next to the kitchen, the route the locals took to get inside. The restaurant glowed with an aura of cozy warmth. The aromas of baked bread and grilled beef and onions were interwoven like a braid.

At first, Torie's eyes passed over the old man in the corner with his back to the wall. Then she realized who it was. Adrian's silver white hair had lost its sheen, had become a lifeless dried-up lemon-pith color. His pasty pallor showed every bit of his age. He used to pass for someone ten years his junior. He looked so much older than he had a few days earlier. When had he aged so?

The restaurant didn't have a window on either side of the corner so Torie could have her back to the wall as well. She didn't feel safe in front of a window. Thoughtful Adrian had chosen the table wisely. He knew full well she was still insecure and edgy, though Carr's assault had occurred a year earlier.

Adrian had transitioned from lover to mentor five years back, but he'd remained very considerate. He would have liked to continue their relationship. Torie was the one who had ended it. Not only did guilt often overwhelm her, but she wanted more out of life, a political future she could never have had if her immoral behavior were discovered.

She lifted her hand but knew he'd spotted her in the moments she'd assessed him. He was an all-knowing kind of person, like her father, always seeming to know what she was going to say before she said it. When they'd been seeing each other, they'd gotten to the point where they could finish each other's sentences. They'd had to be careful not to give any indication they knew each other better than any other lawyer and judge. Any hint of intimacy could have brought scandal down on their heads like a crashing chandelier.

Discovery wouldn't have been as bad for her, at the time, as it would for Adrian. She was having an affair with a married man, bad enough, but she was divorced. People would have talked about his being the judge when her ex kept dragging her back to court fighting for custody of their daughter, no matter that the affair hadn't even begun then. Face facts. It would have been awful all the way around if they'd been found out. And certainly she could never have run for election.

It would have been totally disastrous for Adrian since he was married. A married man with a wife and two, albeit grown, children. And embarrassing for the governor since the governor had appointed him as Presiding Judge for the Tenth Judicial Region. She pulled off her gloves as she reached the table.

Adrian stood and pulled out her chair. "Hello, Victoria."

"Hello, Judge." They shook hands, Adrian holding hers a tad longer than customary. Torie withdrew her hand and unbuttoned her coat. She draped it over the back of the adjacent chair and laid her purse and gloves on the seat. She didn't feel anything for Adrian any more, no tingling of her skin where his hand had touched hers, no thrill of any kind. She perceived their relationship as that of uncle to niece or a friendly ex-husband—who hadn't dragged her through the mud—or a true mentor to a student. Nothing more than affection for a good friend.

"You're looking well." Torie let the lie roll off her tongue. She always said something inane when they met, to cover that initial awkward moment when memories would flit through her mind. She picked up the menu and pretended to study it, hoping he couldn't see in her eyes that she'd lied, that she thought he looked ghastly. "You're like Sergio, you like the winter weather. Have you been skiing with your family this year? I should know that but must apologize because I don't remember if you told me."

"I never said I liked cold weather. I said I liked cold weather sports. And yes, we've been skiing twice, Colorado and Vermont." His eyes roved over her face. "Remember that scene from *White Christmas* when the two couples are in the dining car? 'Vermont can be lovely this time of year.'"

"Bing Crosby, I believe. Wish I skied. I might not mind going downhill, but it's the ski lift I can't manage. I'll stick to tennis where my feet never leave the ground." How many times had they had that conversation over the years? He knew she was afraid of heights and had been trying to overcome her fear for years. Why did she say stupid things? Okay, so she still felt awkward around him when they were alone. She admitted it. Though never to him.

"How long before your next hearing?" Adrian tented his fingers. "Do we have time for a nice long visit, or do you have to rush back?"

"Gotta be back by three." She scanned the menu and glanced at the blackboard for the specials.

The waitress took their drink orders. "Iced tea, unsweetened." To Adrian she said, "Yes, I know it's the dead of winter, but I like my iced tea."

"Coffee," Adrian said. After the waitress went away, he said, "They have beef stew today."

"Have you tried the quail?" She ran her finger down the menu, checking for all the things she liked.

"Quail is good. The special is trout."

Torie was fairly bursting, wanting to broach the subject of the Supreme Court, wondering what he'd have to say. She wanted to get the ordering out of the way before she asked him about it. She didn't want to wait until they finished eating. She knew not to rush Adrian, though. He was a very deliberate person, getting to everything in his own good time. Torie often wondered whether he sometimes dragged his feet to provoke others. She didn't want to believe he'd do something just to annoy *her*, not after what they'd been to each other. When the waitress returned with their drinks, Torie ordered the trout, added lemon and sweetener to her tea the way she liked it, and sat back in her chair, waiting for the appropriate time to speak her mind.

"So how've you been?" He wrapped his hands around the sides of the coffee cup.

"Still feeling frustration with the commissioners and the county judge about security, but okay. Carr will be getting out of jail soon. I'm still thinking of bringing my gun to chambers and getting one of those latch thingies under the desk, so I can reach under and unsnap it the minute I see him." As she spoke, his lips whitened.

"Don't do that. You'd only be inviting trouble. Besides, Carr is crazy and hot-tempered, but my guess is he's not stupid enough to come after you at the courthouse again."

"Thanks for that. Now I won't be able to sleep, worrying about him finding me at my house."

"Are you sleeping now?" He reached out his hand and pulled it back as though suddenly remembering he didn't have the right to touch her in that way any more

"Not unless I take something, which I do most nights." She sipped her tea, feeling the cold as it filtered down her throat. She squeezed her napkin to warm her hands after holding the glass. Every action seemed to be in slow motion, though she couldn't have said why.

"You've increased security at your house?"

She raised her eyebrows. "Put in an alarm system."

"Maybe you should get a dog."

She snorted. "I don't have time for dogs, Judge. You know what my schedule is like. It would be cruel and inhumane, though I wouldn't mind a little dog." In her mind's eye, she saw a fluffy bundle greeting her at the door, bouncing at her feet. "But I wouldn't do that to a dog. And I won't be one of those people who carries a dog around in a large purse."

"Too bad cats don't bark at strangers. A cat wouldn't mind being home alone all day."

"Yeah—a watch cat. She'd go *meow* when some unauthorized person came near the house." She tapped her fingers on the tablecloth. "Anyway, I have something else I'd like to talk to you about."

Adrian stretched his neck like a turtle, his lined face grim. Should she let him speak first? But no, he sat quietly, didn't seem to have a pressing need to tell her anything.

"We missed you at the regional lunch," she said to fill the silence. "You may have heard there was quite a discussion."

He didn't move or even draw a breath. His eyes followed her face, her hands.

"We discussed it at the regional lunch—Justice McWilliams' death and the opening on the Supreme court."

Adrian's eyebrows separated and drew back together. He pulled his hands under the table and sat up straighter.

"Judge—Adrian—do you think I have any chance of getting the appointment?"

Adrian remained poker-faced. She wanted a reaction from him, but he sat motionless. She, too, sat still, waiting and wondering what his response would be.

"So you're interested?" He ran his tongue across his lower lip.

"Isn't that what I just said?" She could have bitten her tongue the moment the words were out. "I apologize. I'm so tense." She sighed. "Do you know how much I want this?" She didn't know what she could say to make him understand how important it was.

"Of course. How many years have we known each other?" He picked up his coffee.

There was something about his tone. Something tickled the hair at the back of her head. She reached up and scratched. "Would I have a shot? Judge Dobbs and the others—well, not Beth—were ridiculing me again about family law and said I wouldn't stand a chance."

"I'm not sure this is the right time for you, Victoria." He peered into his cup.

She gripped the table's edge. "It is. It's just the right time. I'm forty-five years old. If I can get this appointment now, I could get a federal judgeship before I'm fifty. I've got years to work my way up. Don't you see?"

"There's a lot of competition out there. Tough competition."

"I'll do whatever I have to, Judge. With your help and my dad's, and since our senator likes me, I don't see why I shouldn't have a chance."

"I have this gut feeling …" He wouldn't meet her eyes.

"Oh, *a gut feeling* . . . I want this, Judge. I think I can get it." Her words came out like a challenge.

He fingered the coffee cup. "Victoria, this is just not the right time for you. You need to trust me on this."

Something wasn't right. His expression. His tone. The way he looked at her. "I don't understand. Why wouldn't you want me to go for it? Are you interested yourself?"

He shook his head. "It's not that."

"What is it then? Don't you want to help me? You always said you'd do anything for me—support me in all my dreams and ambitions."

His eyes focused over her shoulder. His chest inflated as though bursting with something he wanted to say. "Are you sure this is the right time of your life for a jump to the Supreme Court? You just got re-elected. What does Sergio say?"

"Sergio's known since before we were married that this is what I wanted." Sergio had always given in to her in the past. He knew she didn't want to have a baby and be stuck at home when all the action was out in the world. In the courthouses. In the political back rooms that still existed, would always exist no matter what the rhetoric to the contrary. Sergio. She'd told him when they'd dated, let him know she was ambitious, that children didn't fit into the picture. He knew what she wanted, how high she was aiming, but then she'd found out after they'd been married that he really didn't understand. He'd heard but hadn't comprehended. *No entiendo.* She'd reiterated. She didn't want a family. She'd had one, and it hadn't worked out. As much as she couldn't quit thinking about it, a baby just didn't fit in with her plans.

The waitress came with their order and both clammed up until she was gone.

"Something the matter?" Adrian asked.

"I was just thinking of Sergio. Can I confide in you, Judge?" She picked up her knife and fork, her eyes on her plate as she sought the words.

"Of course, my dear. That's what I'm here for. To help you."

"Sergio wants me to have a baby." There. She'd said it aloud. She glanced at Adrian.

Adrian's eyebrows shot up again. "But you don't want to?"

"Of course not. I told him about Cassie's suicide when we first started dating, that I'd never risk having another child, but now he's after me to change my mind. I think he's having a mid-life crisis."

She glanced at her watch and forked a Brussels sprout, afraid to see in his face that he would not support her goal.

"I'm afraid that would affect the appointment, Victoria. You'll have to make a choice—the bench or the baby." His hand quivered as he picked up his fork.

Did that mean he would support her? "It's no real choice for me, Judge. I don't want a baby. I want that bench, and I'm willing to do whatever I have to."

They spent the next twenty minutes discussing the issue, and Torie couldn't help but feel she was getting nowhere with him. What was he not sharing with her?

"You do have other options," Adrian said finally. He put a forkful of food in his mouth and stared at her as he chewed. He swallowed and slurped his coffee.

She stopped eating, waiting to hear what he thought her options were.

"You could forego this appointment and have the baby now. Then later, when you're a bit older and the child has started school, for example, you could vie for an opening. You'd have a chance to lay some groundwork, allay any suspicions that you'd be leaving the bench to be with your child—you could rearrange your docket to deflect the arguments that are sure to come up that you're a family court judge, that there are already enough family court judges on the higher bench." By the time he stopped talking he was leaning halfway across the table, jabbing his fork in her direction.

"Sounds like you've given this a lot of thought. So you did think of me when you heard McWilliams died."

Adrian wouldn't meet her eyes. He cut his food into very small pieces and put more in his mouth.

Torie put her fingers on his knife hand. "Are you trying to discourage me? I thought you would be on my side. You know one of the reasons I want to be on the Supreme Court is that I can do more for families. I'll have more power and can help more people."

"I *am* on your side, Victoria. This just isn't the right time for you." He stared above her shoulder as if there were an interesting painting on the wall behind her.

"Is there some reason you don't want me to have it? Are you already committed to helping someone else? If you are, just say so."

Adrian went back to his food. He took several bites, chewing and swallowing, still not looking at her. Eventually, he said, "I can't explain my reservations. Could you just take my word for it and wait for another opportunity?" His eyes finally met hers.

Flames licked at her cheeks. "Not if you can't tell me why."

"Trust me on this." His words came out like a plea.

"I'm confused. You want me to give up the idea, I get that, but I have to know why." She stared him down. "Don't I deserve an explanation?"

Adrian's head wagged. "I can't give you one, Victoria. All I can do is ask you to trust me."

Fury filled her throat. She swallowed several times. "Why don't we just skip lunch?" She knew she wasn't behaving well, but at that moment, she didn't care. She wadded up her napkin and threw it on the table as she rose.

Adrian grabbed her wrist. "Don't go, Victoria."

She stopped and stared at him. There was something in his eyes, they seemed very sad, but as quickly as it came, the look disappeared and a fierce expression overcame his face.

"Don't be angry with me, Victoria. It's against my better judgment, but I'll help you. If you want it that badly, I'll help you."

"All right!" Knowing she was too loud, she glanced at the people at the nearby tables to see whether she'd alarmed anyone. "Now you're talking." She dropped back into her chair and picked up her napkin. "Thank you, friend."

"You do realize it'll be a lot of work securing the appointment? You'll have to get support from business owners in the party as well as the bench and bar. People will have to write letters to the governor in your behalf. You need to meet with the Germania County party chairman as well as the state party chairman. And, of course, the governor. He likes to meet with as many of his potential appointees as time permits."

Torie listened with awe. She'd persuaded Adrian to help her. She could persuade the others. She knew it. "That's a good thing, isn't it?"

"He appoints a huge number of people to boards and benches."

"Well, none of this is a problem, Judge. I told you I'm willing to do anything I have to. We can discuss it more." She replaced her napkin in her lap and picked up her fork. "Let's finish our lunch. I, at least, need to get back to court this afternoon." She was having trouble maintaining her dignity. Gleeful thoughts threatened to run rampant. If Adrian was going to help her, she knew she'd get the appointment. He had a lot of influence. Soon she'd be Justice Victoria Rawlings Van Fleet instead of plain old judge.

A frown stretched across Adrian's face. "We'll have to get busy right away. You'll have to talk to your father, get his immediate assistance, as well as that of the coffee club group he's been such a part of. And Sergio. He's got to be onboard." He followed those statements with a huge sigh and a look in his eye that Torie had never seen, almost as though he wanted to cry.

Delight filled Torie. Her father was definitely in her corner. And Sergio. She could be persuasive. He'd come around. "No problem. No problem at all." She finished her meal with relish. "Hey, you said you had something you wanted to talk to me about?"

"Oh, yes, on a different subject." He hesitated. "I was wondering about what you said yesterday when Karl Hawkins and I were having lunch."

"What did I say?" She couldn't remember saying anything out of the ordinary.

"About giving that attorney from Karl's firm a continuance so he could take his family on a skiing trip."

"Yes, Steve Merritt. You know him?"

"No, that's not the point. This is awkward, Victoria, and I hate to put you on the spot."

Torie felt like a match had flared in her abdomen. "Judge, what is it?"

"Well, Karl thought—wondered—and so I thought I'd just come out and ask you. You can decline to answer if you like."

What was Adrian getting at? "What did Mr. Hawkins *wonder*? And what are you *wondering*, Judge?"

Adrian waited until the waitress had topped off his coffee. "Uh—you didn't grant that out of time Motion for Continuance because—uh—their firm had made a hefty contribution to your campaign?" Adrian held his cup between them, his elbows on the table.

Torie shivered. "Of course not. I would never do that. Never.

What's going on? That's the second time I've had an allegation made against me."

"It wasn't exactly an allegation—just the way Hawkins' mind works. Let's forget it."

She had a bad feeling about what Adrian said. She couldn't put her finger on it, but something wasn't quite right. "No. This morning an attorney filed a Motion to Recuse me from hearing a case because the firm on the other side had given me sizable contributions last November."

"That's disturbing. But I didn't get a fax from your office this morning—a referral on a recusal from you."

"That's because I denied it. They didn't have any grounds—the rules don't apply in that instance."

Adrian cleared his throat. "No, of course they don't."

"I've never been so insulted. How could they question my integrity like that?"

"Have you looked at the underlying issue? I mean, it's not grounds, but you should have referred it to me as the Regional Presiding Judge to rule on it."

"Well, I would have, but it wasn't verified, so I didn't have to."

"What was the underlying issue they were so worried about?"

"Water rights, what else these days?" She gave him a wry look. "Let's say XYZ Corporation filed a Motion for Summary Judgment against ABC Homeowners group claiming ABC doesn't have any right to interfere with them building a golf course for their new development. And they can't force them to take gray water instead of regular water."

"I see. How are you going to rule? Have you decided?"

"I'm still thinking about it, and I have a little more research to do, but as angry as I am I can still be objective. I'm probably going to rule for ABC, anyway. Deny the Motion for Summary Judgment."

"Is that a wise idea?"

"If it went to trial, it could go either way."

"Then why not rule for XYZ?"

"If I rule for XYZ, there won't be a trial. If I rule for ABC, then a jury can decide, if they've paid their jury fee, which I feel sure one of them has—though I haven't looked."

"You don't think the law favors XYZ?"

"What are you getting at, Judge?"

"Just asking a question, that's all."

A chill filled the air. Adrian was behaving oddly—very oddly—questioning her like that. The case was her problem, not his. If she needed to discuss the facts with anyone, she would, but now was not the time. She changed the subject back to the Supreme Court appointment. She wasn't going to let Adrian influence how she ruled in that or any case. But she would let him help her get on the high court.

Chapter 13

A S SHE DROVE BACK TO HER OFFICE, TORIE mulled over Adrian's behavior during the latter part of their lunch. They'd dissected all the possible scenarios and who her competition likely would be. Something wasn't right with Adrian, though, but she hadn't been able to discern what it was. He seemed on edge, not the smooth-talking, self-confident senior statesman she'd known so well.

When he'd walked her to her Mercedes, she took his arm. "I can tell something isn't quite right with you. Problems at home or with the kids?"

He brushed bits of ice off her car door handle. "No." He opened the door for her. "There's something going on I'm not free to discuss with you, my dear."

She'd had the brief impression he wanted to follow up that statement with one like, *"Don't worry your pretty little head about it."*

She looked into his face for some indication he wanted to talk more, but his eyes were lidded.

"I'll be in touch about the next step you need to take." His lips had continued to move, but no words came out, like he was silently repeating what he'd said. Then, "Oh, and Victoria, do what you can to find out in your own courthouse who your opposition is." He'd shut the door and stepped back. "*Drive safely*," he mouthed, and his lips did that moving thing again.

Definitely something was up. His aloofness and strange mannerisms left her feeling uneasy, but she could only assume it was nothing to do with her and none of her business. She had her own problems to worry about, including how to tell Sergio of her decision.

She was on her way, her plan beginning to gel. Adrian was firmly in her corner. Now she needed to solidify Sergio's support in light of his recent efforts to convince her to have a child. Getting him to see her viewpoint could take some persuasion, but she would remind him of the discussions they'd had prior to their marriage, of her specific statements of her career goals, of his stated understanding and support.

It also wouldn't hurt to get Beth's backing. Beth was a good friend and had some connections Torie didn't have. She wanted Beth on her side, putting in a good word for her, garnering support for the appointment.

After Torie arrived at the courthouse, she peeked through the window to Beth's court. A jury populated the box, and Beth was on the bench. Torie had several hearings that afternoon, so she didn't have a chance to speak with her before the end of the day when she traipsed across the hall and closed the door behind her.

Beth was on a conference call, first one voice coming from the speakerphone, then another—two males sounding like they were playing one-up. She waved Torie to a chair. Torie made herself comfortable and glanced at the diplomas and certificates gracing the walls.

Beth had graduated summa cum laude from her undergraduate school and cum laude from law school. She'd been in office five terms, since she'd been in her late thirties. There was a photograph of her with the governor who'd appointed her when her predecessor had died in office of a heart attack. She'd been re-elected every election, having been opposed only once. Beth—who was steadfast, honest, trustworthy, and well read—was loved by the bar. She'd never expressed any ambitions past the district court bench until the recent teasing at the luncheon with the other judges. She would probably die right there in the Germania County Courthouse following in the footsteps of her predecessor.

Beth hung up the phone. "God, I hate telephone discovery hearings. You can never tell what's happening on the other end of the line."

"I know. You wonder if the whole law firm is sitting in the office with the attorney, passing notes commenting on your rulings."

"Are we both paranoid?" Beth scribbled in the file and closed it, setting it to one side of her desk.

"I know I am."

"So what did you want to see me about? Charlotte told me you'd called several times. Why didn't you text me?"

"I didn't want to put anything in writing." Torie glanced at the door. "Will we be undisturbed?"

Beth's brow wrinkled when she looked at Torie. She walked

to the window and glanced out. "Everyone else's gone home. The parking lot's empty except for our cars and the security guard's."

"I don't want this to get out yet. I mean, I haven't even told Sergio."

"What is it? Is something wrong? Are you pregnant?"

Annoyance surged through Torie. "God, no. What would make you ask that?"

"Something you haven't told Sergio. I just thought—"

"No," she stressed again. "It isn't that, but Sergio *has* been after me to have a baby. Has he been talking to you?"

"What would make you think that?"

"He has, hasn't he? When?"

Beth laughed. "At the Bar Christmas party. Torie, he wants a child so badly. Your child. You know a lot of women have babies and go back to work. A lot of women judges. You've seen them at the judicial conferences pregnant out to here." She held her hand a foot from her belly button.

Torie crossed her legs. "I know he does, but I'm not in the baby-making business anymore. I'm too old and have other plans."

"He loves you so much. Don't you want to make him happy?"

"You sound as chauvinistic as most of the men I know." She repositioned herself in the chair, anger tearing through her like wildfire. Couldn't anyone understand where she was coming from? She'd had a child. The child had killed herself. Torie couldn't and wouldn't risk having another child. "This isn't what I came to talk about."

"Don't get angry. I'm not the one who wants to see you barefoot and pregnant."

"It's not a joke. I notice you don't have any children."

Beth reared back like she'd been hit. "Torie . . . that was mean. Some people haven't been lucky enough to have one husband, much less two."

"Oh, I don't know what's the matter with me. I've been so on edge. I'm sorry. I apologize for that remark. But can I tell you the news? And it has nothing to do with a baby."

"Well, sure. The baby is a discussion for another day."

"No, it's not. At my age it's not even a consideration. You forgive me?"

"Women your age are having babies every day, but anyway … what is it?"

"Well, you know that opening on the Supreme Court?"

Beth's eyes had become a darker gray-blue, a color that Torie had only ever seen when Beth was upset about something.

Torie didn't want to leave anything to doubt. "I think I have a good chance of getting appointed by the governor. I'm going for it. I think I can cinch it, but I'm going to need your help."

Beth studied a notepad as she doodled on it. "Who's backing you?"

"Adrian. I met him for lunch. Did you already know?"

Beth put her pen down. "I'd heard. I think a lot of people have heard the rumors. Does Frothingham know when the governor is going to make the appointment?"

"In the not too distant future. There's so much to do. I need letters of reference from the legal community as well as the political community."

Beth nodded. "Yes, I know." Her voice held an odd tone.

"You weren't . . . "

"Thinking of going for it? It had crossed my mind."

"Really? So many years on the district court bench. I didn't think—"

"You didn't think I had any ambition past here? It never occurred to you I might want more out of life? No husband, no kids, just stuck on a district court bench until I died? Is that what you thought?" A frown pulled at the corners of her mouth.

Torie's face grew warm as Beth parroted her thoughts almost exactly "Beth—"

"I understand where you're coming from." Her eyes had changed to steely gray. "I'm not demonstrative like you. I don't fight with the commissioners. I go along to get along. Torie, I was picking my battles in this courthouse when you were still practicing law—maybe before you ever got your law license."

Torie cupped her elbows, her hands on her stomach holding back the smoldering sensation she felt as she heard Beth out. "Why didn't you ever say anything? Why didn't you go for an appointment before?"

"I did. You just didn't know about it. I tried for the court of appeals about eight years ago. It didn't even get off the ground."

It was true, Torie hadn't known. She'd thought they were good friends, but there was so much she didn't know that dated back way before Torie took the bench. "What stopped it?"

"I didn't have the connections. But, Torie, I've been working really hard to make contacts, laying the groundwork, doing everything one is supposed to do to get the nod." She pounded on her desk pad. "It's been behind the scenes, quiet, but I've been doing the hard work for years now."

Torie's throat tightened. "And so we're going to be competing with each other."

"Did you think you were going to waltz right in and take this from me?"

Her face grew hotter as Beth chastised her. "I didn't know—it never occurred to me you'd go for it."

"It's not just me. There are others, a lot of people sick of being stuck out here in central Texas with not much action going on. You thought it was going to be easy?"

"I never said that. This is terrible. I don't want to compete with you. You're my best friend."

"So don't go for it." She arched an eyebrow in a challenge.

Torie huffed. "You can't expect me to do that."

"I was pulling your leg." Beth pushed back in her chair and leaned down, rubbing her stockinged feet together and putting on her shoes.

Torie rounded Beth's desk. "We've never been in competition before. We've always supported each other."

Shrugging, Beth said, "Never been anything to compete for. We've always gone after the same things that would benefit both of us. Staff raises. Better working conditions. Increased car allowance. New furniture. We've always asked the commissioners for the same things. You were always there for me."

"And you for me. So what are we going to do?"

Chuckling, Beth stood and grasped Torie's arm. "We can argue for each other in the alternative. I'll go for the position and tell the governor that if he doesn't choose me, to pick you."

"Ha. Ha." Like either of them would get the opportunity to do that. It didn't work that way, and they both knew it. Still, she'd play along. She knew that's what Beth was doing as well. "I could do that. It'd be the next best thing. If I don't get it, I'd like for you to get it. It'd be fun having you review my rulings." It was hard to be jovial when tears tugged at her. She didn't want anything to come between them. How much more awkward could it get?

"Yeah, right. Honestly, sweetie, this isn't a terrible spot we're in. It's not deadly." She reached for her purse and a tote bag. "I'll walk you out."

Torie hooked her arm in Beth's. "It's just so uncomfortable. You're such a good friend."

"I feel the same way."

"Well, I know one thing, we need to stick together even when we're competing with each other. The judges in the other districts have probably already heard the news that both of us are interested even though we were noncommittal with them. Sometimes I wonder whether our phones are tapped." Torie glanced at Beth's desk phone and pretended to lift it and listen.

"Everyone has their contacts, insider knowledge. But let's make this a strictly professional competition," Beth said. "Let's not let it come between us, girlfriend."

"Sometimes I feel like you're the sister I never had," Torie said.

"I feel that way, too. So, I guess I can't support you. Can't write letters on your behalf and vice versa."

"Right. Give me a hug." They stopped outside Beth's office door and hugged each other like close friends who had been apart a long time.

"I needed that," Beth said when Torie stepped back.

"May the best lady win."

They both laughed. They sighed in unison. Their eyes met. Both looked more than a mite tearful then.

"I guess I'll go home now and face the music with Sergio."

In a softer tone, Beth said, "I still think you should consider the baby thing. You were a good mother and are young enough to go for a higher court later."

"You sound like Adrian—and my mother, but thanks."

"Look, I know what you're thinking, Torie. You need to put all of that out of your mind. It's ancient history. You were a good mother. You know you were."

Why did everyone insist on telling her she was a good mother? That wasn't what she wanted or needed to hear. She'd thought she'd been a good mother right up until the time Cassie had died. She'd had to reconsider since then.

"Take care. See you tomorrow." She crossed the hall. Quiet enveloped the offices and courtroom. She picked up her messages and saw one from her husband saying he had to work late. Relieved, she plopped into her chair. She had a lot to think about. The Supreme Court and babies and what she was willing to risk in order to achieve the former. How could she please her ever-loving, wonderful, *young* husband without becoming a mother? All of it threatened to overwhelm her.

And that included the Motion for Summary Judgment. She pulled the file off her credenza and separated the supporting documents into two piles. She would study both and make a decision with no help from Adrian or anyone else. And she didn't care what anyone said. She knew she'd never show partiality to one side or the other no matter what.

Chapter 14

TORIE MEANT TO TELL SERGIO ABOUT THE opening on the Supreme Court that Friday, but he had problems at the resort and arrived home after she'd gone to bed. She meant to tell him on Saturday. Again her plans were thwarted by his having to literally put out fires at the resort. He didn't return until late Saturday evening, exhausted from all the commotion, and would have fallen right into bed, but Torie made him shower first because he smelled like smoke. Sunday morning was a scramble to get to church so Torie put it off once again, targeting that night when they'd finally have some time together.

On Sunday afternoon, when they'd gone to her parents' home for lunch after church, Torie was hoping to have a private conversation with her father, but things didn't turn out right for that either. When they arrived, they found her brother, Howard, and his family there.

Torie raised a hand at her brother as she leaned down and kissed her dad on his unshaven cheek. He smelled like bacon. "Missed you at church," she said.

"Didn't sleep well last night." He squeezed her forearm. "You see the Rockets' play the other night?"

"No, Dad," she said. He would never realize she didn't follow sports, no need reminding him. "Sergio's been working a lot," she said, as if that had anything to do with whether or not she watched a game.

"Sergio, how's it going?" Howie glanced up from the game they were currently watching. Sergio shook the other men's hands and stepped past them, settling onto the sofa next to Howie.

"Hey, Sis. You like this TV Dad and I went and got?"

Annoyance tugged at Torie. "Where's Mom?"

"Back in the bedroom doing something, ask Mary," her brother said. "You missed a great play, Sergio. Just a minute ago."

"Who's winning?" Sergio asked as Torie walked away. She didn't even know who was playing. Didn't know. Didn't care.

She stopped momentarily in the kitchen to greet Mary. "Hey, sweetie." Steam filled the air from boiling potatoes and onions. "You've got it all under control, I see. Where're the kids?"

"They're in the playhouse in the backyard. You know kids don't feel the cold like us old folks."

"Speak for yourself. I've got a lot of life in me yet. I'll see them later. What's for lunch? Pot roast?" When Mary said yes, Torie almost laughed. Mary's standard meal, but she was a good mother, a good wife to Howie, and one of the nicest people in the world. Torie headed down the hall to see her mother.

Her mother sat at her sewing machine with yards of flowery

fabric in her lap and more laid out on a large cutting table set up in the middle of the room.

"Hi, Mom. What's all this?" Torie kissed her mother's cheek.

White and yellow daisies were everywhere. "I'd promised Lily I'd have the new curtains for her room ready when she came today but didn't get them finished, so I called Mary to fix lunch while I finished them. How do you like the fabric Lily picked out?"

"Certainly cheerful. I'm surprised she didn't want white and yellow calla lilies."

"She said, and I quote, 'Eww, I don't want my room to look like my name.' She wanted daisies. She wants her room to look like a field of daisies. When I finish the curtains, I'm to do a bedspread. And Mary's buying yellow sheets and a white rug to put beside the bed."

"Do I want to know what she wants on the walls?"

"She's a strong-willed little girl," her mother said. "Like her aunt."

Torie responded with a smirk. "She's a little doll. I'm fixing to go outside and see what both kids are up to."

Her mother finished running up a seam and clipped the threads. "You doing okay, honey? You look a bit tired."

Her mother knew nothing of politics, so Torie wasn't going to tell her just yet what was going on. And she'd never mention she didn't sleep well when Sergio had to be at the resort. She saw no reason to bother her mother with that information. Like everyone else, her mom thought she should have recovered from Carr's beating. No one but Sergio knew about Torie's nightmares, and even he wasn't aware of how little sleep she actually got. "Stayed up too late last night is all."

"Well, run along and see if you can help Mary with lunch, dear."

"Okay, Mom." Torie walked back into the den and knelt next to her father, "Dad, I desperately need to talk to you."

He patted her hand and dragged his eyes from the TV to her face, but his attention was not on her. He glanced back at the screen, his body jerking in response to a play.

Torie stood. "Maybe after lunch, after you're through watching the game."

"Thanks, honey child." He patted her arm again but didn't look at her.

She had two choices. One of them she knew was expected of her. Help with the meal. At what point in a woman's life would she not be expected to prepare the meal for the menfolk while they did their manly thing—whether it be frying the fish they brought home for dinner, watching basketball, or working on a car? Her other choice was to take part in the men's activities.

Part of her felt guilty if she didn't help with the meal and the cleanup, and the other part of her resented it. The resentment side far outweighed the guilt side. But usually she just chipped in and helped.

Wait, she had a third alternative. The children. Torie grabbed her coat and went out into the backyard where the kids were still playing. "Stevie, Lily Ann," she called when she opened the door to the playhouse. "May I join you?"

They rushed to her and encircled her with their arms. "Cold, Aunt Torie. I want to go inside," Stevie said.

"He's such a baby," Lily said. "Is lunch ready?"

"Why don't you show me what you've been doing in the playhouse for a minute?" Torie shivered and rubbed her hands together.

"Okay, Aunt Torie, but then can I go inside?" Stevie raised his face up to her.

"You're not that chilly, are you?" She tousled his hair. The children ran back inside the playhouse, and Torie stooped down to follow them, not that she was that much taller than they were. Inside, under a pretend window, were a tiny table and chairs. Lily Ann pulled one out and sat down on it. Torie did the same.

Stevie sat on a little plastic sofa. A little boy-size football lay on the floor beside it. He put his feet on the football.

"We're playing house," Lily said. "Stevie is the Dad. He plays football and watches TV."

Torie nodded. "And I guess you're the mom?"

"I fix lunch and read my book." She picked up a well-used children's book from the floor and pretended to read.

"You know, I'm wondering something," Torie said. "What do you want to be when you grow up? Stevie?"

He got up from the sofa. "A coach. I want to coach my little boy's team like Dad."

"You could coach your little girl's team," Torie said.

"Yeah, I guess. At our school the girls have girl coaches. Can we go inside now?"

No surprise there. "Lily Ann, what do you want to do when you grow up? Want to be a judge like me?"

Lily shook her head. "I want to be a nurse."

Torie's back ached from only a few minutes in the little chair. "You could be a doctor."

"Okay," Lily Ann said, jumping up and running into the yard. "Let's go eat."

So playing with the kids didn't work out. Torie ushered them inside and removed her coat again.

"You two wash up. We're about to sit down," Mary called when she stepped out of the kitchen. "Want to give me a hand here, Torie?"

The table was already set. Torie poured the vegetables into separate bowls and placed them at the table's far end. Once the food was out, her father took his place at the head of the table. He just about always was a traditionalist, but he also could keep an eye on the television from there. Her brother sat to his left. Torie sat to his right. It would have been the perfect time to speak to her father about the Supreme Court, except she hadn't told Sergio. And the basketball game was still on.

They all joined hands. Torie's father said grace, ending with their traditional hand squeeze before beginning to eat.

"Looks good, Mary," Torie's father said. "Thanks for helping Debra out." Torie had placed the serving dishes next to his plate. He served himself and passed the dish to his left so Torie's brother was next. That always irritated Torie. Why should her brother get the next best slice of roast? Not that she really cared about roast. But it galled her that her brother always had second choice right after her father. The food always went to the left. For once she wished her father would pass the food to the right.

She was no less a person than her brother because she was female. She recalled the meeting with the other judges a few days earlier and their statements that another family law judge didn't need to be on the Supreme Court bench. First of all, that was a sorry attitude whether or not she was a family law judge, which she was not. Secondly, it shouldn't matter where a judge's focus had been as long as the candidate had half a brain. Third, their whole attitude infuriated her, but she couldn't let on any more than she already had.

She remembered what the female justices of the U.S. Supreme Court had gone through at the confirmation hearings. Any little statement, any little thing said as an office holder or even before, could be captured and used against a person in perpetuity.

Ergo, Torie had to keep her mouth shut.

And so she waited for the pot roast, the onions, the green beans, and the potatoes to circle around the table and finally arrive. Though simmering inside, she exchanged pleasantries as they ate. And as soon as her father could choke his food down, he abandoned them and his dirty dishes at the table and went back into the living room to watch the rest of the basketball game.

A few minutes later, Howie did the same.

Sergio, however, knew better. He finished his meal, picked up his plate, utensils, and glass and took them into the kitchen where he rinsed them and put them in the dishwasher. Sergio had been raised by a working mother who insisted all her children be treated the same. Everyone pitched in. Howie had been raised by a stay-at-home mother who believed the man was the king of the castle.

Finally, the basketball game having come to an end, Howie packed up his family and went home. Of course, by then Mary and Torie had cleaned up the table and the kitchen. And Debra had kept sewing in the back room, determined to send Lily home with the curtains.

"If you don't mind, Sergio," Torie said as soon as the door closed on her brother, "I'd like a few minutes alone with my father."

Sergio started to get up, but Torie stopped him. She took the remote and gave it to him. "Dad, let's go out onto the porch." The porch was enclosed and had a space heater, which she'd turned on before their late lunch. They could close the door and have some privacy. Excluding her husband was awkward, but it was politics. Her father, who had been active in party politics since he'd been a young man, had always given her his guidance when it came to politics. He might be a traditionalist, but once she'd made up her mind to run for judge, he supported her one hundred percent.

"We'll be back in a few minutes. You don't mind, do you?"

Sergio shrugged and followed her with his eyes. "I'll find the news."

She pulled on her father's arm until he climbed out of his recliner. They walked arm-in-arm to the porch where she opened the door, hit the light switch, nudged her father in, and closed the door behind them. He sat on the glider, and she pulled up a chair opposite him, knee to knee.

"Dad, I have a chance to be on the Texas Supreme Court," she blurted. She watched his face for a reaction, hoping for a favorable one.

His eyebrows flew up. "You mean an appointment?"

"I met with Judge Frothingham on Friday. Justice McWilliams was killed in an accident. You may have seen it in the paper. Adrian says if we play it right, I have a chance to get the appointment from the governor."

Her father rocked back and glanced at the ceiling. "Whew. What a feather in your cap. It's what you've always wanted, isn't it, honey child?" He took her hand in his warm one.

"You know it is," she said, unable to keep the elation out of her voice. She was on the verge of giggling like a little girl. "Are you pleased?"

"You bet. Just to be considered is an honor. Those good old boys in the other courts will wet their pants when you get the nod."

"I've had a run-in with them." She told him about the lunch conversation a few days earlier.

"I've never understood that attitude. Seems like most of the people in the world go to family court for one reason or another."

Annoyance tugged at her once more. Not him, too. "Thanks, Dad, but I'm not a family court judge. I hear other things. Beth and I just have an agreement about the cases we hear in this county. It's not like I haven't had other experience—like I don't hear other cases."

"You don't have to protest so much. I understand. What does Beth say about all this?"

Beth was one of his favorite people. He always called her the rock; said she was as solid and good as they come.

Torie cleared her throat. "Beth's vying for it as well."

Her father's lower lip stretched over his teeth in a grimace. "That's too bad."

"We're okay with it. I wouldn't be as happy if she got the nod, but I'd rather her than one of those goofballs. God, I can't believe their constituents keep electing them. Except Bo. He's not so bad."

"Beth's a fine lady and a finer judge."

"And a good friend."

"But we want you to get it, don't we? So, tell me, what can I do to help?"

Torie grabbed her father and hugged him. "I'm so excited I can hardly stand it." She pulled a piece of paper from her pocket. "Here's a list I made for you." She laid it on his lap and went around behind him so she could read over his shoulder. "You'll recognize the names. You can start by contacting every person on this list and see if they'll recommend me. If they'll do so without a meeting with me, all well and good, but if they want to meet with me, fine. Whatever it takes. I'll need a whole network of people to speak to the governor. And eventually, I'll be meeting with him myself."

"That's my girl. Already organized. Good going. I'm ready to get started, too." He flexed his fingers like he was ready to get to work.

"Just one thing, Dad. Don't mention this to Sergio. I haven't had a chance to talk to him about it."

"I'm sure he'll be as pleased as the rest of the family." He rose from his chair and pressed his hand to his stomach.

Torie grabbed his arm. "You okay?"

He cleared his throat. "Too much beef, I suspect. Indigestion." He hugged her. "I'm very proud of you."

Her father's arms were warm and firm. She snuggled against him like she used to do when she was small. At that moment, there was nowhere she would rather be.

Chapter 15

ON THE DRIVE HOME, SERGIO SAT SO STIFFLY IT looked like rigor mortis had set in. Torie touched his gloved fist, which lay on the armrest between the seats. "You enjoy the game?"

He didn't respond.

She tapped his arm to get his attention. "I said, 'Did you enjoy the game?'"

He jerked his arm away. The headlights of an oncoming car illuminated his face, revealing a twitch at his right eye and lips pressed tightly together.

Was he cross because she'd asked for some alone time with her father?

When she and her father had come in from the porch, they'd found Sergio in the back bedroom, in deep conversation with her mother as she straightened her sewing things. In the three years Torie and Sergio had been married, Sergio had developed a close relationship with her mother. His own had died from cancer at a relatively young age. He frequently spent time with her mother, even stopping by sometimes during the week to see her and Torie's father. Torie had interrupted their conversation, but Sergio had seemed okay when they were saying their goodbyes.

Now, startled, she twisted in her seat and leaned over, trying to see his full face. "What's wrong? I do something to make you angry?"

He shook his head. A vein throbbed on his temple. "Now is not a good time, Victoria. It's late. We're both tired."

She blew out a long breath. Sergio never called her Victoria unless he was beyond angry, and then his voice sounded like a parent's. Straightening in her seat, she heeded his advice and stared out the windshield. When he pulled into the garage, she let herself out and headed inside, into their warm, cozy house that still smelled like wood smoke from the fire she'd lit the night before. He was right. She was tired. But she hated to go to bed without knowing what she'd done, hated to go to bed with either of them angry.

When they were inside and had shucked their coats, he stalked toward the bedroom and spoke over his shoulder, as though he didn't want to look at her. "I feel like I've been hit with a knockout punch, Victoria. Twice this week you talk about me—about our relationship and our lives—with your parents, and you don't include me in the conversation."

She started to respond, but her words wouldn't come. She followed him. She wanted him to face her eye to eye when he was accusing her of something. She reached for his elbow. "What are you talking about?"

He twisted away, thumbed the buttons of his vest out of the buttonholes and threw it onto a chair all in one swift motion. "Don't pretend you don't know. I heard you on Tuesday with your mother. I know you don't want a baby. I know that. But do you have to discuss it with your mother with no consideration for how I feel?" His face was a dark brown.

Remembering her father and his football metaphors—the best defense is a good offense—she said, "You listened to our conversation? You eavesdropped? How could you?" She tried to look into his eyes, get him to stop peeling off his clothes, to stop and discuss what was bothering him.

"Don't try that stuff with me. I didn't listen on purpose." He sat on the chair and pulled off his shoes and socks, not looking at her. "I went back to tell her hello. I couldn't help hearing what you said." He pulled off his pants.

Late on a Sunday night was not the optimal time for another argument about a baby. If that was all, she should be able to smooth it over and get some sleep pretty quickly. "I'm sorry, Sergio. My mother and I have always discussed things—I admit more intimate things than maybe I should sometimes—"

"What about your father? You really think closing that porch door makes it sound proof? You are sadly mistaken. Just when were you going to tell me you are trying to get on the Supreme Court? I'm your husband, Victoria." He scooped up his socks and pants and stalked into the bathroom where he threw them into the hamper along with his shirt. She followed and stood in the doorway, trying to find an appropriate reply. He took two steps until his face was only a few millimeters from hers. She could smell pot roast and onions on his breath. "A woman is not supposed to put her father before her husband." His teeth clacked when he clamped them together. His eyes pierced hers.

Torie's throat filled with hollow, airy shock that caused her mouth to go dry. She backed up a step. "Sergio, I—"

"There is no excuse for that. I'm your husband," he said again, the piercing look hardening into something more, something glinty and steely. "You should confide such things in me first. What kind of marriage do we have if you don't talk to me, if we don't share our hopes and dreams and joys with each other?" *Wham.* He slammed the bathroom door in her face. The lock clicked.

Her breath caught. On a second try, she was able to get air into her lungs. This fight was the worst ever. She tried the door handle, but it wouldn't budge. She knocked. "Sergio, I made a stupid mistake. Let me in. Please."

What had she been thinking? He was right. He was her husband, so why did she do it? He was absolutely right. He'd taken care of her when she'd been injured, beaten by that maniac Carr. He'd taken a leave of absence from work. He'd stayed home and nursed her and held her in the night, trying to make sure she felt safe and secure.

He was right. At his behest, the alarm company quickly installed an alarm system. He'd even bought her the gun, *The Judge,* for her to carry in the tote she took back and forth to the courthouse.

He was absolutely, positively right. Now if he'd just let her tell him she was wrong.

From behind the door came the sound of the shower. Torie sat on the edge of the bed and took off her shoes. If he'd just listen. Let her explain. She didn't mean anything by it. She'd always relied on her father for political advice. But she could understand Sergio's being hurt and angry. Early on, they'd discussed how they wanted to keep as much negativity as possible out of their relationship and that some of the ways of doing that would be to spend time together, communicate, and celebrate as frequently as possible, even the little things, the little successes. After she'd been assaulted, they'd reaffirmed that intention.

When she'd been upheld on appeal, they'd celebrated. When he'd been promoted to general manager, they'd celebrated. Of course they'd celebrated birthdays and their anniversary, though she still felt humiliated she'd forgotten the last one.

When the shower stopped, she stood outside the door and spoke again. "I'm sorry for what I did. I know you must be really angry. Don't ignore me, Sergio. Don't act like I'm not here."

When he came out, wrapped in a robe, he said, "I don't think I even want to be around you. I'm sleeping in the guest room tonight."

"Sergio, I—what—" The hair stood up on her arms.

"I don't have to tell you how disappointed I am in you and your low esteem for me. We need to rethink our relationship."

When she started to speak, he held his hand in front of her mouth to stop her. "Don't say anything. I need some time. We'll talk tomorrow night. Don't make any plans." He scooted around her and out of the bedroom. She followed him as far as the stairs and watched him climb them and disappear into the guest room. The locking door echoed in the quiet.

She sat for a minute on the carpeted bottom step. Her stomach had passed queasy and settled on tumultuous. She could be getting an ulcer. That would explain a lot of things. Picking herself up, she dragged into the bedroom where she hung up her clothes, performed her nightly rituals in a bathroom that smelled of Sergio's rosemary and orange scent, before crawling under the covers. Much as she thought she wouldn't be able to relax, even her bones felt weary and, in spite of her stomach issues, she fell into a deep sleep.

Sergio remained in the guest room the following morning. He knew her schedule. If he didn't have to be at the hotel, there was no reason for him to get up unless he wanted to be with her. Evidently that was not the case.

She'd never seen him so angry. Fear gripped her as she remembered the expression on his face, the clenching of his teeth. If he would only talk to her, she was sure she could make things better. She tapped lightly on the guest room door, but he didn't hear or refused to answer. She tried the handle and found it still locked, so she went down to breakfast.

The toast she made tasted like cardboard. The orange juice was so acidic she upchucked it into the sink about thirty seconds after swallowing. With shaking hands, she filled a to-go cup with black coffee and left for work, hoping whatever was on the calendar would distract her from what lay ahead with Sergio when she returned home.

When she reached her office, Torie breezed past Nettie with a simple "Good Morning," stopping only to pick up the day's docket. At nine-fifteen, she had an additional civil hearing squeezed between some criminal pleas and preliminary motions on a jury trial. Nettie knew better than to set motions like that. It gave Torie no chance to review the files for later in the day.

"What's this about?" she asked.

"A Motion for Sanctions." Nettie stopped what she was doing and looked up at Torie. "You okay, Judge?"

"Sanctions are heard on Friday afternoons. You know that." Torie had made that rule on the theory that no one wanted to work on Fridays. Setting them on Friday afternoons would encourage settlement.

"One of them insisted. Marc David. Said he knew you wouldn't mind since it was him. Something about LLE?""

"What's that supposed to mean? I don't understand."

Nettie shook her head. "I didn't either but . . ." She held her palms up and shrugged.

Torie took the file out to the bench. She would have liked to read the motion before argument. After the two pleas of guilty, one for delivery of cocaine and one for aggravated assault, she glanced at the motion. Another attorney from yet another law firm that had supported her re-election. One of the larger firms. Was he the one who had said something about LLE, whatever that was?

"Marc David for the Movant, Your Honor," a burly, brown-haired young man said as he stood next to counsel table.

"John Esprey, for the Defendant." One of Germania County's icons, he halfway rose from his chair.

"Okay, gentlemen, I have pretrial hearings in a protracted child custody jury trial, so one of you please tell me why this motion couldn't wait until Friday when I always have sanction hearings scheduled?"

"I asked it be bumped up, Judge," David said. "We have video depositions scheduled in thirty minutes at my office. They're rescheduled from a month ago when Mr. Esprey and his client didn't appear. Remember we had a hearing wherein you ordered him to pay the costs of failure to appear the last time?"

She remembered very well. Not that it was hard. Esprey never did anything in a timely fashion, and he never paid the costs that were assessed. He had been a constant adversary of hers years ago.

He had the mistaken impression that he was a privileged character. "Yes, I remember Mr. Esprey being so ordered. Did you pay what you were ordered to pay, Mr. Esprey?"

Esprey, who had sat back down, slowly stood again. "Your Honor, my client doesn't have that kind of money."

"I didn't order your client to pay, Mr. Esprey. I ordered *you* to pay and you know it. You admitted you told your client not to appear. You've done nothing but throw up obstacles in this case. *Have you paid the sum that was ordered?* Am I speaking Mandarin?"

"No, ma'am, Your Honor."

"And what do you have to say about this, Mr. David?"

"Judge, we're asking that he be fined and ordered to jail if he fails to immediately remit. Also, we want an order for him to produce his client immediately for deposition, or we'd like you to strike his pleadings."

Torie's tendency was to be lenient in these matters—up to a point. But Mr. Esprey always caused problems, and she was tired of it. "So ordered." She banged her gavel, which was something she was wont to do. "Now you two go out into the hall and make arrangements. I have other things to hear."

"Thank you, Your Honor," Mr. David said with the tiniest wink.

Torie scowled. She didn't like to be thanked for doing her job. It made her look like she was favoring one side over the other, and she definitely wasn't doing that. And what the heck was that wink? Lawyers. Whew.

As soon as the two men cleared out, she beckoned to the attorneys and parties for the child custody case and buzzed Nettie. "Bring me the Becker files," she said when Nettie came into the courtroom. "After that, if you wouldn't mind, find me a very hot, very black cup of coffee."

A few minutes later, Nettie and one of the young women from the District Clerk's Office came in lugging a box of files. "There were more than twenty, more than we could carry in one trip," Nettie said.

"Okay," Torie whispered when they started stacking them on the floor next to her chair. "I guess I really only need the last three or so."

The two women laughed. The clerk, a young woman named Martha, said, "Judge, during the trial we'll keep them in a rolling bin for you like in the Campbell case. So you can look back to some early pleadings if you need to."

"Thanks." Torie picked up the current file and opened it, clearing her throat. Without even reading, she knew the case was every bit as bad as a toxic tort case, only this time it was toxic people who involved a child in their craziness. She ran her finger down the index and flipped to the back of the file, paging to the most recent motion, scanning it, then the previous one, scanning it, until she'd reviewed all pending matters.

Giving the parties and their attorneys the once over, she pushed back in her chair and tried to relax with a legal pad and pen in her lap. At least with the Becker motions to hear, she wouldn't have time to worry about whether Sergio would have cooled off by the end of the day. And if not, what lay in store when she got home.

"Good morning, ladies and gentlemen. Are both sides ready for pretrial motions?"

Chapter 16

THE DAY WAS ONE FOR PHONE CALLS, GOOD and bad. After lunch, when Torie was on the bench and in the middle of a hearing, a chat bubble from Nettie popped up on her laptop. "Call from the sheriff."

The back of her neck prickled with dread. She was sure Jim Bob's calling could only be about Wesley Carr. His incarceration must be drawing to an end. Would he be released soon? She wasn't ready—it hadn't been long enough. Not nearly long enough for what he'd done.

She had to steady her hands as she typed a message back, "I'll return the call asap."

As soon as the testimony changed direction, she called a ten-minute recess and left the bench for her chambers. She flexed her hands several times to get a grip on herself before reaching for the phone.

"Judge Van Fleet for the sheriff," she blurted to the secretary and drew a long breath. Thinking the man who had beaten her so severely could come back at any time after he was released shook her to her shoes. She'd had to be hospitalized. Talk about a defenseless female, that had been her. Short. Thin. Not strong like a man. In her next life if she had to be a woman, she wanted to be six feet tall and weigh two hundred pounds.

"Judge? Got some news on Carr."

A tornado twisted in her belly. She drew a sharp breath. "I thought as much. When's he getting out?"

The sheriff cleared his throat. "Well, you'll be glad to know he got into a fight and his release date has been extended."

Gooseflesh rose on her arms. She sank onto the edge of the credenza behind her, cupping her middle in relief. "Thank God. Dare I ask how badly he was injured?"

"Oh, not bad enough as far as I'm concerned, but he instigated the incident so he loses some good time. He's not the brightest bulb—"

"You know, Jim Bob, whether or not you give good time is entirely discretionary."

"You know, *Judge*, I've been sheriff for a long time, and I'm completely aware of the range of my authority."

Torie swallowed twice in quick succession, feeling appropriately chastised. "There I go overstepping my bounds again. I apologize. I know you're well aware of your responsibilities. I just wish you could keep him locked away forever."

"I'm working on it." He cleared his throat again. "Seriously, I wish there was a way I could keep him locked up longer. He should have been given more jail time, but he would have had to beat you far worse or used a weapon, so I guess we should be careful what we wish for."

He wasn't telling her anything she didn't know, but talking to him was reassuring. The sheriff was a friend and an ally, and often she was in need of both. "By the way, while he's been there, has he had a psych eval?"

"Absolutely. Our psychiatrist examined Carr after the psychologist put him through a battery of tests."

"And . . . other than his being angry at me, what did it show?"

"Wish I could tell you. His lawyer could or his file could if you can get the trial judge to unseal the envelope. But I know this, he's not legally insane."

"No one's legally insane under Texas law. Thanks for calling, Jim Bob. At least I'll be able to sleep easier for a while."

After they hung up, Torie released a deep breath and sat down in her chair, rotating toward the window. The blinds were open. The sky clear, sunlight beamed in, lighting up a rectangle of carpet. Carr was one less thing to worry about for a while, which was good with everything else going on. Perhaps the Supreme Court thing would be resolved by the time he did get released.

If she got the nod, she would get an apartment in Austin and spend a great deal of time there, driving home on the weekends. Sergio could come down on his days off. She'd be able to keep the location confidential. Much more secret than living in a small town. In Austin, there was no way he'd find her unless he followed her home. She'd make sure that didn't happen.

She reached for the phone to tell Sergio about Carr, but he didn't pick up. He still wasn't speaking to her. In retrospect, she couldn't blame him. She'd practically given him a written invitation to be angry with her. Not over her mother, a woman should be able to discuss female things with her mother. But he was right that she should have told him first about the Supreme Court, at least before her father, if not Adrian. Adrian was her mentor, and Sergio knew that. What he didn't know, and what she would never tell him, was what she and Adrian had been to each other. If he knew, he might not be okay with their continued friendship. And there was no way she could give that up at the present. She needed Adrian too much.

At the end of the day's hearings, after she'd returned to chambers and sorted through the files stacked on her desk, signing documents that were time-sensitive, prioritizing the others into stacks, her cell phone rang with a phone call from William Peterson. She was always happy to hear from Bill, who had been a big supporter of hers, raising money, putting up signs, working phone banks. He was president of Fathers for Fair Judges, an organization that had worked for Torie's re-election. He thought he had been treated unfairly by a judge in another jurisdiction and founded the group as a result.

He immediately dispensed with the pleasantries, which was unlike him. "Hey, this is Bill. I heard you're trying to get appointed to the Texas Supreme Court."

"Where in the world did you hear that?" A shiver ran down her spine.

"Never you mind, young lady, but if what they say is true, I'll tell you right now what I think about that. You'll have to run for election to that job eventually. You know we helped you get elected and re-elected to this one because of your reputation of doing the right thing in family law cases. If you leave your bench, we'll never help you again."

"But Bill—"

"Don't bother denying it or arguing with me. After all my friends and family have done for you, and you repay us by trying to go to Austin? I'm warning you." He coughed into the phone. "Think about it, Judge, before you make a bad mistake."

"Wait! Are you okay, Bill?"

"Don't worry about me. I'm fine. You'd better think about what I've said."

"Please don't hang up. Why don't you come in, and we'll talk about it? You don't understand the good I can do from Austin for all the people of Texas, not just those in my district."

"I don't care, Judge. Just remember what I said. *Adios*." He disconnected.

Torie threw her cell on a pile of papers. The day had been a series of ups and downs that were wearing her out. Anxiety ate at her. Nothing she did was right. She leaned back in her chair and stared at the ceiling, hoping to find some answers. When she didn't, she picked up her things and shut off the lights as she headed home to mix herself a martini. She hoped she'd have time for one drink before Sergio started in on her.

Chapter 17

"GOOD MORNING, MRS. WAGNER," TORIE SAID TO the Perdido County District Clerk the following morning in as cheerful a tone as she could muster. Perdido County was one of her four counties, and one she seldom went to more than once a month. The sparse population was made up of large ranches with few people living in the tiny county seat.

She'd had a miserable night alone. Sergio hadn't come home. When she phoned him, his curt tone told her he was still angry as he informed her he'd be spending the night at the resort.

"Good morning, Judge," the clerk, a middle-aged, wiry-haired woman said. "A few things of note. We have several protective orders on the family docket, and after that, the criminal docket." She held her hand up like a fan, concealing her mouth as she whispered, "The biggest thing is a bond reduction hearing in that murder case, the one where the police officer killed his brother's wife."

From behind her own hand, Torie said, "Allegedly, Mrs. Wagner.

Allegedly killed his brother's wife." She settled on one side of the ancient executive chair that sat behind the bench, avoiding the spring pushing through the stuffing. She smoothed her slacks and robe down beside it so nothing would get caught and torn and, with the toe of her shoe, clicked on the small heater under the bench.

Mrs. Wagner chewed the corner of her mouth. "Of course, allegedly."

Scanning the faces of the people seated in the gallery, Torie picked up the first file from the stack the clerk had set out for her on the edge of the bench. "23,044 Lucia Wilson v. Clarence Wilson, Application for Protective Order."

Two of the faces in the gallery were people who had worked on her campaign in the last election. Did they have an interest in a case, or had they just come to watch? Didn't matter. Wasn't supposed to matter. Still, she was annoyed that recent events caused such thoughts to enter into her mind. Probably they were there to see her on her first day in that county since the January first swearing in.

"John Drake for Applicant, Mrs. Wilson." Drake, a huge man Torie remembered—but wished she didn't—having given a small contribution to her re-election campaign, loomed in front of the bench. His client, a tiny, dark woman in a thin sweater and a long skirt, came from behind counsel table and stood next to him.

A man, wearing a long-sleeved plaid shirt and jeans and holding a black Stetson in one hand, stood up in the back of the courtroom.

Torie asked, "Sir, in the back, are you Mr. Wilson?"

"Yes, ma'am, Your Honor." He stepped into the aisle. "But I ain't got no lawyer. Could I just pay the fine and go back to work?" Holding his hat in front of him, he walked toward the bench.

Fear filled Torie's chest as he approached. Her eyes darted

from the hat and his hands to his face and his eyes. Did he have something under that hat? A gun or a knife? She clenched the gavel in her right hand. "I'm afraid it's not that easy, Mr. Wilson. This is a civil matter." As he grew close, she braced her feet flat on the floor and pointed the gavel at him. "Stop right there. What do you have under your hat?"

The man stopped and glanced up at Mr. Drake, who dwarfed him. He held one palm out and gripped his hat in the other hand. "Nothing, ma'am." The whites of his eyes reflected the courtroom lights.

Torie's breath quietly escaped as she rested the gavel on the pounding block and let it go. She felt like a fool, but he could have been concealing something. "An application for protective order doesn't have a fine, though it may have attorney's fees and court costs, Mr. Wilson."

"I—I didn't know that, ma'am," Mr. Wilson said, his lips quivering.

Torie looked at Mrs. Wilson's attorney, "You ready to proceed, Mr. Drake?"

"Yes, Your Honor. And we have a witness out in the hall. The rancher these folks work for."

"Tell you what, Mr. Wilson, why don't you visit with Mr. Drake here and see if y'all can't reach an agreement while I call the rest of the docket? It may expedite matters. When I get to the end, if you still need a hearing, you'll be first."

Drake's frown couldn't be missed.

"Have you seen the size of this morning's docket, Mr. Drake? Yours is not the only case. It's not even the only protective order." She pointed at Mr. Wilson. "At a minimum, Mr. Wilson, I'm going to require you to go into San Antonio and take a family violence class."

"But, ma'am—"

"Required in every case, Mr. Wilson. Wish we had a program up here, but we don't. Now y'all go talk."

"Can Mrs. Wilson stay inside the courtroom?" Mr. Drake stood between the couple.

"Absolutely. Mrs. Wilson, you sit down in the jury box and make yourself comfortable. Your attorney and your husband are going to see if they can come to an agreement. If not, we'll get to your case in a little while."

"Gracias, señora," Mrs. Wilson said.

Torie picked up the next file. "Cause number 22,675, Lucinda Martinez versus Hector Martinez, Motion for Summary Judgment." She made a notation of the attorneys' names on the docket sheet where she'd be able to read them easily. Thankfully, neither of their names sounded familiar nor did they look like anyone she'd ever met. "Good morning, counsel."

"Good morning, Judge," the first one said. She appeared to be younger than Torie, very tall with long brown hair, brown eyes, and a pockmarked face. "Judith January for Mr. Martinez." She indicated her client who stood behind the bar. Gleaming red hair, together with his very dark brown eyes, betrayed a mixed heritage.

The second attorney, about six feet tall with spiked black hair, clear sky blue eyes, and a build even Sergio would kill for, said, "Matt Tiller for Mrs. Martinez." He stepped up to the bench and shook her hand, his cologne smelling as good as he looked, a musky manly aroma. "Nice to meet you, Judge. I'm from San Antonio with the Eggleston, Meyer firm. I just moved from Orange, Texas. "

Her heart sank. The Eggleston, Meyer firm had been a large contributor to Torie's re-election campaign. She wished she didn't know that, but she'd reviewed every contribution to be sure she wasn't accepting money from anyone she shouldn't. In their case, the contribution was large in the sense that every attorney had given the maximum allowed by law.

Was he telling her the name of the firm to send her a message they had been her supporters, and she'd better remember it? She hoped not. She hoped they'd supported her for good government and for no other reason. And she hoped she'd have their support in her aspirations to the Supremes. She glanced around the courtroom and wondered how many other supporters were out there and whether every single one of them in every county expected something from her. She'd never really thought about it until that Motion to Recuse. Now, she couldn't get it out of her mind.

Judith January, not to be outdone, walked up to the bench and shook Torie's hand as well. Her grip was far firmer than Tiller's and warm to the touch. "Judge, we met when you were campaigning out here last fall. At the reception at the Western Art Gallery? I'm a solo practitioner. Remember we talked about the need for a visitation exchange center somewhere in your district?"

"I do remember that conversation. That's on my list of things I want to get done this term."

"If I can help in any way, please call me. I have some ideas for locations." She held her file in front of her chest like a schoolbook.

"Great, then let's do lunch sometime soon. Dutch treat, of course."

Tiller cleared his throat, and Torie could see he wouldn't be outdone either, he said, "I know the director of the exchange center in Bexar County, Judge. If you'd like, I'll hook you up with her."

Smiling at the competing attorneys, Torie said, "Okay, you two, I'll take all the help I can get. Now let's take up the reason y'all are here today. Motion for Summary Judgment? I hardly ever see these in family law cases. What's the deal?"

"I filed that, Judge," Judith January said, her back stiffening. "I know it's rare, but in this case it's appropriate. My client, who is the petitioner in the divorce suit, owned a substantial amount of separate property at the time of the marriage. Respondent seems to think it magically converted to community once the marriage certificate was inked."

"We dispute that, Your Honor. Petitioner is mischaracterizing the property. That's why we made a jury demand. Let a jury decide what the nature of the property is."

Torie said, "Well—"

"Regardless of the jury demand, summary judgment is appropriate in this matter where it's clear that certain property is separate. You can cut down on the issues at trial, Judge, if you'll grant summary judgment, even a partial summary judgment in favor of my client."

"But if he's disputing the facts—"

Her voice raised, Judith January said, "They can dispute everything, Judge, but that doesn't make it community."

Torie's face tightened. "Miss January, stop! I don't like to be cut off in mid sentence."

Tiller looked smug when Judith January apologized. Torie was glad she didn't practice law anymore. Having to tolerate rude behavior from the lawyers was a pain. Fighting wasn't one of her favorite things. Then why, her father had asked, had she gone into litigation? There were so many other areas where a law degree would be useful. But Torie knew the answer to that, unexpressed though it was to her father.

As a litigant herself, she'd seen many places where the justice system could be improved. As a family law practitioner, she'd observed even more. She'd felt she could make a difference. And she wanted to make her father proud. She wanted him to see her as a fighter, just like he had always said to her brother. *Get out there and fight. Make that touchdown!* In her case, it was *pass the bar exam, win that case, win the election, then re-election.* And now, the Supreme Court.

January interrupted her reverie. "Judge, are you ready to hear argument?"

"How many parcels of property are we talking about here?" Torie asked as she placed the file under the stack to her right.

"I delineated it in my motion, Your Honor." Ms. January brushed at her hair before draping her hand behind her back.

"Tell you what, why don't the two of you go back to your respective offices, and when I rule on the summary judgment I'll e-mail or fax you."

"You don't want argument?" Tiller asked in a tone of voice that said *I came all the way up here for nothing?*

Torie toyed with saying something sarcastic then thought better of it. Miss January's face was drawn up in a scowl as well. "Now I'm not saying you can't argue. You can. It's just that I have a very long docket this morning. I thought you might not want to wait for me to call the whole thing before you argued."

"I don't mind," Miss January said. "How long are we talking

about? An hour, two?" She glanced at Tiller out of the corner of her eye.

"An hour?" Tiller said.

"You're second, after a protective order. I won't know if they've been able to work that out until I get to the end of the docket. I sent them outside. Why don't y'all go have a cup of coffee and come back in about ten minutes? I'll be better able to calculate how much time you'll have to wait then."

Tiller glanced at his watch. "I'm used to doing summary judgments by submission. You go ahead, Judge. Rule on it at your leisure. I'm sure I can count on you to read our response and give it the attention it's due."

Tiller's patronizing statement rankled Torie. When she shot him a look, he wore a poker face. "What about you, Miss January?"

"I'm confident you'll do the right thing, Your Honor, without taking up thirty minutes—"

"Ten," Torie said. "I never give more than ten minutes for argument on summary judgments even if you have to wait all day for me to hear it."

Ms. January's lips pressed against each other in a crinkled line. "Okay then. You've just saved Mr. Tiller and myself a lot of time, Judge. Thank you for your forbearance. May we be excused?"

"Certainly."

Tiller approached her again and stuck out his hand. "Nice meeting you, Judge."

Torie shook his hand and nodded at Miss January and both of their clients. After writing a sticky note to herself to make sure she'd remember what the discussion had been about and sticking it to their file's docket sheet, she placed the file into a third stack. And picked up the next one.

Completing the family docket took another fifteen minutes. Then she came to cases, which were civil, non-family.

"22,917, Barrow v. Doran." Two men, one past middle age but as robust as a man half his age and the other young but on a walker approached the bench. Torie glanced at the file. "I remember you gentlemen. Mr. Barrow, you're suing Mr. Doran because he sold you his dental practice which you allege didn't have the business he held out it had. Mr. Doran, you're suing Mr. Barrow because he quit paying you, correct?"

"Yes, ma'am," Barrow said. "He told me his dental practice would be enough to supplement my retirement if I gave up my practice in Houston and moved up here."

Mr. Doran rolled his walker closer to the bench. "Judge, I need that money to pay my medical bills. My disability isn't cutting it."

"Aren't y'all set on the jury docket in the next few months?" she asked.

"Yes, ma'am," Doran said. "But Judge, I've filed a Motion for Summary Judgment, if you'll look on your calendar. I'd like that heard today because if you grant it, we won't have a trial."

She glanced from one to the other of them. "Okay, no problem. Have you hired an attorney, or are you wanting to argue it yourself, Mr. Doran? I could review the motion and your supporting documents and e-mail or fax my ruling to the two of you."

"That would be fine with me," Barrow said.

"I'd like to argue if you don't mind, Judge," Doran said. "I know you'll do justice by it, but this has gotten to be very personal. There are some things I'd like to point out to you in argument. It's rather complicated. That is, if you don't mind."

"I don't mind, but you gentlemen better go for a cup of coffee, because it'll be a while."

"You can't get to us right now?" Barrow asked.

"No sir, I can't. Why, are you in a hurry to go someplace? As you said, you're retired."

Barrow shifted his weight from one foot to the other. "I'll wait if I have to."

"You have to," she said. "By the way, I thought you had an attorney, Mr. Barrow. I didn't see in your file that your attorney has asked to withdraw."

"No, Your Honor, he had court in Austin today, and I thought since it's just a summary judgment hearing he wouldn't need to be here—since we're supposed to have a jury trial."

"Well, it's your case. You can do what you please. Why don't y'all go for a cup of coffee and come back in ten." She laid the file to the side and picked up the next one from the foot high stack in front of her.

The remainder of the civil docket call only took a few minutes, but then there was the little matter of the criminal docket call which included status conferences, motions for discovery, writs of habeas corpus, and settings for pleas of guilty and trials.

Torie enjoyed criminal cases. The defendants intrigued her. She pondered their motivations, their backgrounds, and their upbringings. Contrary to popular belief, not all of them came from poor families. Sometimes it was shocking to find a defendant who was just plain mean, just plain bad—a bad seed. No explanation. No testimony as to mitigating circumstances like having been a victim of child abuse or neglect or of a life-changing event in his youth. That's where the nature versus nurture argument came from. People like that—the bad seeds—she found the most interesting of all. Sociopaths and psychopaths, which sometimes were one and the same, were a curiosity to her. Could be that Wesley Carr fit into one of those categories. She didn't know, and it wouldn't make her feel better if she did.

Picking up the first red file, she called, "State of Texas versus Reed, aggravated assault with a deadly weapon."

"State's ready," the district attorney announced from his place at counsel table, leisurely standing up to his full height of well over six feet.

"Defense's ready subject to a Motion for Discovery. I really need to know what evidence they have, Your Honor." The defense attorney, a white-haired man who looked older than Zeus, had been bent over the bar in a muted conversation with a very well-endowed, redheaded woman. When Torie called the case, Tom Sherwood approached the bench with a huge grin on his deeply grooved face. Torie didn't know what he was so happy about, but it was nice to see someone who wasn't dour, who didn't look like he had gotten up on the wrong side of the bed.

"Good morning, Mr. Sherman," she said. "Nice to see you today."

"It's a beautiful day, Judge. A beautiful day."

It was another overcast day, at least when she drove over a few hours earlier, flurries sailing in the wind.

The district attorney, Billy Ray Raymond, hurriedly followed Sherman up to the front of the courtroom. "I think it's a beautiful day, too, Judge. Just wanted to be clear on that for the record."

Jennifer, the court reporter, snickered.

"All right, you two." The criminal side of the bar frequently was much more irreverent than the civil side. "For the record, on my drive down here I found the day to be beautiful, if wet, as well. So now that we've got that out of the way, why does Mr. Sherman have to file a Motion for Discovery when your office has an open file policy, Mr. Raymond?"

"Overzealousness on the part of a new young attorney?" Raymond said.

"I'll accept that. So if we don't have to have a long, tedious hearing on Mr. Sherman's motion, what else is going on with this case?"

"Bond reduction, Judge," Sherman said. "You previously set it at three hundred thousand. We'd like to take some testimony on what Jimmy Reed can afford."

"You're opposed to the reduction, Mr. Raymond?"

"You betcha, Judge. The defendant is a rapist who belongs behind bars until trial."

"I thought this was agg assault."

"It would have been rape—aggravated sexual assault—except before he could act on his impulses, someone heard the victim's cries and came to the rescue. The defendant, who had been holding a gun on the victim, then pulled up his pants and tried to make good his escape. Fortunately, he tripped over his own feet and fell, hitting his head on a tree trunk dazing himself just long enough for the witness to get the gun out of his hand and hold him at bay until the police could get there." After that long recitation, he exhaled.

"Are we trying the case to the bench here today?" Sherman asked. "If so, I'm prepared to make my opening statement as well."

Torie raised an eyebrow, tempted to burst out laughing. "Okay. Okay. When is the trial set for?" She rummaged through the file.

"Month after next, Judge," Sherman said, and then in a lower tone, "but if you'll lower the bond, my client can get out of jail and go back to work and make some money to pay me."

"Aren't you a little bit old to still be taking cases like this where you might not get paid?" Torie whispered.

Sherman nodded. "Way too old. So can we have a hearing on bond reduction?"

"Get in line at the coffee machine and be back in ten minutes."

The D.A. laughed. "Bring me back a cup, Tom. I've got to do the rest of the docket."

"Sure thing." Sherman raised his hand in a wave as he headed down the aisle to the back of the courtroom.

Torie called the rest of the docket. She set the pleas and motions for that afternoon and calendared some trials. By the time she got to the end, she took a ten-minute recess before beginning the hearings.

The judge's chambers at the little Perdido County Courthouse left a lot to be desired. The bedroom closets at her house were larger. The outer office barely supported a desk and chair. Since there wasn't a court coordinator or even a receptionist, Jennifer set up camp there. Inside the judge's personal office, there was at least a private restroom. One of the other counties didn't even have that. She had to use the ladies' room out in the hall. In still another, she had to share with the clerks and anyone else privy to the coffee room including jurors in deliberation.

After a stop in the restroom, Torie placed a call to Sergio, but it went to voice mail. She'd never known him to take so long to come around. Should she worry that he was re-thinking their relationship?

Chapter 18

B Y THE TIME TORIE FINISHED THE HEARING ON the protective order and the summary judgment argument, it was time to break for lunch. The judges were meeting at a restaurant just twenty minutes into the next county, so she decided to attend.

The sun finally showed its face, the day becoming seriously beautiful and clear, with not a cloud in the azure sky. Early spring days like that she loved to tool around in her Mercedes on the two lane roads in the Hill Country, around the valleys and the curves, even if she had to drive more slowly since the roads were wet. Only ten minutes late, she bounced inside and found the usual suspects, including Beth, at a table for six in a private room.

"Y'all didn't start without me, did you?" Slinging her coat onto the rack by the window, she took her purse and walked to the table, all smiles. It wouldn't do for that gang to see any crack in her demeanor.

Jack Dobbs and Randolph Stewart, who sat beside each other,

looked at her with the guilty expressions of little children. Bo, who sat at the end of the table where she would have expected to see Jack, jumped up and pulled a chair out for her. She nodded at Adrian, who sat opposite Bo, before patting Beth on the shoulder and sitting next to her. "Have y'all already ordered?"

"Just," Beth said. "Glad you could make it."

A waitress took Torie's order and brought her a glass of iced tea. "So how is everybody? Did I miss anything?" Everyone was quiet, more subdued than usual. Suspicion crept into her mind. Had she been the subject of discussion or was she being paranoid? She glanced at each of the judges. No one said anything. She mixed her tea and took a swallow.

Jack Dobbs said, "We were talking about everyone who's throwing their hat in the ring for the Supremes."

Torie nodded. "You guys decided what you're going to do?"

"It's not for me," Bo Calhoun said.

"I'm too old to do all that work," Randolph Stewart said. "But if I wanted it, I'm sure I'd have a good chance."

"I'm sure you would," Torie said. "So what's going on? You're all too quiet."

"Well, if you want to know the truth, Judge Van Fleet—"

"Jack," Adrian said in a warning tone.

"What?" Torie glanced from one to the other.

Beth said, "Of course you already know I'm going for the position."

"Right, and I know Adrian is not going for it." Torie spread her napkin on her lap and faced off with Jack. "So, Jack, what about you?"

"And we all know you *are* going for it, Judge," Jack said. "And that's what we were talking about."

"Jack, don't start anything," Adrian said in that warning tone again.

"You're correct, I am," Torie said, "but you still haven't answered as to yourself."

"Thanks to you girls sewing up so much of the support around the Hill Country already, us fellas aren't getting much traction," Jack said.

"Yes, we have been working hard, haven't we, Judge McGruter?"

"That's affirmative," Beth said. "Night and day."

"You're angry because Beth and I didn't let any grass grow under our feet?"

"Don't, Torie," Beth said in a cautionary tone. "It's not worth arguing over."

The waitress brought salads and set them before each person. Jack waited until the waitress left before saying anything else. Torie picked through the greens, taking out the cucumbers and peppers, which she didn't like. She'd told the attorneys she'd be back by two-thirty, so she was going to go ahead and eat. "Adrian," she said, "do you have any kind of agenda? Anything *else* anyone wants to talk about? I have to get back pretty quickly."

"Some of the district clerks requested a meeting to discuss modernizing the way we handle our dockets, schedule our cases, and so forth," he said. "I wanted to get feedback from y'all on that. We'd all have to learn some new software and probably get new computers if we could get the commissioners to pay for them." He glanced around the table. "We might be able to get a grant for our region."

"Why do we need that?" Randolph asked, slurping his drink.

"The attorneys have been asking for it," Adrian said. "Especially the ones from the big cities, like San Antonio and Austin, where their district clerks already have it."

"If we can't get a grant, our commissioners sure won't like it," Beth said.

"Mine, either," Bo said. "Now if it was a new road or bridge—"

"We're not the big cities, and I don't see why we need it," Randolph said.

"I'd like to have it," Beth said. "It would make things easier."

"Me, too," Torie said. "Let's bring our smaller counties into the twenty-first century."

Jack said, "You're always full of bright ideas."

"Jack, if you have something to say, spit it out and get it over with," Torie said.

"Okay, you asked for it. What we were talking about when you came in is that no one wants you on the Supreme Court. You're too young. You've just started your second term. There's already enough family law experience on that court and enough women."

The blood drained from her face. She glanced at Beth for support, but Beth stared at her salad bowl. Adrian shook his head slightly. Randolph and Bo didn't say anything. "Who is 'no one'? Who are you speaking for? Is he speaking for you, Randolph? Never mind, don't answer. I'm sure I know how you feel. And certainly I know my worthy opponent would like me to drop out of the race." She elbowed Beth and grinned. "So is he speaking for you, too, Bo?"

"Well, Torie, you *are* kind of young—"

"And for the record," Jack added, "if I have to support a woman, which I don't, Beth would be my first choice and you'd be last on any list, short or long."

"I'm pretty sure Tom Phillips and Wallace Jefferson were

younger than I am when each of them was appointed *Chief Justice* of the Texas Supreme Court a number of years ago."

"Well, BFD," Jack said. "You're still a family law judge, and no one wants another family law judge."

"I know what BFD stands for, for your information, Mr. Big Shot Judge, but you don't have to be so crass. Anyway, today I've been hearing a bunch of different matters, the rest of my day will be tied up solely with other civil and criminal cases. Just because in Germania County I do most of the family law doesn't make me a family law judge. What a snob you are. Just because some people specialize in family law doesn't make them any less a judge than you."

"And you're a bitch," Jack said.

A shock of adrenalin lit her up. "How dare you?" She half rose from her chair.

"Whoa!" Adrian piped up. "This has gotten out of hand. Can it, Jack."

"I don't need anyone to take up for me, Adrian." Torie wanted to stop him before he said something that might be misconstrued. Jack would be just the person who would carry tales around the whole Hill Country about Adrian coming to her defense. Her body flushing with anger, Torie also knew she couldn't back down from a confrontation with Jack or he'd use it against her any chance he got.

"I know Jack doesn't like me, but for the life of me I've never known why. What did I ever do to you, Jack?" She glanced at each of the other judges, hoping someone, if not Jack, would speak up. Outside, the wind whipped the American and the Texas flags around on the flagpole at the entrance to the parking lot. A sharp light reflected off the windshield of one of the cars and lit up a spot on the wall behind Jack's head, making only his silhouette visible. The muted commotion from the rest of the restaurant came through the closed doors.

The waitress and a waiter arrived with their food, setting it on a buffet behind their table. Garlic permeated the air. They served the judges, refilling water and tea glasses. There were murmurings of thanks and the rattle of silverware.

"Bring me another rum and Coke," Jack told the waitress.

All eyes were on Jack. He cut into his steak with relish and stuffed a gob of bloody meat into his mouth, chewing with his mouth half-open.

"Well, I'm going to clear the air if no one else will," Randolph said. "When you ran for office the first time, Torie, your opponent, the man you defeated, was Jack's best friend—his best friend since junior high school."

Torie frowned. "I didn't know that," she said. "But that's politics, Jack. It's tough to lose, but don't you think it's time to move on? It's been four years."

"'Bout what I'd expect from you," Jack said with his mouth full.

Torie shook her head. "You want me to apologize for winning an election?"

Adrian said, "Why don't we change the subject or just eat? I'm sure Victoria is not the only one who needs to get back to work." He cut his eyes at Jack and the rum and Coke the waitress had placed in front of him.

"Adrian," Bo said, changing the subject, "if you have some information about this system the clerks want, send it to me, would you? I'm not opposed to it but don't know much about it either, just what the attorneys have mentioned." He raised his eyebrows at Torie as if sympathizing with her.

Torie had lost her appetite. She took several bites of her fish and excused herself. "I've got to get back. See you guys another time." She covered her plate with her napkin, gathered up her purse and, taking her coat off the coatrack, headed out the banquet room door, her heart feeling like it had taken a beating. She paid her tab on her way outside. A cloud had covered the sun. The wind had stopped blowing, but a chill in the air said the temperature had dropped in the past hour, indicative that spring hadn't quite arrived.

Things picked up in the afternoon. She disposed of more cases than she'd thought possible, the attorneys having worked out agreements during the lunch hour. Later in the day, she felt even more optimistic when she pulled into the garage and parked next to Sergio's Mercedes.

Sergio had given her a scare. Ordinarily, they didn't fight. Not like she and Bert had. There hadn't been much to fight about. Before they'd married, they'd had long discussions. Neither of them had wanted their relationship to end up like her prior one. They'd agreed on most everything and when they hadn't, they'd agreed to discuss things like rational human beings and compromise.

The hood of Sergio's car was still warm. She took a few moments to gather her thoughts before searching him out. Her stomach fluttered with anxiety. She'd decided to apologize, to let him know she understood why he'd been so angry, even beg his forgiveness if she had to.

When she entered through the back door, there was no sign of him. Fear clutched at her. Normally he'd be in the kitchen putting together some dinner or mixing drinks. She glanced at the bar and saw no indication he'd made himself a drink. She hoped he wasn't packing a suitcase in the bedroom. Surely he'd give her a chance to apologize. She hurried from room to room, not even stopping to take off her coat. He was nowhere to be found.

"Sergio!" Torie called from the top of the stairs. Nothing. Finally she went back into the kitchen for a drink of water, bewildered at his absence. When she took a glass from the cabinet, she glanced out the kitchen window. Sergio, still in his general manager's clothes—suit and dress shoes—with his overcoat unbuttoned and blowing in the wintery breeze, was pacing off what they jokingly called the back forty.

Torie put the glass down and buttoned her coat. Outside, she picked her way over the clods of dirt. Their eyes made contact. Sergio's cheeks, nose, and chin were red with cold. Torie continued her trek toward him. She should have changed her shoes. Her five-inch heels weren't designed to maneuver over earth and rocks. She took his ungloved, frozen hand in hers, and he let her. Looking up at him, seeing a look of determination, she chose her words. Just before she spoke, he put his other hand up to her mouth.

"Before you ask, I'm counting paces. I don't want to forget the number. Walk with me." He stretched out his legs and pulled Torie along as he continued counting. She did her best to keep up. What was he doing?

Finally, he stopped. "I think I would like to place the pool right here."

"Pool?" Torie laughed, a tiny shiver enveloping her.

"I think we should have a swimming pool. A patio off the kitchen with a wooden deck leading up to the pool." He gestured toward the house, drawing pictures in the air.

"You do, do you?" She couldn't think what to say.

"Yes, *mi amante,* and next to the pool we'll have a pool house.

The downstairs will be showers and changing rooms. The upstairs will be your home office. When you are a big, important Supreme Court justice, you will need an office larger than the little one you have in the house now, so you can work from home if you want and even have space for a clerk."

She threw herself at Sergio, wrapping her arms around his neck. "You crazy hombre. I love you so much. I'm sorry for what I did. Does this mean I'm forgiven?"

Sergio pulled her close and squeezed her tight. "My hot temper got the best of me."

Torie kissed his neck. "You were right to be angry. I should have told you first, talked to you first. I meant to, but you were so busy—but enough with the excuses. I should have made it a point to tell you before my father."

"I know how much your father's approval means to you." He stroked her cheek.

She didn't respond. He understood more than she knew, but now was not the time to get into a discussion about her relationship with her father. "You do forgive me?"

"Of course I do, my darling little judge. But could we do this inside before we freeze to death?"

While they'd stood there in each other's arms, snow flurries had begun to spin in the air and settle on them. She shivered and gave Sergio a mushy kiss. He tasted like warm sugar. With relief rushing through her, she headed for the house, selecting the path with the fewest rocks and slushy spots. He steadied her and gave her a little pat on the bottom before slipping an arm around her waist and helping her pick her way back. She hoped that little love pat foreshadowed the remainder of the evening, and that he would be pleased when he found the drawer full of condoms she'd left for them.

Chapter 19

ADRIAN PICKED UP HIS DESK PHONE TO ANSWER a call from an unidentified attorney whom Viola, his administrative assistant, had put through, an odd thing for her to do but not totally unusual.

"You don't know me," the female voice said, "but Karl—you know the Karl I'm talking about, right?"

It could only be Karl the corrupter. "Yes, Karl—"

"He told me you were responsible for our firm getting a ruling on a particular case in Perdido County."

Goosebumps rose on Adrian's arms. "Who is this? Kindly identify yourself." He pulled the phone away from his ear and looked at it as if he could see through to the other end. Surely Karl wouldn't go about saying any such thing. And if he hadn't, who put the voice up to making the call?

"Doesn't matter who I am. Just wanted you to know we appreciate your judge—the judge of Perdido County—well, the *district* judge who has Perdido County—ruling in favor of our associate last week."

Adrian's throat felt hollow, like air rushed through it. He had trouble verbalizing. "I don't know what you're talking about, Ms.—"

"Don't be so modest, Judge. We wanted to let you know that we're grateful. And you can pass that along to her. Goodbye." The phone went dead.

Sweat broke out in his scalp, his armpits, his hands. He hung up and rested on his elbows, his breath nowhere to be found. The door to his office was closed, thank God. He wouldn't want Viola to see him like that, to see the sweat dripping off him, to see the fear that must be written on his face. He pulled his handkerchief from his breast pocket and mopped his head and wiped his hands.

By telling people Adrian was getting Victoria to do his bidding, Karl's dangerous behavior could get them all taken before the Commission on Judicial Conduct or worse, brought up on charges. In all the years they'd been connected, Karl had never been so reckless. Any idiot knew even the appearance of impropriety could be a violation of the rules.

How careless of the caller, whomever she was, to have phoned his office. What was she thinking? Viola, who was completely in the dark about everything, could have overheard. It was a government phone line. Not that he had any reason to believe someone was listening in on his calls, but why take a chance?

Adrian picked up his cell and tapped in Karl's number. When he answered, Adrian said, "What the hell, Karl? Have you been putting our business on the street? Are you crazy?"

"Whoa, boy," Karl said. "What are you talking about?"

"Don't pretend you don't know. I just got a call from some woman expressing her appreciation for her firm, or an associate in her firm, winning some case before Judge Van Fleet in Perdido County."

"Oh, is that all?" Karl chortled.

"Is that all? The idiot woman called me on my county line. What are you trying to do?" He gritted his teeth.

"Okay, listen, it's not a big deal. I'll tell her not to call you again, especially not at the county number."

"How about not ever." His face was hot with anger.

"Don't worry about Aiden. She's on the Lawyers for Lawsuit Equity board of directors. She's okay."

"So you did tell her that? You knew she was going to call? For years I'm dealing with you and Gray and suddenly a woman calls me out of the blue—"

"I may have mentioned something like that. Calm down. I'll talk to her."

"See that you do," Adrian said and cut Karl off with one quick punch of a button, plunking his cell down on his desk. Stepping to the window, he watched the wind blow leaves about the parking lot. The old adage from World War II, "Loose lips sink ships," floated through his mind.

He didn't like it that he'd gotten that phone call, that someone named Aiden thought it all right to call him. He didn't like it one bit. He chewed on his thumbnail, breaking it off, ruining his manicure. He reached into his desk drawer for a file, going at it with fierce determination until he realized what he was doing. He'd filed his nail down to the quick.

He retrieved his cell and punched in Victoria's number. "How's it going?" he asked when she answered.

"I had a rotten morning, but this afternoon's better, how about you?"

"Fine. Making any progress on support for the appointment?"

"Yes, my father's making contacts with some of his former business associates."

"Good. Say, I wanted to talk to you about Jack Dobbs." Not first on his list of things he wanted to talk about, but he thought he would ease into the subject of Perdido County. He didn't want to raise her suspicions.

"I'm not worried about Jack," Torie said. "Jack's just . . . well—Jack."

"The conversation before you arrived at the luncheon was really not all that bad and not all about you. Just so you know."

"It's okay—"

"Jack was ranting, but when is Jack not ranting about something? Surprised he hasn't had a heart attack."

"We couldn't be that lucky."

"Victoria, that's not like you."

"That's my dark side speaking, but keep it just between us. I get tired of him picking on me all the time. His friend lost, so what? If you can't deal with politics you shouldn't be in it."

"You're right. That's true. By the way, how'd it go in Perdido County?"

"What do you mean?" Her tone changed.

"Wasn't that where you were when you came over to lunch?"

"Yes. Why, what's going on?"

"Oh, just heard some things about a ruling you made, that's all." He tried to keep his voice light.

"Really? What ruling?"

"I'm not sure. Did you have any unusual cases?" It was hard to question other people with legal backgrounds. They were always so suspicious.

"Not really. A bunch of summary judgments. You know, I'm thinking I may do all summary judgments by submission, not allow argument on them at all anymore. What do you think?"

"The lawyers in the big cities would like it, unless they're coming to this neck of the woods for a hunting trip and want to write it off."

"I didn't think about that."

"I don't know about our country lawyers, though. A lot of the ones my age are old-fashioned. They think they need to argue everything."

"Yeah, I know. Speaking of old men, do you know Dr. Barrow from Perdido County? He was a dentist in Houston who thought he was going to retire to the country and have a part-time dental practice."

"He's the one who bought the practice from a crippled dentist?" Adrian vaguely remembered an old case that had begun before Victoria had ever been elected.

"That's the one. I got rid of that dog of a case through summary judgment. I'm thinking someone in San Antonio's helping the *pro se* litigant. Finally the guy presented a compelling motion so I could dismiss it."

That could have been what the Aiden woman had been talking about, but there was no way he could find out without asking a lot of undue questions. He'd have to let it go.

"The facts and the cases were pretty clear and, get this, Barrow and his attorney never even filed a response to the Motion for Summary Judgment. How crazy is that?"

"How many years had it been going on?" He knew the answer already, but he didn't want to give away too much.

"Five, at least."

"Why, all of a sudden, did the guy file a Motion for Summary Judgment?"

"I don't know, unless someone felt sorry for him and decided to help him out. The motion and research were very well done, though."

That had to be the case the woman had called about. "What was the name of the law firm that helped out?"

"Dunno because it was filed *pro se.* Only the dentist signed it. Is there some reason you want to know?" Her voice had grown high-pitched.

"Just wondering."

"I think I'm *persona non grata* in Perdido County for a while. Dr. Barrow's developed quite a few friends in the old boy network, but I don't care. When it got right down to it, Dr. Doran had been treated unfairly."

"Well, I wouldn't worry about it then. Anything else going on?"

"Nada. I have a heck of a custody case brewing here—reminds me so much of mine—but I can handle it now."

"Okay, just checking in. Keep me posted if anything comes up I need to know about."

"Like what, Adrian? Are you expecting something to come up?"

Adrian realized his blunder. There was no reason she would need to contact him. "I meant—well, you know, about the appointment. Never mind. Take care." He hung up and lay back in his chair. He needed to get ahold of himself. Anyway, the Barrow case must be the one. But he didn't see how he could identify the attorney who had prepared the motion. He'd have to forget it.

That evening, though she was feeling worn out and wanted to go home and get to bed early for once, Torie stayed at the courthouse for the first of a series of meetings with her supporters. She had scheduled the meeting two weeks earlier. The agenda included an array of programs people were interested in establishing in all four counties in her district, programs designed to assist families with children. Although some of the ideas were farfetched, and some would require so much money it would be virtually impossible to fund them in the current cash-strapped economy, several were quite doable. She was eager to get started.

Carrying a stack of computer-generated agendas, she entered the courtroom from her chambers. People overflowed the room. Not only were the chairs at the two counsel tables occupied, but the jury box and the benches in the gallery as well. People lined the walls.

Applause broke out as everyone stood. A thrill enveloped her, and she grinned at the crowd. One of the ladies, who had hosted a house party and sent a mailing to friends and neighbors during the election season, gestured to the only empty chair at one of the counsel tables. "We saved this for you."

"Thank you, Patti." Torie projected her voice. "And thank you all for your support, for helping me during the election, and for coming tonight. Please sit, those of you who have a place, and if you could scoot together, maybe one or two others could squeeze in."

She stood by the chair. "It's gratifying to know y'all sincerely want to help the families and children of our district." Applause broke out again. "Before we get started, Patti, would you hand out this agenda?" To the group she said, "Here's a sign-in sheet for you to give us your contact info." She gave Patti a stack of pages. "If we don't have enough, we can make more copies.

"During the campaign, when people approached me with ideas, I saved them and combined them with my own. What I thought we could discuss tonight is which ones are feasible, which may not be, ideas for funding sources, etcetera."

"Judge Van Fleet," a man in the back stood. "I'm Ben Carrington from Santa Fe County."

"Good to see you, Ben."

"What if we have some ideas for programs that aren't on the list?" He retook his seat.

"By all means, let's get everybody's input. Patti, why don't you take one copy and write Master List at the top of it. We'll circulate it, and if anyone wants to add something, please put it down. And also, y'all, when you get the master list if you see something you'd like to work on, put your name next the program you're interested in.

"This is only the first of what I hope will be many meetings. I hope we'll have a working relationship with each other for the benefit of the families of our counties for years to come."

Torie scanned the people row by row as she spoke. "Let's go ahead and start at the top of the list. I think this will be one of the easiest projects in terms of support from our communities. National Adoption Day. Carol Braun, do you want to speak to this one?"

A short, stocky brunette who sat on the front row stood. "I—I'm not much of a public speaker, Judge."

"It's okay. Just tell them like you told me when we first talked about it."

The paper in the woman's hands wavered, and she held it to her chest as she looked from Torie to the people behind her. "Okay if I talk from here?"

Torie nodded. She felt so tired the last few days. The lack of sleep was catching up with her. She sat in the chair Patti had saved for her.

"Well," Carol said, facing the crowd, "my sister lives in Galveston and she and her husband were foster parents and when the court down there freed the children for adoption, my sister and brother-in-law adopted them." She looked back at Torie.

"You're doing fine." Torie gave her a thumbs-up.

"Well, um, in Galveston they gather up all the people who are adopting and on a Saturday their judge comes out and does all the adoptions in one day." She dropped her hands to her sides as she warmed to the topic. "Then they have a big party with balloons, kind of like our county fair. They have it at a special place, Moody Gardens, and get sponsors and have a big celebration with pony rides and cotton candy and whatever they can get people to sponsor."

Torie said, "Thanks, Carol, nicely done."

Carol beamed, her eyes lit up. "I—I was thinking we could have it at the Germania County Barn the first year or at the city park. The judge could be in the gazebo and do the adoptions there, and we could have booths like at Oktoberfest."

Another woman stood two rows over. "I'm Marty Akers from Worth County. Could we change the county that hosts it from year-to-year so that every county in the district gets a shot at it?"

"Sure," Torie said, standing again. "Whatever the group decides."

Marty said, "I've read about this. I'm all for it. Maybe ours wouldn't be as big as Galveston's or some of the really big counties, but we could sure put on a nice event."

Torie said, "Is there anyone in the room who would be opposed?" At that point, she made eye contact with Bill Peterson from Fathers for Fair Judges. A jolt swept through her. She braced herself on the table and hoped he hadn't picked that venue to fuss about her possible appointment. She focused on the woman who was speaking.

"I'd be glad to head up a committee," Carol said. "You want to join me, Marty?"

"I'm thinking we should have at least one person from each county to coordinate it," Marty said. "I'm from Worth County, you're from Germania, who else might be interested?"

Several people raised their hands so they sent around another sign-up sheet, which took awhile. Torie made small talk with Patti as best she could, all the while knowing that Peterson could cause her a problem at any moment. When the sheet made it back to Carol, Torie stood again.

"The next thing I'd like to bring up is a visitation exchange center. I don't think this will be nearly as easy as National Adoption Day. What I'm talking about is not just a place where parents in difficult cases could exchange their children for possession times under the supervision of an impartial adult, which would be costly enough with a salary and rent, utilities, and all, but a place where people who are allowed only supervised access to their children would be able to visit with their children under the supervision of impartial people. In some places it's a franchise, and the parents have to pay quite a bit." Her knees went weak, and she gripped the back of the chair. What was wrong with her? She swallowed several times in quick succession. "We have so many poor people in the four counties in this district, but poor people ought to be able to see their children . . ." She looked at the ocean of faces. Some blurred. "I don't know how we'd accomplish it, but we sure do need it around here."

"What I'm wondering, Judge," came a male voice from the back of the room—Bill Peterson's voice—"is whether you're going to be around to help get these programs off the ground?"

He rose, arms crossed, face glowering. Dressed in a red plaid, long-sleeved shirt and jeans, he looked like he'd just come into town from the farm. Torie knew good and well he was a business owner, an insurance man. Did he dress that way on purpose so he could fit in with the crowd? And what did he think he would accomplish by interrupting the meeting? Could he possibly think she would change her mind if he embarrassed her?

Nausea gagged her in the back of her throat. Her feet felt bolted to the floor. Not that she could flee. She had to face her friends and supporters and explain what was going on, but if ever there was a time when she needed a few moments to pull herself together, this was it.

"What does he mean?" Patti asked. Her face wore anxiety like an insult.

"Okay, Mr. Peterson, you've got my attention. You can sit down now." The warmth of pleasure at seeing her courtroom filled with her friends and supporters changed to the heat of anger. How dare he? She swallowed several times again as she felt more nauseated and gripped the back of the chair so hard her fingers ached. She'd like to tell him exactly what she thought of his little stunt.

"Folks, I didn't want to mention this because quite possibly it won't come to pass, but one of the justices of the Texas Supreme

Court died in a tragic accident a few weeks ago, and it's up to the governor to appoint his replacement. I've applied for the job."

"But you just got re-elected," one woman called out.

"You'd abandon us?" a man asked from her right, at one of the counsel tables.

Other angry voices piped up from around the room.

"Well, I think that's wonderful," Patti said. "Hey, everybody, let the judge explain."

"Come on, y'all," a male voice bellowed, drowning out the others.

Torie wished she had a bailiff to settle everyone down. After a few moments, when the room grew quiet, she addressed them again. The situation couldn't be more awkward as she faced angry, questioning faces.

"Well, first, thank you for giving me the opportunity to explain. The deal is that the governor wants to have someone from the Hill Country on that bench. Most of the justices, if not all, are from large cities. He thinks the state needs justices who represent all our people.

"Secondly, if I were on that bench, I'd be in a position to do more for you all. Justices do more than hear appellate cases, they head up committees and studies and task forces. There are grants and—"

"Would you move to Austin, Judge?" another man at the counsel table to her right asked.

"No, definitely not. If I get the appointment, I'll get an apartment in Austin for when I have to be there, but my husband and I love our home here. If I'm appointed, he's going to build me an office behind our house. And besides, he works here in the Hill Country." Her hands were clammy, and sweat had broken out under her arms.

Mr. Peterson stood again. "I don't like it one bit. You asked us to support you in the election and we did. Now you turn on us—"

"I'm not turning on you, Mr. Peterson. I'd be here on weekends, at the very least, still able to participate in all the activities and programs we're talking about."

"But some other judge would be our real judge, right?" a woman at the counsel table where Torie stood said.

The door at the back of the courtroom opened, and two people left.

"Let's talk about this. Please hear me out." The mood in the courtroom had definitely shifted from one of exhilaration to one of sullenness.

"But there would be a new judge, right?" the woman asked.

"The governor would appoint a new district judge for this district."

"And we wouldn't have any say-so in who was appointed, like someone who cares about families like we thought you did."

The blood rushed out of Torie's face. The room faded into black and white. Dizziness swirled around her head. She stumbled as she tried to sit in the chair. "I do care about you. I could do so much more from there—"

"You don't look so good," Patti said. "I think you'd better sit back down." She took Torie's arm and helped her ease into the chair.

"I don't see that at all." Mr. Peterson pushed his way past the people down the row from him and stepped into the aisle by the back door. Jabbing his finger in her direction, he said, "You made promises during the election, promises you never intended to keep. And I'll tell you one thing, you'd better hope you get that appointment because if you don't and you run for re-election again,

I'll find someone to run against you." There was a collective gasp in the room. He swung the door wide and stormed out, two more people following him.

A metallic taste coated the back of her tongue. She drew a deep breath, trying to clear her head. "Please, folks, if you could give me a few minutes to explain my rationale . . . " She knew if they would listen, she could explain better the importance of having a local person on the highest court of the state, she could explain how she wasn't letting them down, she could explain she'd be helping not just them but other families. "This would be a feather in the cap of everyone in the Hill Country."

The room grew quiet again.

"I don't know what's the matter with me," she whispered to Patti. The light-headedness had grown worse.

Patti said, "Folks, I, for one, support Judge Van Fleet. If she says she'll still be around to work on those programs with us, she will. We have to trust that things will work out for us the way they're intended to."

Torie glanced at the blurry faces of the people who had been her friends and supporters. She hoped they'd understood.

Carol Braun stood and said, "Is the sign-up sheet back up here? Did everyone get a chance to sign the sheet and give us your phone number or e-mail?"

A thin, thirty-something man she recognized from Perdido County handed it to Carol and said, "Okay. I, for one trust Judge Van Fleet to do the right thing, so I propose we schedule another meeting. Anyone have a problem with that?"

"Thank you," Torie said. She tried to appear stoic in light of the situation, but in a matter of a few minutes, she had begun to feel bad all over. Maybe it was the flu.

"Otherwise," the man said, "let's adjourn."

Muttering, some sounding angry, others placated, people filed out into the hall.

Patti leaned over Torie. "What is it? Can I get you some water?"

"I'm so sorry," Torie said. "I haven't had much to eat today. My stomach's been upset lately, and I've been really tired." She felt totally humiliated. The one thing she'd never wanted to do was appear weak. "If you'd wait and walk me out to my car, Patti, I'd appreciate it. I'm sure I'll feel better tomorrow after I get some sleep."

Chapter 20

STANDING OUTSIDE THE SAN ANTONIO OFFICE of her OB-GYN, Torie overheard the conversation of two women. The daughter told the mother how scared she was, and the mother reassured the daughter. Many years earlier, Torie's mother had accompanied her to the doctor, holding her hand, both of them as full of awe as the two women with whom she'd just come into contact. She'd been filled with elation coupled with a bit of fear, the normal anticipatory fear, the not-knowing-what-it-would-be-like-to-be-the-mother-of-a-child kind of fear, but knowing her own mother would be there to advise her and help her and assuage that fear.

Now, she was there for a different purpose. To get new contraception, to prevent an unwanted pregnancy, to insure that nothing would interfere with her hopes and dreams of being on the Supreme Court. Her well-woman exam was past due, but getting in to see the doctor was no easy feat between the doctor's busy schedule and her own.

Life would be easier if she'd use a local doctor, one in Bremerhaven or even in one of the neighboring towns. Since she'd first taken office, she'd gotten all new doctors not only out of town but out of her judicial district. Bad enough as an attorney she'd often come into contact with litigants in the grocery store, the fitness center, or church, but as a judge it could be even more delicate. One of them could be testifying before her in the morning and looking up inside her in the afternoon.

The office, which smelled like rubbing alcohol, was filled with women in various stages of pregnancy, including one who could go into labor at any minute. Torie sat as far from the women as possible, hoping it wasn't catching, her stomach in a knot at the idea of stripping down to a hospital gown for the exam. She'd borne a child and still minded being examined. Was she a prude because she didn't want to expose her genitals?

She hadn't told Sergio of the appointment. Talk of birth control, when he wanted to have a child, was not high on their list of dinner topics. She'd scheduled the appointment after the almost-disastrous anniversary night. They were back on intimate terms, but a smidgen of coolness had seeped into their relationship. Something she couldn't quite grasp. She took responsibility for it, for everything that had gone wrong lately.

After she'd found him pacing off the backyard, they'd had deep discussions about their relationship. She'd promised not to put her father before him, though truth be told that was going to be excruciatingly hard when it came to discussing politics. She and her father had never been as close as Howie and her father, but her goal was that one day they would be. As she'd progressed professionally, he'd been more attentive to her. And politically, they had a lot to talk about. Her father had always been involved in politics as a behind-the-scenes person, coordinating local campaigns from the time he was a young man. He'd been her main organizer the first time she'd run for judge. He loved hearing about the muckraking, the plotting, the planning. That was a good thing.

After a while, the nurse called Torie's name and ushered her into the corridor to be weighed. Torie slipped off her shoes and stepped on the scale. A five-pound weight gain, two pounds more than her usual weight fluctuation. She gasped, stepped off, and stepped on again. Was that a bad omen? Her body telling her something? Her body signaling that she hadn't lost the weight from the campaign—all those spaghetti and rubber-chicken dinners—and to not get involved in another complication?

She followed the nurse into a private room where the nurse sat down at a computer and recorded Torie's answers to a series of questions. "And the reason for your appointment today is well-woman?"

"Well-woman and to discuss what else I can take for birth control since I was having problems with the pill I was on." Torie described her symptoms, trying not to leave out even the slightest concern.

"I see." The nurse made the entry. "Okay, let me get your blood pressure and other basics, and then you'll get undressed and get on the table."

Torie nodded and sat still while the nurse recorded her vitals.

"There's a gown and a small sheet on the table. I assume you know the drill."

"Oh, yes, ma'am," Torie said. "Every woman of childbearing age knows the drill." And every one of them wished they didn't know the feeling of putting their feet into those icy stirrups.

The nurse nodded and went out. Torie stripped, donning the gown, tying it in the front as requested. She folded her clothes into small squares and stacked them, her pantyhose and bra hidden under her outerwear and her shoes resting beside the chair.

The room was chilly, so she took her coat with her as she climbed up on the table and covered herself with the smaller sheet over her lap and the coat draped over her whole body. She would have liked it better if she'd been able to discuss birth control with the doctor before she had to get up on the table and spread her legs, but this wasn't her office, and she didn't make the rules. She was just another patient, and every doc did things differently.

After a while, Dr. York, a tiny Asian woman whose age range was anywhere from forty to seventy, came in. A white coat was layered over black shirt and pants. A few tinges of silver graced the ebony hair at her temples. She wore large black-framed glasses that made her face look like a little mouse, deep smile grooves around her mouth, and a wide, friendly smile.

"So, Judge, been a while." She shook Torie's hand.

"Yes, ma'am, the past year got away from me with the election and all. But I'm here now. How are you?"

"Same as always. But we're here about you." She pressed a buzzer on the wall. The nurse returned. "I'll do the exam first to get it out of the way, all right?"

One of the things Torie liked about the doctor was her no-nonsense approach. She never wasted time on chitchat. Torie handed her coat to the nurse and shook out the sheet that she'd held in her lap, covering her legs with it.

The little doctor stood next to the table and looked up at Torie. "We're doing a well-woman exam, and you want different birth control."

"Yes, Doc. I quit taking the pill I was on last year."

Dr. York frowned and shook her head.

"Well, I had some issues with it and meant to get in here. I wondered if one of the new pills I read about on the Internet would be better for me, especially at my age."

"You're how old?"

"Forty-five." Torie squinted at her. "Perimenopausal, right?"

"Let's get your feet into the stirrups, and we'll see. Sara?" Dr. York glanced at the nurse who assisted Torie into the correct position.

Torie stared at the ceiling. She wasn't the only woman in the world who disliked gynecological exams, but at that moment she didn't care about any other woman. At least this doc had small hands.

"You're married again if I recall," the doctor said as she rolled a stool to the foot of the table.

"Yes, very." Torie tensed her body as the doctor began the procedure.

"Just relax," the doctor said as she probed and prodded. "And you don't want children?" The doctor pressed down on her abdomen.

"Not at this late date."

"Had you ever thought about getting a tubal ligation?" Dr. York manipulated Torie's abdomen a bit more and murmured something.

"Pardon me?" Torie said.

"You sure you don't want children?" The doctor stood and stepped around the foot of the table toward Torie.

"Yes, positive." No way was she going to give Dr. York the lowdown on her political plans, but she didn't want to get into some argument about whether or not she should have another child. "This is awkward, Dr. York. Do you usually question your patients' decisions like this?"

"Not usually." She pushed her glasses up on her nose.

"A baby doesn't fit into my life any more. I've got things I want to accomplish before I'm too old." Cassie had died before Dr. York became her physician, and she'd never talked about her to the doctor. Anyway, it didn't matter why she didn't want another child. It was her decision to make.

"Uh-huh, well if you don't want a baby, then we have something to talk about." She examined Torie's breasts, her gloved hands cold. "I'm going to squeeze your nipples to check for discharge." She pinched the nipples then patted her shoulder. "You can sit up."

Torie folded her legs against each other and struggled to rise to a sitting position. The nurse's face wore a blank look as she assisted her. Torie wrapped the sheet around her waist and legs. "So you have some suggestions for me?"

The doctor put her stethoscope to Torie's chest and moved around to her back, asking her to cough, take deep breaths, the whole routine, but didn't engage in conversation for a few minutes. She checked Torie's ears, throat, and eyes and looked up her nose. When she finished, the doc looked Torie in the eye and sighed. "We'll do a urine test to confirm, Judge, but I'm afraid you're pregnant."

"No. What? That's why I'm here. So I won't get pregnant." Images of herself with a baby flashed in her mind. A vision of her young self with Cassie. She pushed them away. She didn't want to remember what it was like to have a baby and lose her years later.

"Well, you are, Judge. You came to me too late."

Torie's stomach twisted inside out. "I—I—am? Pregnant?" Her

head spun as her body melted onto the table. "No." She started to say *That's not possible* until she remembered it was *very* possible. Too many martinis plus no birth control equaled a baby. A martini baby. She let herself fall back onto the table and stared at the doctor's face.

"Yes, Your Honor, you're about two months." The doctor's mouth formed into a pencil-thin line as though she'd given the news of a fatality, a death, rather than an impending birth.

A small cry escaped Torie. She squeezed her eyes shut. No wonder she constantly felt nauseous. *Oh God, Oh God*—what was she going to do? She couldn't move. Couldn't open her eyes—to do so would make what the doctor said real, and it couldn't be real. *What was she going to do? What was she going to do?*

Dr. York patted her shoulder, "Okay, come on, sit up. Take a few minutes. When you're dressed come into my office." She left the room, the door clicking behind her. The nurse handed Torie a box of tissues and left also.

Torie lay still for a few moments, trying to make some sense of her situation. Why now? Why, when she'd laid out a plan for her future? After a bit, she cleaned herself up and climbed off the table. How could she have been so reckless? She was an extremely educated woman who saw people who did dumb things every day, turning their lives inside out. She was right in there with them. She was an idiot.

After dressing, Torie found Dr. York sitting in her office and making entries on a computer. Her office was standard institutional except for a ginormous teak desk with carvings down the sides and across the top under a thick layer of glass. She looked up at Torie. "Close the door and have a seat."

Torie did as she was instructed. Her limbs were stiff, wooden.

She held her purse in her lap and stared at the doctor, unseeing, as images of people, courts, and files marched through her head.

"You don't want this baby, Judge?"

"I certainly didn't plan to have a baby." Her stomach roiled. Thoughts swirled through her head. She needed time to think.

"I think we have established that. What I'm asking is whether you want to terminate the pregnancy?" Her lips pressing together, her black eyes peering at Torie through glasses that were too big for her face, she tapped on the desk pad with a mechanical pencil.

Torie stared at the doctor and wished she had an answer. "I don't know. I have, what, about two months to make up my mind?"

"About that. I can make a referral if that's what you want to do. Otherwise, we need to set you up on a plan for prenatal care." She licked her lips and reached into her desk drawer where she retrieved some lip balm and applied it, never taking her eyes off Torie's.

"I understand." Torie stood and reached out to shake the doctor's hand, which was even smaller than her own. "I'm going to take a bit of time to think it over."

"Well, until you make a firm decision, I hope you'll at least take a really good vitamin. You're a bit rundown." She pushed a slip of paper toward Torie.

Torie closed her eyes for a moment and shivered. When she opened them, she took the paper, which had the name of a vitamin hand-written on it. "Okay."

"You'll give us a urine specimen before you leave, then you can make another appointment on your way out if you want. Otherwise, good luck, dear lady." Dr. York turned her attention back to her computer.

As Torie drove back to her county to the courthouse, her head spun. She had known her period was late, but that had happened before. She blamed stress. In her heart of hearts, she didn't really believe she could get pregnant from just one night without protection. Not her. Not when she'd been so determined not to have a baby. How could she have been so stupid?

And now she had to make a decision. If she kept the baby, she might as well give up the idea of being on the Supreme Court. Adrian had made that clear. And it was a good thing she'd just been re-elected, because if she was up for election and pregnant at the same time, her opponent would be spreading the lie that she intended to have the baby and quit, or ask the voters what kind of a judge was she when she wasn't even home taking care of her own child? And on top of that, she had Bill Peterson already saying if she didn't get the appointment, he'd find her an opponent the next time she ran. Could things get any more complicated?

If she terminated the pregnancy, things would be even worse. First of all, even though her party took the opposite view, she believed a woman had a right to choose whether or not she would have a child, not let the government decide.

Secondly, though that was her view, she wasn't sure whether she wanted to apply it to herself. Could she live with herself afterward?

Thirdly, if Sergio ever found out, she was sure he would leave her for good. She could just hear him say, *"You killed my baby."* He would hate her. Their relationship would be over.

On the other hand, she could imagine what a lovely baby it would be, with Sergio's dark looks and maybe her own blue-purple eyes. You never knew.

If her parents found out she terminated the pregnancy, they

would shame her. So would Howie and Mary. She'd never hear the last of it.

Finally, if the public ever discovered it, her political career would be over, at least in Texas. She would be as good as dead.

Her head pounded and her fist ached from beating on the steering wheel. What was she going to do?

Fortunately, she didn't have to decide at that moment. She'd think it over, like she'd told the doctor. Sleep on it. See how the next few weeks progressed before she made a decision. Her chest hurt, and she couldn't get a deep breath when she considered that this was one choice she'd have to make all on her own, but one that could affect many other people in her life.

Chapter 21

TOWARD THE END OF ANOTHER WEEKNIGHT AT her parents' home, her mother asked Torie to come into her sewing room. There was something she wanted to discuss. Torie was wary when her mother wanted a talk. She didn't ask to speak to Torie privately very often, but when she did, the subject was usually something that made Torie uncomfortable. However, she acquiesced, curiosity piqued.

"Sit down, dear." Her mother pushed aside a stack of folded fabric and patted the foot of the bed next to her.

After closing the door so Sergio couldn't overhear should he come down the hall and try to listen like he had several weeks earlier, Torie perched on the edge of the bed.

"Your father and I have noticed you and Sergio seem distant from one another." Debra's face was lined with concern.

Annoyance nipped at Tori. She'd often had a hard time discussing her relationships with her mother. She thought it was because they held such different outlooks on life. Her mother was a traditional wife and mother. The homemaker. Torie was the career woman. "Mom." Torie stood. "We're not having this discussion."

Her mother pulled her back down, her hand soft but her grip firm. "You know we don't ordinarily interfere in your relationships, but Dad and I wonder if we were wrong in not trying to help you and Bert before everything got out of hand."

Torie's throat grew tight. "I'm not rehashing Bert and me at this late date."

"I don't mean to do that. Water under the bridge and all that. But you and Sergio—maybe we can help." She gave Torie a look that said I've-got-something-to-say-and-you're-going-to-listen. "Sergio is such a lovely young man."

Torie exhaled and settled onto the bed. There was nothing for her to do but let her mother have her say. "I can't disagree with you there." Should she follow up on the *young man* comment or let it ride? Her mother's soft face held no malice. Torie was the one who feared criticism, whose insecurity made her want to read something into almost every sentence, if not every word.

"Would you like to confide in me what the problem is?" Her mother mimicked Torie's posture down to holding her own hands in her lap. A corner of her mouth twitched.

If her mother had something particular in mind, she should come out and say it, not dance around the subject. Torie covered her mother's clasped hands with one of her own. "No, Mom, I wouldn't. At least not right now. Maybe later. Another time."

"It's about having a baby, isn't it?"

Torie's neck flushed. She fought to keep from rolling her eyes, a habit she'd never completely broken since she'd been a teenager. She might have known the baby thing would come up. She wasn't ready to discuss her dilemma with anyone, especially her mother. For her mother, the decision would be simple: keep the baby.

Her mother had always wanted Torie to have more children, a little brother or sister for Cassie. Before Torie decided to further her education. Before Bert became so threatened and insecure. Before she and Bert began having serious problems in their relationship that eventually led to their separation and divorce. "Has Sergio been talking to you? I know how you feel about each other. Maybe he should have married you."

"Don't be hurtful, honey. This is serious." Her eyes crinkled as she smiled a wistful smile. "You make such nice babies, Torie. Dad and I think you really should consider giving Sergio one, just one."

Torie reared back as though hit. She crossed the room and pushed the curtains aside to look out the window, as if she could see anything beyond what the backyard light illuminated. Anger and annoyance competed in her. She fought a rude retort. As if she didn't have enough pressure on her without more from her mother. And her father. What was he thinking? He knew what she wanted. Was he really not as much behind her as she thought? He was such a traditionalist in so many ways, but she'd thought he'd come into the twenty-first century—agreeing that women were equal to men.

No, this must be coming from Sergio. It didn't even matter when he'd discussed the baby thing with them, just that he had. And after he'd addressed her about her own behavior. His was no better. "I can't believe this. Does Sergio think he can get you to persuade me to have a baby? Is that what he thinks?"

"No, honey. He's just confided in me, that's all."

Torie ran her fingers across the windowsill, coming up with only a bit of dust. She brushed off her hands and straightened a pillow on the easy chair next to the sewing machine. How easy it would be to plop down and confide everything to her mother, to confess the surprise pregnancy—that it had created a dilemma in her she didn't know existed, that she had only known about it for a few days but already she was exhausted, her appetite had changed, and she frequently felt tearful. "And Sergio's talked with Dad, too?"

"Briefly, Torie. He dropped by one afternoon." She still clasped her hands in her lap.

Torie stood with her hands on her hips and glared. "Mother, we had a heart-to-heart before we got married. Did he tell y'all that? In fact, the first night we had a real date I told him, and I quote, 'If you're looking for someone to have your babies, you're looking at the wrong girl, because I'm way past that stage in my life.'"

"Really?" Her mother looked at her and straightened nonexistent wrinkles in her slacks.

"Yes, really. And he laughed and said that was okay, he didn't have to have kids. That I would be more than enough for him." She remembered how pleased she'd felt when he'd said that. She'd liked him but hadn't wanted to get involved with someone who would expect her to produce children.

"Apparently he's changed his mind."

"Apparently." Torie clamped her lips together.

"Don't be sarcastic. It doesn't become you."

"Look, *Mother*, I'm sure Dad has told you my plans by now. I mean, he must have since he's been rounding up letters of support for me. Can't you see I have a future that requires all my time and attention?" She glanced away. Hiding something from her mother had always been hard. Her mother could read her like the pages of a book the printers' ink hadn't even dried on. "Besides, there's always Cassie to consider."

"You can't bring her back." Her mother clapped her hand to her mouth, her eyes wide and frightened. "I'm so sorry. I didn't mean to say that."

Adrenaline shot through Torie's insides leaving her feeling as raw as she had after she'd found Cassie's body. She clenched her fists, forcing down her feelings. She didn't want to erupt in an angry outburst. That she still felt so much grief, even though it had been five years, was not a new feeling but one she kept hidden, pushed down deep inside until someone mentioned her daughter. Or she heard a hotly contested case involving children. Or she saw a blonde girl on the sidewalk. "I know I can't bring her back. But I don't want to make the same mistakes."

She wanted to cry and throw-up at the same time. She wished there were some way she could reset the clock. Do something different to change the course of her life, of her daughter's life.

Debra held out her arms. "Don't call Cassie a mistake, honey. She was a lovely little girl."

"I didn't say Cassie was a mistake." Torie choked back a sob. She went down onto the foot of the bed and into her mother's arms. "God, how did we get on the subject of Cassie? I thought that chapter of my life was closed forever."

"I'm so sorry I started this conversation. I just thought . . ."

Torie fought tears, but they were beyond her control as they pushed their way out and flowed onto her mother's shoulder. "I can't go through it again. I can't. If for some reason Sergio and I split up, I couldn't go through what Bert put me through again. The fighting. The lawyers. The court battles for years on end."

"That's not going to happen. Sergio loves you too much."

Torie slipped from her mother's grasp and onto the rug on the floor and looked up at her mother. "See, Mom, if I had a child and it did happen . . . if Sergio left me or I him . . . well I know so much more now than I did then." She looked into her mother's eyes. "And I would never do what Bert and I did to a child again. Never fight like that. Never drag her into court. Make her choose between her parents. I know now how damaging that is to a child. I would simply give the child to Sergio to raise and accept whatever time he would allow me with the child."

Her mother's lips knitted together. She opened her mouth, but no words came out.

Torie sat back on her heels and squeezed her eyes shut tight like she could erase the images of her lost daughter. "I've given this a lot of thought since Cassie died." She wrapped her arms around her knees. "I don't want to lose another child." She shook her head and said in her firm judge's voice, "I can't take the loss of another child. I won't chance losing another child."

She didn't consider the fetus she was carrying to be a child, just a mass of cells. She had no feelings for it yet. It hadn't moved, hadn't kicked, hadn't drawn a breath. She hadn't heard it cry. Once it did those things, life would never be the same.

Chapter 22

A FEW DAYS LATER, AT LUNCHTIME WHEN THE building was mostly deserted, Torie crossed the hall to Beth's chambers. She didn't stop for the startled Charlotte, who was eating a sandwich at her desk, to see if it was a good time for her to enter. "Beth, you won't believe—"

One of their mutual friends, Jean Boswell, a judge from Austin, sat opposite Beth. She wore a pantsuit, but had her shoes off and one foot tucked under her.

"Hi, Jean," she said. Jean pulled herself up and glanced from Torie to Beth. She looked like she'd like to find a place to hide.

At the back of the room, the restroom door clicked open and another of their mutual friends, Cynthia Van Skyke, a judge in San Antonio, emerged, drying her hands on a paper towel. Cynthia was a former college cheerleader and always looked like one, a perkiness about her. Her eyes flared, but she recovered quickly. She finished drying her hands and bounced toward Torie with a look that said she was going to wrap her in an embrace.

Torie's breath caught, and she stepped back. Her eyes skipped from one woman to the other. Jean wouldn't look at her. A little pain struck Torie right next to her heart.

Beth's chin jutted out in a defensive, defiant *you-caught-us* look.

Something was going on, some kind of meeting, and Torie had not been invited. A flush swept up her neck and into her face.

Her friends. Their so-called *mutual* friends.

"We were just talking about you," Jean said, finally looking at Torie, sizing her up. "You're looking well."

Torie knew she looked anything but well. She'd been hugging the toilet every morning, unable to keep even saltines and water down. Sleep had finally come to her after all the time she'd lain awake worrying about Wesley Carr, but now the pregnancy was making her constantly fatigued, feeling like she'd been drugged. She wanted nothing more than to stay in bed and sleep. Her face was puffy, always looking like she'd just woken up.

Directing her words at Jean, Torie said, "Yeah, I bet you were talking about me." She realized she had happened onto a meeting of some of the people—some of the judges—who were supporting Beth's application for the Supreme Court. She held a palm up as Cynthia approached. Cynthia stopped and looked from Torie to Beth.

"What did you want?" Beth asked, her voice indignant, her hands flat on her desk as she started to rise.

"Never mind." Torie did an about-face, pulling the door closed behind her. Her vision blinded by anger, she felt her way past Charlotte. The pain of betrayal swirled inside her.

She didn't get as far as inside her own door across the hall when a third woman-judge friend of theirs rounded the corner from the elevator. Kathy Turnwell carried take-out bags of Chinese food, the aroma of moo goo gai pan and fried rice filling the hall.

Torie hadn't been invited to lunch with them this time. She'd always been included before. She was positive she was correct. Those three judges were supporting Beth for the Supremes. She waved at Kathy and fled inside her own chambers, shutting the door behind her.

How could her friends do that to her? She hadn't contacted them yet, that was true, but how could they automatically become supporters of Beth's without even talking to her? And if they weren't there for that reason, why were they there? If they weren't there to rally around Beth, wouldn't they have asked Torie to join them? If they'd forgotten to invite her, why didn't they ask her to stay? Or come after her when she left?

No, throwing their support to Beth had to be why they were there. How humiliating to have friends, alleged friends, her friends—well, Beth's friends too—meeting in support of Beth right across the hall. Didn't they realize she'd find out? She leaned against her chambers' door for a moment. How utterly humiliating. Her head throbbed. Her face radiated heat.

Her stomach heaved, a sour taste pushed its way up the back of her throat, and she slammed past the restroom door in time to upchuck into the toilet. Once, twice, the third time dry heaves.

When she was through, she leaned back against the wall and wiped her mouth. She patted at the perspiration on her face with a brown institutional paper towel, her knees weak. She gripped the side of the sink and splashed water on her face. That was all she needed, to be sick in the afternoons as well as the mornings.

Thankfully no one else was around. Nettie had left for lunch. The lawyers knew better than to bother her during her lunch hour. She'd established those boundaries early on.

She stumbled back into her chambers and dropped onto her couch, kicking off her shoes and pulling a throw over her legs in hopes the chill of fear would subside.

Her friends must not care if she saw them at Beth's. Either they didn't think she'd be there, or they didn't think she'd see them. Or they figured she would find out anyway, so it didn't matter. But it would have been so much nicer of them to hold their little meeting at a restaurant or at Beth's home, where Torie wouldn't be treated so rudely. More than anything, they had hurt her feelings. Not one of them had called and told her they were supporting Beth, that they still wanted to remain friends but felt Beth was the better candidate. Not one.

How many others were doing the same? She dug her hands into her hair. Her scalp was damp and hot. Just goes to show you never know a person as well as you think.

Her stomach rumbled. It had just emptied, so there was nothing to rumble about unless her stomach had a mind of its own and now wanted to be fed. No way. She couldn't face running off the bench to puke. And having to make up excuses. Claim she had a virus. Or, worse, food poisoning and everyone would want to know what she had eaten and where. And had she reported it to the health department? No. There'd be no lunch for her that day, or any day at work, until her body settled down or until she had the procedure. Which she hadn't decided on. Which she couldn't think of right then. The pain of her friends' betrayal was just too great. It made her sick in a completely different way. Sick with fear. Sick at heart.

And lonely. Very lonely. She couldn't focus on more than one issue at that moment.

Still, she needed to put something in her stomach. She found a bottle of fizzy water in her small refrigerator and took a few small sips. The water was too cold. She shivered. Her stomach rebelled. She barely made it into the restroom before she lost the water as well. She'd never had any kind of illness when she'd been pregnant with Cassie. Of course that was twenty years earlier. She'd been young and, besides trying to finish her undergraduate degree, under no stress. That was the difference. Dr. York had warned her that a forty-five year old pregnant woman's body would react differently from a twenty-something's.

When she emerged from the restroom again, someone knocked on the door to her chambers. She opened it to find Beth standing there.

"See, that's what you're supposed to do before entering a judge's chambers. Didn't anyone ever tell you that before?" Beth held up her fist, mimicking someone knocking. "Knock. Knock. Knock."

"Yeah, I get it," Torie said, dropping onto her sofa. "Knock, knock, knock. Like the old song says." Her limbs felt weak, and she still had that awful taste in her mouth. "I've never had to knock before, and you've never had to knock on my door either. Now I know there are new rules, I'll follow them." She pulled the Afghan over herself again.

Beth's voice softened. "I'm sorry you had to see us. I didn't want it that way. The meeting came up so quickly, I didn't get a chance to tell you."

Torie didn't reply. She draped an arm over her eyes.

"I said I'm sorry. You have your supporters, and I have mine.

You don't see me getting all huffy because Adrian Frothingham is helping you." Beth had moved to stand over Torie, her hands in her skirt pockets.

"Do you see me getting all huffy?" Torie asked, peering above her arm. "I don't think my lying here is tantamount to being all huffy."

"Torie you can't burst into my chambers anymore like you used to. We each have confidential communications we don't want the other to see, right? I mean, surely you have stuff you're collecting to give to the governor? Letters of support—"

"Those women in your chambers were supposed to be my friends. Not one of them had the decency to call me or e-mail me and tell me they'd decided to support you. Not one."

"I'm sure they would have in time. Would you take your arm down so I can see your eyes? What's wrong with you?"

Torie moved her arm and sat up. "You could have called or texted me. It was bad enough when Jack had his little rant at lunch—"

"I had nothing to do with Jack's rant. And I never asked him for his support, because I figured neither he nor the others would back either of us. I would have told you if I had."

"Like you told me about Jean and—"

"I would have told you. This is really our first meeting. I invited them to a long lunch, and they were all able to make it today. They volunteered to bring the food."

"I'm sure they knew what they were coming for."

"Of course they knew."

"It's not right. They're my friends, too."

"Did you call them? Have you bothered to call anyone, or are you relying on Adrian and your father to do all the legwork for you?"

"How dare you? I'm making calls every night." Torie leaned her head back.

"Sure you are." Red-faced, Beth stared down at Torie. "Anyway, I don't want to argue with you."

"Oh, right, so why'd you deign to cross the hall and come see me?"

"I've never seen this ugly side of you, Torie. It doesn't become you."

"Who are you, my mother? Just go back across the hall where you belong and tell my ex-friends they can kiss my patootie." She knew she sounded like a pouting teenager, but at that moment, she didn't care.

Beth reared back. "What's gotten into you?"

"Betrayal, that's all." Feeling dizzy, she flopped back down. "Just get out."

"Gladly," Beth said, her face drawn up into a fierce scowl. "And may I add, before I go, you need to see a doctor. You look like shit." She walked back to Torie's chambers' door and slammed it behind her.

Chapter 23

ADRIAN SLOUCHED OVER A COLD CONTAINER of coffee and stared out the picture window overlooking the river, the murky green water drifting past the leafless, almost lifeless, oaks. He still wore a lightweight coat, because he didn't intend to be there long. The Coffee Haus, a short walk from his office, was devoid of any other customers as often was the case in the middle of the day.

A few scraping steps came toward Adrian, and a suit slipped into the adjacent chair. A man named Gray, wearing a gray suit, matching the gray day, and Adrian's gray mood. Many of the attorneys in Lawyers for Lawsuit Equity often wore gray suits, gray silk suits. Why was that, so they could disappear into a crowd?

"Good afternoon, Judge," the suit said.

Adrian nodded almost imperceptibly, his eyes following the water flow, his arms resting on the edge of the table, his fingers drumming, *thrum—thrum, thrum—thrum.* He well knew the voice and the man, though he didn't know him well.

"How's your lovely wife?" There was a slight lilt in the suit's voice, what Adrian thought of as a false lilt, a lying lilt.

"Fine. She's fine." His voice a monotone. "Just returned from a health spa."

"Glad to hear that." The suit slurped from his steaming cup of coffee, a hint of hazelnut wafting into the air. "I hear our girl is doing well."

Adrian nodded, still watching the scene framed by the window. "You could say that." If push came to shove, he'd rather deal with brash, boisterous Karl than this guy. Gray made him think of the paper dolls his sister played with as a child. A paper doll man, tall, thin, flat-affect most of the time, nothing inside. Adrian knew little about the man other than he was an attorney. He'd seen him in court over the years, but Adrian had never so much as conversed with the man except for LLE matters. Never had, never would.

"We have a *small* problem." With emphasis on small, which told Adrian it was not so small.

Adrian finally looked in the direction of the suit, an eyebrow arched, an eye narrowed. "In what way?"

The suit reached down and pulled his chair closer to the table, closer to Adrian. "She has yet to rule on a summary judgment. Do you know what's hanging her up?"

Adrian's lips stretched across his teeth. "She doesn't discuss her cases with me. You know better than that."

The suit's voice never varied from a tone of passive pleasantness. "Have you discussed her responsibilities with her? Does she know what's expected?"

"Not specifically. I've given her encouragement."

"Well, I suggest you *specifically* do. And soon."

The sides of Adrian's face twitched, his sideburns, his ears. He grimaced. He wished he could hit the man. Slap him. Push his face in until he fell backward out of his chair and onto the floor.

"We need that ruling." The suit's jaw flexed, which Adrian knew would be the extent of any public exhibition of emotion. Paper doll people rarely showed any reaction to anything.

A muscle twitched at the edge of Adrian's eye. "You made that clear."

"Look." The suit leaned closer, his coffee breath in Adrian's face. "We appreciate her giving our man a break on his vacation, but that was just a warm-up."

"Must have been routine." Adrian flexed the fingers of both hands and spread them on the table. That had been a couple of months ago. He wished they'd quit dwelling on it like it was something special.

"Family ski trip. No vacation letter on file. Continuance granted."

"I heard. She'd help anyone out if it wouldn't be detrimental to the other side."

"We prefer to think she favored our man out of gratitude. If you say she didn't, fine. Then there was the case involving two dentists where she poured out our friend's opponent. Our friend is very grateful for that, as well. But we still need that ruling on the summary judgment. You'd better talk to her."

Adrian choked down his coffee before answering. "She's not the type to be rushed. You can hang in there another few days."

"Our client is losing money every day your girl sits on that case. The engineers are ready to go forward. The workers are lined up.

We need a ruling, and we need it now." He jabbed the table with his forefinger.

Adrian wanted to grab it and bend it backward until it broke. "You think I can interfere with her docket? Tell her she needs to rule in their favor? Are you insane?" Adrian gripped the edge of the table to stop himself from punching the man.

"That's exactly what I think," the suit said in a fierce whisper. "It's just a little thing. The law and the facts are on our side. We'll win in trial anyway. This will speed up things and save a lot of money on both sides. So you see, she'd be doing a favor all around."

"You're mad."

"Remind her of the contributions that were made to her campaign. She had to know why she had so much support."

Adrian shook his head and looked into his lap. "I can't do it. It'll break her heart."

"Listen, Judge. She's going to rule in our favor, anyway. As I said, the facts and the law are on our side. It's no big deal. And while you're talking to her, remind her we're supporting her for the Supremes. Tell her we have a lot of contacts in the governor's office and a lot of sway with the governor. You've experienced that. Remember how you got this job in the first place?"

Adrian crushed his paper coffee cup in his hand, the dregs popping out onto his fingers. He was past being humiliated. They'd finished him off a long time ago. They might think it was necessary to remind him, but Adrian would never forget. It haunted him.

But now to force him to jeopardize Victoria's very soul? He hated to do it. Why had she been so insistent? Why was she so determined to get the appointment? He'd tried to reason with her. Tried to make her understand without showing his hand. Everything in her manner had told him she'd terminate all contact with him if he didn't sponsor her, help her. He should have let her. When she had risen from the lunch table in anger, he should have let her go. But he didn't. He didn't want to lose the small bit of relationship they still had. He didn't want to go from mentor-mentee to the formality of Senior Administrative Judge to sitting District Judge, speaking only when required by legal duties.

He was selfish. And now he had to do it. He had to turn her. He rose and shuffled to the wastebasket where he tossed his coffee cup. He'd become an old man in the past few years, older in the past few weeks. The life he'd chosen had taken its toll. He could almost feel himself aging as the days clicked by.

Without looking back at the suit, Adrian left The Coffee Haus. He knew what he had to do. He would do it, because he knew not to would cause him to forfeit something significant. He wasn't sure what, but LLE was capable of wreaking havoc on his life. They'd managed to let him know that over the years.

Chapter 24

THE FOLLOWING DAY, TORIE RECEIVED A CALL from Adrian asking her to meet him at the new coffee house in Bremerhaven. It was the grand opening, and they were promising free tastings. Personally, the thought of sipping a mocha-this or a latte-that made her want to escape to the ladies' room and throw up her guts, but she agreed to meet Adrian mid-morning during an opening in her calendar caused by a cancelled hearing.

She would walk over. She needed to get more exercise, needed to shed those two pounds—probably more than that now—before she started showing.

Ditching her stilettos for tennis shoes, she struck out toward the creek where the shop was located. The town was making an effort to develop a miniature creek-walk like San Antonio's Riverwalk. The coffee house was to be the keystone at one end and an ice cream parlor, which she secretly hoped would be a *Ben and Jerry's* even though she would probably only patronize it once or twice a year, would anchor the other.

Adrian was waiting for her. He had taken a table on the terrace overlooking the creek. He'd always had a thing for tables on terraces.

"Hey, Victoria," he said, getting up and kissing her cheek. "What'll you have? Want an espresso mocha?"

She shook her head. "I don't know what that is, but no. How about a plain cup of black tea. I could use the caffeine, but I don't want anything sweet. Thanks."

Adrian left to get in line, and Torie took his chair. The chill had left the air in the last few days. Now it was warm and breezy on the terrace. A weeping willow tree stood only a few feet from the creek, its draping branches like braids almost brushing the ground. The wind blew the boughs one way, and then sucked them back the other. An emerald green lawn ran all the way to the creek and to the property lines on both sides, not something seen frequently.

Lawn grass required a lot of water, like golf courses. Water was a precious commodity in the Texas Hill Country and, as she well knew, often the subject of litigation. Still, it was pretty. Some kind of flower bulbs planted at the borders were pushing their way up. No doubt as spring came to Bremerhaven in full force, the flowers would bloom, perhaps in conjunction with the celebration of Easter.

The idea of making the creek a commercial area was a good one and long in the development stages. She had first heard it mentioned when she'd been a little girl. She didn't really know what it entailed, since she stayed out of city politics, but the city had owned the banks on the North side of the creek for as long as she could remember. The hold-up had probably been getting the South side freed up. Anyhow, once the walkway was complete, it would be a nice place for tourists to wander about in shops and restaurants in addition to Main Street.

Adrian returned and set a cup of tea in front of her, taking the chair opposite. "The creek looks pretty good, doesn't it?"

She nodded and sipped her tea. Though it wasn't even lunchtime, she was ready to call it a day. She'd started bringing her lunch—something she thought she might be able to keep down—eating in chambers, and lying down for a few minutes' nap afterward. She needed to make a decision about the baby soon. It was wrecking her both emotionally and physically.

"How're things going?" She put down her cup, studying his face. "Have you heard back from anyone? When will I get my meeting with the governor?"

"There are some things I wanted to talk to you about. You've got a lot of support. I must say some of it has come as quite a surprise."

"Beth has a lot of support also." She glanced at the creek. The pain of seeing her friends in Beth's chambers was still with her. She hoped the hurt she felt didn't appear on her face. "The other day some of our friends in the third and fourth region came to have lunch with her. And obviously Jack Dobbs supports her."

"Don't let that worry you, Victoria." Adrian had a very large paper cup of something foamy. After he took a drink, some of it stayed on his mustache. In past times she would have reached out and wiped it away. Now she kept quiet, mildly amused at his appearance. "Having other judges' support is okay, but they don't really hold a lot of water with the governor."

She hunched forward in a confiding posture. "That's good."

"You've got my support, and that has weight." His eyebrows

rose, and he pulled a smiley face, made funnier by the foam he didn't know he wore.

"I can't tell you how much I appreciate all you're doing for me."

He leaned toward her and whispered, "I'd do anything for you. Don't you know that?"

A shock swept through Torie. She did know that, though the last few years she'd come to think of him as a father figure. She knew he still had feelings for her. She'd hoped he realized he'd never be more now that she had Sergio. She knew he'd never gotten over her, but that kind of talk was dangerous, had been off-limits for years, and if anyone overheard, they'd know he had once been more, much more, than a mentor. Maybe his feelings, the words he wanted to express, were some of the reasons he chose a table outside on the terrace where no one could hear them. She was able to handle their past relationship, but was Adrian having regrets?

She kept her voice low. "Adrian, please, let's keep this on a professional level."

He sat back. "I'm allowed a little slip now and again, am I not?"

"I suppose, so long as it's only verbal." She was too worn out to argue.

"Anyway," he said, "you also have the support of a group called Lawyers for Lawsuit Equity. Have you heard of them?"

She shook her head. "I'm not sure. It sounds vaguely familiar. The name is similar to so many other organizations."

"LLE's members contribute great sums of money to campaigns around the state, hell, some even to those in Washington. You had some contributions from them last fall when you ran for re-election."

"I did? How come I didn't know it?"

"Well, because the organization doesn't contribute. The

members meet and decide who they're going to support and the individual attorneys contribute."

Maybe their actions weren't odd, but there was something about it that made her uneasy. It wasn't that different from political parties asking their members to support particular candidates. For someone who had already served a four-year term and run in two elections, she was just coming to the realization that she was politically naïve, ignorant even. She frequently heard of new pranks, for lack of a better word, being pulled by one group or another.

She'd had so many contributions this go-round she couldn't remember many of the donors, not even all of the high-dollar ones, even though she'd reviewed them and written thank you notes to each person. She probably wasn't supposed to, but she had a copy of her final contribution list in her desk drawer. She'd taken it to the office after the Motion to Recuse was filed, the one where the attorney said she couldn't be fair because of the size of the contributions she'd received.

When she thought back on it, she remembered an incident that took place after she'd taken office in her first term. An attorney who had given her a campaign contribution of five hundred dollars had come to court with his young associate and sat in the back of the courtroom watching the proceedings. Could he have attended court just to remind her of that contribution? Could he have thought she was bought and paid for? Bad enough for anyone to think she could be bought at all, but for a mere five hundred dollars made it even more laughable.

"What's going on in that pretty little head of yours?" Adrian's eyebrows were drawn together.

Torie laughed. "Do you know how sexist that question is?"

"Just trying to get your attention. What are you thinking about?"

She pursed her lips. "Do you know which attorneys are members of LLE?"

"I'm not sure of all of them. Hell, I don't even know how large the group is anymore. It started out as a closely knit bunch from one law firm who wanted to get judges that had the same philosophy elected."

"Could you name some of the ones who supported me last fall?"

"Why?"

"If I showed you my list of contributors, could you pick them out?"

"I've seen your list of contributors. It's available at the Secretary of State's office, remember? And I know there are several on it."

"Do you think all those lawyers who gave me the maximum contribution are in LLE?"

"Probably most of them."

"And what, they contribute to the governor as well?"

"Oh, absolutely. I daresay if one or two particular attorneys called the governor, he'd take their calls with no hesitation."

"So they're putting a good word in for me with the governor?"

Adrian nodded. "They're not the only ones. I've contacted other supporters of his—"

"My father has contacted old business associates of his, too. He's collected letters. He's going to send them all in a packet."

"Well, tell him to go ahead and send what he has. Your meeting with the governor is next week. It would be good for the governor to have them at his fingertips if he wants to look at them before you get there."

Anxiety beat in her chest. "Next week? So soon?"

"You know the governor appoints hundreds of people to positions on boards and commissions and God knows what in the State of Texas. This governor moves through the process as quickly as humanly possible. He doesn't want his enemies to be able to say he held up progress in the state."

"Just the thought of it makes my insides jittery."

"You'll be fine. I'll meet you there, and we'll see him together. By the way, are you fixing to rule any time soon on that building construction case, the one with the motion for summary judgment that you took under advisement?"

She was taken aback. Her cases were none of his business. Raising one eyebrow, she asked, "Why do you want to know?"

"A friend asked me to inquire, that's all. And, Victoria, now is not the time to fall behind in your rulings. Don't give the opposition anything to use against you with the governor."

"Like what?"

"Like that you drag your feet when it comes to making decisions."

She didn't like the sound of that. "I'm not dragging my feet. I've been really busy and have a lot on my mind. I need to discuss something with you, too." She rested her hand on her abdomen. "Something I'm wondering about in regard to the appointment. Can I tell you in the strictest of confidence? The very strictest of confidence?"

"Certainly. What is it?" He pulled his chair a tad closer.

He sounded concerned, but in a moment he would be angry. She whispered behind her hand, "I'm PG."

"PG—what? Pregnant?" His tone of voice was one that would make an attorney wish to melt into the courtroom floor.

She pressed her fingers to her mouth and spoke between them. "It surprised me, too."

"Jesus, Victoria, what were you thinking?"

"Never mind that."

"Why didn't you tell me sooner?"

She shrugged and glanced at the creek.

"You're not planning on keeping it, are you?"

"I haven't decided."

"Have you told Sergio?"

"God, no."

"You can't have this appointment if you're pregnant," he whispered. "You'll have to campaign hard as soon as you get it, since you'll be on the ballot when McWilliams' term expires. Terminate the pregnancy right away, and don't let anyone find out or your career is over."

A little pain pinged in her heart. Easy for him to say; he wasn't the one who would have to do it. Could a man even imagine what it was like to climb up on a table and put his feet into stirrups, much less spread his legs wide and let someone suck his insides out? She didn't think so. She pushed her tea away. "That's mighty harsh, Adrian."

"Pardon me for being so blunt." His voice hissed like that of a large, mad cat. "It's certainly your decision, but do you want to be on the Texas Supreme Court or don't you?"

She stared at him. She didn't know what response she'd expected. Anger? Disappointment? But his harshness, his command, and that last question didn't deserve an answer. "I have to go." She rose.

He grabbed her arm. "Just do it. And rule on that case, goddammit."

Chapter 25

THE NEXT MONDAY, TORIE GLANCED AT A COPY of the commissioners' court agenda and found courthouse security listed. Just like the county judge and commissioners' to give her no notice. She didn't expect three days' notice as if it were a legal requirement under the regular court rules, or even the same courtesy one might give a girl they were asking out on a first date, but didn't their good old country mamas teach them any manners? They were nothing but a bunch of underachievers. Had it ever occurred to them that courthouse security was for their safety, too?

She had an hour before the meeting. She slipped on her robe and went into the courtroom to see whether the attorneys on another custody case from hell, or "high-conflict" custody case as the experts called it, had been able to reach an agreement.

Knowing dizziness could strike her at any moment, knowing she often was not careful when she darted up or down the stairs to the bench, and not wanting to take a chance on losing the baby in a fall when she still hadn't made the decision about whether or not to keep it, Torie picked her way carefully, holding the handrail with one hand and the court file with the other. Until she made up her mind, she would behave as though she were going to have the baby, take better care of herself, eat healthy food, and avoid alcohol. She'd miss her nightly martini, which was what caused her to be in that condition in the first place—pregnant with a "martini" baby.

She'd keep up with her regular exercise. Exercise was good for an expectant mother, especially exercise that worked the muscles from her thighs to her chest. Her worst fear about her body was seeing herself in a mirror after the baby was born and looking like a deflated basketball. That is, if she did have the baby. And she definitely hadn't made up her mind. No, she hadn't. In spite of the negatives of having a baby—fatigue, the weariness, the upchucking— she was still mulling it over.

She scowled at the parents sitting at their respective counsel tables. Each faced away from the other. Each scribbled on a legal pad. She could imagine the notes they were writing to their lawyers, questions they wanted to ask.

Back when she had practiced law, she had always given her clients paper and pen so they'd have something to do. No lawyer wanted distractions when she was examining a witness. Nothing was worse than being in the flow, about to get an important point across, and having the client tug her sleeve or elbow or lean forward and whisper in her ear, totally derailing her train of thought.

Now, she addressed the people at the counsel table. "One of you fetch your attorneys. I have just about enough time to hear the pending motion, and if I don't do it today, it's going to be continued again."

The father jogged down the aisle to the back of the courtroom and out the door. The mother looked Torie in the eye and smiled. When Torie didn't smile back, the woman put her head down over the legal pad and began writing again.

Torie glanced through the file—number five, which meant the parents had been fighting for quite a while. There were three children, an eighteen-year-old boy, a sixteen-year-old girl, and an eight-year-old girl. The father wanted temporary orders changing custody of the children pending final trial.

The door to the back of the courtroom squeaked as the attorneys and the father entered. She waited until they stood in front of the bar before she addressed them, pointing at the large black-framed clock on the wall. "I have fifty minutes to hear your matter today, before I have to leave for another commitment. Do you want to go on negotiating, or do you want the hearing to proceed? It makes no difference to me."

The father's lawyer, a man about the size and shape of an acorn, buttoned the second button on his blazer and stepped in front of counsel table. "If you don't hear us today, Judge, when will you be able to give us another setting?"

"Without looking at my calendar, I'd say a month, maybe two." She clamped her lips together and raised her eyebrows.

Each man spent a moment speaking to his client, before turning back to the bench. The mother's attorney, a seventy-something rail thin man who could pass for a willow switch and, Torie knew, was minutes away from retirement, glanced at the other attorney. His lips shuffled back and forth across his teeth as though he ached to say something to the man. Instead he spoke to the Court, "Let's have the hearing."

"Okay, no problem. Whoever's going to testify, stand up and raise your right hands."

After Torie swore everyone in, the father took the stand. He was alleging the mother let men sleep over when the children were there. Further, he said, "One of the men had hit on the oldest daughter." The daughter had told the father, and the father had filed the motion to change custody.

Once he got on the stand, the father hovered over the microphone, twisting in his chair toward Torie, his eyes wide, his hands shaking as he testified from notes he'd brought with him. She studied his demeanor. She listened to him describe the visitation problems. She watched the mother scribble notes next to Willow Switch at counsel table.

Torie leaned back in her chair and stared at the father with as blank a look as she could muster. Her job was to try to fathom the truth of the matters before her. She always said there was the bride's side, the groom's side, and the truth was somewhere in the middle. The man on the witness stand resembled Bert, her ex-husband. Same jaunty walk. Same physique. Same grim determination to win at all costs. She remembered Bert well, even though it had been several years since she'd seen him. After Cassie's death, he'd moved to Dallas and as far as she knew, never came back to her neck of the woods.

She wouldn't hold it against the witness that he resembled her ex; she couldn't. And the fact that he assumed a certain demeanor didn't mean he was like Bert, either. She'd seen many men with that jaunty cock-of-the-walk walk. It wasn't anything more than false bravado, a way to hide their insecurities. For all she knew, the man was sincere. His daughter may very well have been hit-on by one of her mother's boyfriends, fondled, kissed, whatever. The mother might really sleep around a lot. She might even be a paid professional. The testimony would reveal what was really going on.

She remembered Bert's making allegations against her every chance he could. Would this be such a situation? Every time Bert dragged her back to court, she'd had to live with a daughter who didn't sleep well at night, who was haunted by nightmares, whose grades dropped in school, and who developed discipline problems. There was no end to it. But Bert either didn't see what he was doing or didn't care. Now, she looked from the father on the witness stand to the mother sitting at counsel table. Was that what was going on with the daughter in the instant case? Or was what was going on actually what the father described?

She nodded at the father as he left the witness stand. Acorn testified as to his legal fees, the amount he wanted the judge to order the mother to pay should the judge decide the case against the mother, and rested his side of the case.

Although she had never discussed the problems between Bert and herself with Cassie, Bert had sent messages home by Cassie. He told Cassie when he was filing suit and when the court hearings were. He complained about Torie to Cassie every chance he got. Cassie would come home and cry her heart out. She would want to tell Torie about it, but Torie wouldn't let her. She didn't think it appropriate to discuss adult matters with a child. Even when she took Cassie to a counselor, Bert took Torie back to court and complained that she hadn't consulted him before she had chosen someone and the divorce decree said *blah blah blah*.

Willow Switch called the mother to the stand. Torie sank back into her chair and watched the mother testify. The woman kept her eyes on her attorney, nodding as every question was asked. At one point her eyelids fluttered, and Torie wondered if that meant something about her answer. Was she being untruthful? Was she remembering something or making it up as she went along? She had an annoying habit of smiling with her teeth clenched and talking through her teeth. Torie wished she could interpret this odd behavior. The woman denied everything her ex-husband had said. Where was his proof?

On cross-examination, Acorn took her through a list of alleged infractions, date, time, place, manner—every detail he could come up with. The mother denied them all. After she left the witness stand, Willow Switch testified as to his own fees and asked that the motion be overruled.

"Just a moment before you rule on that, Your Honor," Acorn said, shifting about as though standing on hot asphalt. "We have a rebuttal witness."

Willow Switch's face looked like a blanched almond. He whispered to his client, the mother.

"Proceed," Torie said, relieved her decision would be aided by more than a swearing match between the parents.

Acorn called the daughter's name and, since there was no bailiff, hurried outside to get her. He returned with a petite brunette wearing glasses, jeans, and a too-large olive drab unbuttoned sweater that revealed a T-shirt with the Bremerhaven High School mascot—a goat— blazoned across the front.

Torie was adamant in her opinion that children should not be put in the middle of their parents' lawsuits and especially should not have to testify, but the law didn't agree with her. She was convinced that her own daughter's testifying was what had finally forced Cassie over the edge.

The young girl took the stand. Torie leaned toward her. "Don't be afraid. Just speak into the microphone and answer the best you can."

As the testimony developed, as the girl began crying, as she began telling about her mother's boyfriend groping her, visions of Cassie's pleading eyes, of Cassie holding her stomach, of Cassie squirming in the witness chair knifed through Torie.

In this situation, the law was right. The child's testimony had been necessary. That hadn't been the case with Cassie. Bert's calling Cassie to the stand in their last modification trial, forcing her to testify, making her say she preferred Torie to him when he already knew what she'd say, allowing his attorney to badger her, had shattered Cassie's fourteen-year-old psyche, though neither parent knew it until days later.

Now, less than five minutes into the testimony, the mother, whose face had become a mottled red, pulled on the hem of her lawyer's suit coat.

He stood and addressed the court. "May I have a moment with my client, Your Honor?"

"Certainly." She pushed away from the bench, her chair rolling back a few inches, and stood and stretched. From what she'd already heard, a moment was all he would need. Unless the mother was stupid or mean or just plain nuts, now was the time to settle the case and get out of the courtroom before someone mentioned the word perjury.

Willow Switch and the mother held a quick conference. He stepped across the aisle and held a second conference with Acorn. Then back to his client. He wrote something on a legal pad. His client nodded and initialed it, her movements stilted and jerky. Acorn and his client initialed it and handed it back. The father reared back in his chair, sagging as though relieved.

"I believe we've reached an agreement, Judge," the mother's lawyer said, tipping forward in a slight bow.

Torie looked at the mother, then at the father, and resisted saying something snide. She almost always wanted to say something snide, but she wasn't a TV judge and wouldn't give in to that desire. "Young lady, you may step down and wait for your father in the hall."

"Yes, ma'am." The girl smeared her tears away with the heel of her palm and scrambled out of the witness chair and down the aisle toward the back door without a look at either of her parents, her head hanging low. Torie remembered that posture so well. She might not be an expert at reading body language, but any idiot could see that was one unhappy little girl.

As soon as the door at the back of the courtroom closed, Torie said, "I appreciate your working this out. It's always better for everyone concerned if the parents can come to some kind of agreement without extended litigation."

She held out her hand for the agreement. The two attorneys approached the bench and stood while she scanned it. The gist of it was the father would have custody of all the children, and the mother could only have possession so long as no men were at her home.

"Entry date for the Temporary Orders is one week from today at nine a.m. Now if you'll excuse me, I have a meeting to attend."

She stepped off the bench with only minutes to spare. She hung up her robe, used the restroom, and, picking up a stack of books, headed for the elevator that would take her to the commissioners' conference room. No more running up and down the stairs in her stilettos in her condition. She shouldn't even be wearing high heels, but so far her back hadn't started hurting like it had in her first pregnancy, and vanity wouldn't let her give them up just yet. Besides, everyone would know something was going on with her. Her trademark stilettos missing? Never.

Commissioner Pig Farmer hadn't been eating anything nauseating that day in the meeting room for which Torie was grateful. Considering her weak stomach, the ordinary smells of honest sweat and too-strong aftershave were about all she could stand.

Judge Johnson had begun the meeting. As opposed to the more formal setting of the commissioners' courtroom, the commissioners sat around two rectangular Formica tables pushed together in the center of the room. Plastic chairs lined the walls, and most were occupied, but her friend, Commissioner Holtzbrink had an empty one next to him and beckoned to her. She inclined her head.

"Judge, I've been saving this for you," he whispered and patted the chair back. "I knew you'd want to be here."

Torie gave him a stealth thumbs up and sat down, placing the stack of books on the table in front of her. "Thanks," she whispered, biting back a reproach about not receiving notice of the meeting sooner.

Her item was only five down from the top so she waited patiently, not having anything else on her calendar until later in the day, and thumbed through one of the books, with which she was already familiar.

The county judge called the courthouse security issue. Instead of being aggressive, which had never worked with those five men, Torie was pleasant, if not cajoling.

"I just wanted a moment of your time, gentlemen. I brought

each of you a copy of a book published back in 2004, *Murdered Judges of the Twentieth Century*. It contains forty some-odd cases where a judge was either murdered or went missing or died under mysterious circumstances." She handed each man a copy of the book.

"If you'll take the time to look through the book, not today—I'm not asking you to do it today—I think you'll find some interesting facts. Even though there are cases where the murdered judge was not on the job, and some, where a relative killed him or her, you'll see in a number of cases if there had been courthouse security, the judge's life, and indeed some bystanders', would have been saved. Though the focus of the book is judges, each chapter talks about the other people who were killed—from police officers to witnesses to lawyers and clerks.

"All I'm asking, gentlemen, in addition to my previous request, is for installation of metal detectors at every entrance to the courthouse. You may save not only a judge or other elected official's life, but a litigant's or a county employee's." Her heart felt like it would burst out of her chest as she looked at each man's face and was rewarded by eye contact from every one of them. Maybe there was something to Harold's idea of her being less aggressive. The book she'd picked up on assertiveness may have helped.

"As you may recall, previously I've given you each a notebook with clippings of courthouse violence across the country wherein victims were spouses or relatives of the perpetrator, as well as child support workers, lawyers, and just about everyone in between, including county commissioners. Just add this book to your collection. If there are no questions, I'll let you get back to your job." She smiled and when none of them asked her anything, she scooted out her chair and left, her stilettos *rap-rap-rapping* on the granite floor.

She was proud of herself. She had wanted to point out to the county judge that there had been a county judge in another state who had been murdered, but since that county judge had not been killed at the courthouse, and since she was determined not to antagonize her own county judge any more than she already had, she'd kept her mouth shut. And she was glad she had. Now all she had to do was wait until their Wednesday meeting to see how they voted. She crossed her fingers and said a little prayer as she took the elevator back up to her court.

Chapter 26

ABOUT TWO WEEKS AFTER WHAT EVERYONE IN the Hill Country decided was the last freeze, spring returned for good. Pale green leaves sparkled in the mornings like dew on grass. Peach buds popped their heads out. Creeks rose and rushed, foaming over rocks and debris. The spreading oaks perked up, no longer looking so forlorn—with the exception of trees affected by oak wilt—and as suddenly as it had come, Torie's morning sickness disappeared. Not only was she sleeping soundly, but she was able to keep down her meals.

This change signaled to Torie that time was running out for her to make her decision about the baby. Adrian could order her to get rid of it, but it wasn't so easy.

She kept weighing all the factors. Would Adrian withdraw his support if she decided to keep it? Would the governor think she'd betrayed him if he didn't know until after he'd appointed her? And would there be backlash? In a campaign to hold on to the seat in the

Supreme Court, would her opponent raise the question about her ability to be a justice as well as a mother? She'd heard the gossip, the talk, about other candidates—national candidates—leaving their babies and children with caretakers in order to hit the campaign trail. Torie had enough battles to fight without giving her enemies fodder for another one.

On the other hand, if it were discovered she'd had the pregnancy terminated, she knew what that meant. Not only did her own party reject a woman's right to choose, but the other party, though they gave lip service to it, had many members who would frown on her decision, who would rail against her, asking, *What kind of example is she setting for our daughters?*

And then there were the independents. Who knew what they thought?

None of that reasoning took Sergio into consideration. Nor did it take into account her own feelings about having another child or having someone take it from her. If Sergio found out she was pregnant, he would insist she keep the child. And if she had an abortion and he found out, it would be the end of their relationship.

When Torie arrived home that Monday, she found Sergio sitting on the sofa, the newspaper spread open on his lap. He did little more than collapse the paper when he spotted her, his face not betraying his thoughts. He didn't wave; he didn't get up.

"Hey," she called and stopped in the doorway as their eyes met. He was not an afternoon paper reader. What was he up to?

"Hey yourself," he said, his smile looking like something a politician would practice in the mirror.

Once, he would have given her a rush. He would have swept her into his arms and kissed the lipstick off her face. He would have pressed himself against her and stroked her back and starting at her neck . . .

He hesitated a beat too long before rising and coming toward her. "Let me take that from you." His hand brushed hers when he took her briefcase, but his face gave no indication there was a purpose, no beginning of a sexual dance. He hung it on the hall tree and returned to kiss her cheek. "How was your day?" He failed to add the "dear" that once had been a little joke between them, about their not being conventional.

"Frustrating, to say the least. Those rock-head commissioners. You won't believe what they've done now."

"Would you like a drink? Do we have anyplace we have to be tonight?"

"Perrier with a twist of lime." She made a little tweaking motion with two fingers. "And no." She shook her head. "Nothing going on that I'm aware of. Listen to what the commissioners' court did. They finally voted, three-to-two, to install a security system. The pig farmer and the ancient mariner voting against." She followed him into the other room, touching the back of his sleeve with the tips of her fingers.

"But that's wonderful, Torie. You won. You'll finally feel safe."

"Well, yes and no. That's part of what I'm angry about. We're going to get metal detectors at the entrances to the stairwells and elevator but not at the entrances to the courthouse itself."

"But the courts will be protected, darling. That's what you wanted."

"Yes, but all the employees who work in the offices in the basement and on the first floor will still be at risk."

He stopped and faced her, pointing a finger at her chest. "It's a start. And you're not responsible for them, anyway."

She backed away from his finger. "I know that, Sergio, but some of them asked me to get the commissioners to give them security, too."

"You did what you could. Be happy with what they are giving you. Are we going out tonight to celebrate or not?"

Spotting small lines of tension at the corners of his mouth, she stroked his cheek, letting her lips lift upwards in a smile designed to get him to let go of whatever was stressing him out. "Home alone, just the two of us tonight. Can you believe it?"

"And you only want water to drink?" His eyebrows gave an almost indiscernible flicker.

"Perrier isn't only water. Isn't that what you told me? It's zany, it's stimulating—" She made a joke out of it, whirling around a little, clapping her hands. Until she decided about the baby, she wouldn't be drinking alcohol but didn't want Sergio getting curious either. "I've had an upset stomach ever since that meeting with the commissioners."

There was something in his grin that didn't seem right, didn't seem natural. "All right, all right. Perrier and lime. You're in a strange mood."

She could say the same about him. She leaned against the bar and crossed one ankle over the other. "I'm angry they didn't give us the kind of security I asked for, but I am happy we got something. And, to make it even better, they voted a budget amendment even this late in the budget year and will be hiring a contractor immediately. I don't know what's gotten into them, unless they finally read all the material I gave them."

"Go sit down, and I'll bring your drink. Take off your shoes. Make yourself comfortable."

"Hey, I like this treatment. Thanks." She moved forward to put her cheek to his before heading into the living room, but he stepped away. Something was going on, and she suspected she'd find out in the not too-distant future. She hoped she hadn't forgotten another important day. His birthday? No. Anniversary of the day they met? No. Her own birthday? No.

She stretched out on the sofa and closed her eyes, remembering the day they'd met at the resort where he was now general manager.

She'd been attending a judicial conference and had first seen him when she'd been signing in. He wore a dark navy blazer over a plain navy round-necked T-shirt, with a chest hair or two peeking out, and well-pressed slacks. His shoes held a glossy shine, as did his jet-black hair. Something drew her attention. Something sexual. Animal. His hazel eyes met hers though he was in conversation with the new executive director. She hadn't looked away. Neither had he until several moments passed.

She hadn't looked at another man since Cassie died, since she'd broken off the relationship with Adrian. She was no longer in the market for a relationship—not interested and hadn't been tempted—but there was something about him that caused her to draw a breath. She'd been momentarily overcome with regret, a strange way to feel, and sadness. She'd become almost tearful, because she'd decided her life had ended with Cassie's death, and she'd never have a relationship again. And that was too bad because something drew her to that man.

Later in the conference, they came into contact again when she went for coffee during a break. He was instructing a staff member about something to do with the beverage cart. Again, their eyes met.

"Madam, may I be of service to you?" he'd asked. She'd declined.

Still later, he was everywhere. Every time she exited the conference room, this handsome stranger, who she learned was the resort's food and beverage manager, was in the reception area. Finally, the executive director had approached her and introduced them. At that point, she learned his name, Sergio Torres.

Now, she kept her eyes closed for a few moments' rest before facing whatever was going on with her husband. As she counted back from a hundred, she heard him come into the room and set her drink on the table next to her. He was so sweet and understanding most of the time. After a few minutes, she opened her eyes and found him watching her from the recliner adjacent to the sofa. He was a man with something on his mind. She sat up and swallowed from the glass of iced Perrier. It was refreshing. It was stimulating. But it wasn't a martini.

Sipping from his glass of red wine, his eyes followed her. Neither of them spoke. Finally he said, "The housekeeper came today."

Torie glanced at the furniture. No dust. Faint vacuum cleaner tracks ran across the carpet. "House looks good."

"She could come more than once a week if we wanted her to. She'll do ironing, also."

"If you want. It's no trouble for me to drop your clothes off in town the way I've been doing. Whatever you want."

He wet his lips and pressed them together, straining to smile, making her wonder what was behind his edginess.

"What are you smiling at?" She reflected his expression, her muscles feeling every bit as taut as his looked.

"You look so beautiful sitting there, the dark chair behind you makes that green suit look good with your skin."

Glancing down her body and back at him, she shrugged. "Well, thank you. I always like compliments, especially from my husband."

"I like your hair that way." He held a hand out as though he would run his fingers through her hair if he were close enough.

Torie brushed at her hair and wondered what he was getting at. Suspicion nibbled at her. "You look nice too." But he always looked nice. Nice and sexy. Handsome and sexy especially with a day's growth of beard on his face.

"Have you gone to the doctor like you said you would in January?" His brow wrinkled.

Torie's stomach quavered. How to answer. She hated lying. "Why?"

"You were going to get a new kind of birth control."

So this was to be a conversation about their sex life. Relief swept over her. "I know we haven't had sex—made love—much lately but when we did, you had condoms. That was okay wasn't it?" She brought herself completely to an upright position and reached for his hand. He let her take it, but didn't otherwise respond.

"So you haven't gotten that new birth control? A new pill?" His fingers closed around her hand and squeezed.

"Yes, it's a new kind of pill and no, I haven't yet."

He squeezed harder and pulled her hand toward him. "You didn't think it was important or why?"

Torie twisted her hand, to get loose, but he didn't let go. "Sergio, I've been really busy with this Supreme Court appointment thing, and with my own court cases, and in meetings."

"You know, we have the money for a nanny."

"Sergio, let go, you're hurting me." She jerked her hand, and he released it. Did he know? How would he know?

"You wouldn't have to take off work for very long. I would decorate the nursery. When my sister had her babies, I helped her purchase furnishings for her nursery, and sometimes I took care of her kids. I would manage everything if you'd have my baby—just one baby—and you could do your judging and politics."

She rose and went to the window, pushing the draperies aside and looking out so he couldn't see her face and she, his. "What are you talking about? What baby?" She spoke over her shoulder.

He followed her and encircled her waist and pulled her to him, her back up against his front where he could speak into her ear. His voice dropped, low and husky. "I thought maybe you didn't get that new pill you talked about because you really, deep down, want to have my baby." His breath felt warm on her cheek and held an acrid, sweet scent of red wine.

Torie cleared her throat. "No, that's not why."

"*Chica*, I know you're scared to be a mother after Cassie."

"You can't know much about that. I never told you the whole story," she whispered. She'd wanted to put her old life behind her, start over with a fresh, new husband. And he'd never pressed her.

"I know more than you told me. I found some papers in the spare room."

A flare of heat swept through her body. She drew a sharp breath. "*Found?*" She pulled away and swiveled on her heel. "You've been going through my private papers?" She backed up as far away from him as she could and still be in the same room.

"No, it wasn't like that. You know I've been working on our taxes, getting things together for the CPA—"

"No. You couldn't have just come across them. What did you think you were doing? What kind of relationship do we have if we don't respect each other's privacy, each other's wishes?" Anger twisted her gut into a tight rope.

His face had become a dark red. His arms still extended from his body as if he were still holding her. He straightened up. "I was up in the spare room looking for something related to the taxes. I'm sorry I looked at your papers. They were sitting right there, and I guess, I mean, the thing is, I want to understand you better. I want to understand why you say some of the things you say and do some of the things you do." The muscles flexed in his jaw.

She studied Sergio's face. What was really going on? This was a man she'd loved and lived with for three years and suddenly he's going through boxes of her private things. Why did he think she wouldn't mind? Or did he think he had a right to everything that was hers? They didn't open each other's mail. She didn't go through his wallet. She hoped to high heaven he didn't go through her purse, just as a matter of principle.

"Just what is it you want to know? You could have asked me anything. You could have asked me if you could see everything I have about my divorce from Bert. *And* Cassie's suicide." Just saying the word suicide aloud made her want to run outside into the evening air to draw a deep breath and push the pain back inside where she could hide it from herself and the world.

Sergio had put down his wine and now stood silent and crossed his arms. "I want to know everything. Don't you understand? You're my wife, and you keep so much from me."

"I didn't want to rehash my life before you. I know I kept a lot of papers from before, papers I could probably throw out, I should have already thrown out. What am I sounding apologetic for? I want to understand this invasion of my privacy."

He shook his head. "I didn't mean to invade your privacy, Victoria. I've been thinking about us, about your refusal to have a baby."

"So that's how you're going to couch it." She didn't need this right now. If he could just wait a few weeks. She needed some breathing room to be able to make up her mind. It would be so easy to tell him, and she'd often been tempted, but once she did, the decision was made. She'd be stuck with it.

"I know we've discussed this before, but I wish to talk about it again. I want so very much for you to carry my child, *our* child."

Torie started out of the room. "I thought I had made myself very clear."

He hurried after her. "But Torie, *mi amante*, I would do everything except have the baby. If you don't win the Supreme Court appointment, you don't have to stand for election until another four years—"

"Technically, but really three. I'll have to start campaigning in another year or so. And besides, I intend to get the appointment. Then I'll have to stand for election in two years, which means I'd have to start campaigning almost as soon as I'm sworn in." She stopped, glaring, but felt deflated, no real argument left in her, her voice sounding like the wind had gone out of her sails. "Sergio, you know how much I love you, but I told you when we met I didn't want any more children. How many times do we have to go through this, have this argument?"

Sergio took two long strides and pulled her into his arms. "I don't want to upset you. You know I want nothing more than to make you happy, but I can't explain this feeling I have. This need I want to fill, to have a child, a girl, a boy. I don't care which." He pressed her to him. "One little person with both our traits who we can teach our values, who we can cuddle with, take fishing, show the world. I know I said I didn't want children, but since we married I found I do."

She rested her hands on his shoulders. "You make it sound so easy. It's not."

"I would make it as easy on you as possible. We'd hire a nanny. My sister would help out. She would probably give you one of those party things. What do they call them?"

"Baby shower." Torie gazed up at him, focusing on the dire seriousness found in his eyes. How had she misread him when they were dating, when they'd discussed children?

"Yes, that's it. She's always doing things like that for people."

Torie shook her head. "I don't think I can go through all that again, and if we, you and I, don't work out—all the fighting over the child—"

He gestured in the air. "*Mi amante*, what are you talking about? Us not working out? We love each other. We would love our baby, our child. It would not be the same as it was for you before, I can promise you that."

"You act like we haven't been having problems. We have. Have you already forgotten that fight we had?" She stood with her hands on her hips.

"That was nada—I love you. I had to think. If we had a baby we wouldn't have fights like that."

Shaking her head again, Torie said, "I don't think I can do it. Don't hate me, but I just don't." She pulled away and rushed to the bedroom. She hated to be put on the spot. She hated that she couldn't make up her mind about what she wanted to do about the baby. Too much was going on. She felt weepy all the time. Tired. She'd just started eating again and feeling a bit better. She went into the bathroom and washed her face, then peeled off her clothes and hung them up.

A few moments later, Sergio strode into the bedroom, walking right up to her, stopping only inches from where she stood in her panties and bra. Torie thanked God nothing more than a thickening of her waist had occurred. She hoped it wasn't enough for him to notice. The expression on his face was startling, though, and made her want to cover herself with her hands.

"What is it?"

"You don't take me seriously." His nostrils flared. "You are always thinking of *yourself* and *your* life." His voice grew louder. "You never think of me and what *I* want or what would be best for *us*."

"That's not true." She backed into her closet and pulled a light robe off a hanger, covering herself with it. "But anyway, Sergio, I told you before we got married what life with a politician was like." She found her voice growing louder, too. She was almost yelling at him. She didn't want that. She liked to have calm discussions. "But now that you've been through a campaign you should really understand."

"I do." He jabbed his finger toward her face. "I understand it's all about you."

Torie's temper flared. "Do you really want to raise a child in that environment?" Her voice filled the room. "Do you want to leave the child at home with nannies or would you rather drag her—it—around to all four counties in my district as I go from one rubber-chicken event to another? Is that what you would want for our child?"

He slapped the bedpost. "It isn't even about that, Victoria. We haven't even gotten to that *issue* yet. The point I'm trying to make is that you don't care what I think. Do you ever give how I feel the least thought in your mind? No. I don't think so."

Torie stepped back. Is that what he thought? That she only cared about herself? Is that how she came across? "I can't believe you think that's true."

He stood his ground. "Did you ask me how my day was today? No, you did not."

"I didn't get a chance." She held the robe's lapels in place across her chest.

"I'm tired of you putting everything and everyone before me. You've had every chance to show some interest in my day. You could call or text me during the day to see how things are going."

"Call or text you? That's not something I've ever done. I don't think my mother and father ever talked to each other during the workday, either."

"We are not talking about your parents. We're done talking about your parents, and how you put them before me."

"Wait a minute, Sergio. I thought we'd worked all that out."

"We did. I'm now talking about how you think everything is about you." He pointed at her again. "I don't know why I didn't see that before—"

"Before we got married, you mean?"

He glanced away, the muscle in his jaw flexing. "I guess I was so attracted by this beautiful, powerful blonde lady that I couldn't see the way things really were."

"So I overpowered you?" Her head shook like a bobble-headed doll.

"I was so surprised that someone like you would be interested in someone like me. Someone who used to be a chef. Who was a waiter before that. A poor boy who worked his way through school. You flattered me." His speech was halting as if he were trying to replicate the language of his youth

"Oh, brother," Torie said, doing an about-face and throwing up her hands. She pivoted back. "What is going on with you? You're sure laying it on thick." She hated it when he started with the poor-boy stuff.

He held his hands down by his sides as if it was the only way to control what they did. "You insult me. You show me no respect."

Something about his demeanor set her on edge.

"This is really about the baby, and you and I both know it. Don't try to hide behind that poor-me stuff. You're trying to manipulate me into doing what you want, don't you think I see that?" She started to walk past him to go to the kitchen, when he grabbed her wrist.

"Don't walk away from this. We're having a discussion about our relationship. You don't just walk away in the middle. Stay and talk."

"Sergio, what do you want from me?" Torie wrenched her wrist out of his grip.

They stood eye to eye for a few moments, close enough to breathe the same air, both of them stiff, clenching their teeth. She could see a minuscule reflection of herself in his shining green and hazel eyes, eyes that at that moment had turned eerily dark.

Confusion muddled her mind. She was caught off guard by everything that had been said since she had come through the door, as though she teetered on the edge of a precipice. Everything in her life somehow had spiraled out of control and was still building like a powerful, swirling tornado sweeping her with it, her professional life as well as her personal life with both Sergio and her parents.

She didn't know what Sergio wanted of her, other than a child. She hadn't changed since they'd married three years earlier. Perhaps his perception of her had changed. He'd thought he could change her. Why did people do that? People were who they were. Unless an individual was willing to change, there would be no change.

Finally, Sergio took a step back and jabbed his finger toward the front door. "I'll be staying at the resort for a while until I can figure things out." He went out of the room, returning a few moments later with a suitcase, and started packing.

"What happened to staying and talking?" She watched him fold clothes into the suitcase, hoping he would say something more. She wasn't going to, even though she realized what his leaving might mean. When he didn't say anything, she tightened the belt on her bathrobe and went to the kitchen for another bottle of water. A few minutes later, as she sat at the bar, sipping and staring into space, striving to get her anger and fear and anxiety under control, Sergio carried his suitcase past her and out the door to the garage without a backward glance.

Chapter 27

TORIE HAD TO LAUGH AT HERSELF AS SHE DROVE back home after meeting with the governor. For a moment she thought of herself as being about as blessed as a woman could be. After all, how many people had the opportunity to meet the governor about a possible appointment to a position? Then she remembered her situation. Pregnant and abandoned. If she let her guard down, she could easily let despair creep in.

But the day was good. The sun shone in a cloudless azure sky. Bluebonnets and Indian paintbrushes blooming beside the highway wavered in the breeze. The day couldn't be more perfect, except for one thing. Sergio was gone. Okay, two things. The baby dilemma and Sergio was gone.

She wanted to share the experience with him, longed to get his take on how well the governor had received her. He hadn't called or responded to her calls though it had been several days. And truth be told, if they had been together, he wouldn't have been pleased to hear how well the interview had gone. She held out hope that he'd take the time away from her to think things over and come home like he had before. She wouldn't go begging. And she sure wouldn't use the baby to get him back.

She'd taken the governor's behavior as a good sign, though he probably didn't treat any of the judge-applicants badly. After all, they were in the same political party and had the same constituents. She wanted to discuss it with somebody, get someone else's opinion—preferably Sergio's. But that was not to be.

She would have shared her experience with Beth, but they each had their own camp and their own supporters.

So she headed to her parents' house. She couldn't wait to tell them, especially her father. He would be so proud. To have been invited to the state capitol to meet with the governor. How many people could say that? Howie couldn't say that.

After she turned off the ignition, Torie placed a call to Sergio again, hoping this time he'd at least speak to her for a few minutes. The call went directly to voice mail. She closed her eyes for a moment and leaned her head back against the headrest.

Squaring her shoulders, she opened her eyes and glanced at her parents' front yard. From the looks of things, her mother had been gardening in the last few days. The beds in the front of the house were much neater than they'd been over the winter, and the soil had been turned over. It was nice and black. When Torie opened her car door, the odor of fresh manure accosted her. No wonder the earth was so dark. She couldn't escape it. It covered the flowerbeds on both sides of the sidewalk all the way to the front door. A few weeks earlier, she would have been upchucking in their garden, but luckily her insides had settled down.

"Mom! Dad!" When she entered the living room, she didn't find either of them, not even her dad sitting in front of the television. She walked through the kitchen and out to the back porch where she found him on the glider, his head back, eyes closed, mouth open. He wore a fleece jogging suit and house slippers, and the newspaper lay on the seat beside him. The air was cool, blowing in through the screen door.

Was he okay? No one had said anything about his not being well. She ran a finger across the back of his warm hand in an attempt to wake him. He smelled like bacon again. She wished he'd change his diet. "Dad," she whispered as she picked up the paper and sat down, careful not to let the glider shift backward. Her father didn't budge.

Was he just taking a little nap? She wasn't often at their house in the middle of the day. Wasn't sure of their routine. A nap on the porch every afternoon could be perfectly normal. She studied his face, trying to remember how many times she'd ever seen him asleep as opposed to how many times he'd seen her asleep.

Once, when she had been in high school, he'd had a heart attack. Her mother sent a neighbor to the school to pick up Torie and Howie and take them to the hospital. When they arrived they learned the heart attack had been that morning after they left for school, but their mother kept it from them all day until the doctors were sure he was stable. When they arrived, their father was in ICU. Only one of the children could go in at a time. Howie let her go first. She walked down a long hall full of nurses and doctors and other people clothed in scrubs. Machines and carts full of medical material cluttered her path. The smell reminded her of worn athletic socks, dank and sour, coupled with rubbing alcohol.

Her father's room was at the end of a long corridor. A large plate glass window looked in on him, and the curtain was open. He lay there with his eyes closed, face pale, tubes running in and out of his body like strings on a marionette. She watched him sleep for a couple of minutes before she went inside. Lying there, he didn't look like the father she knew and loved. Though his face bore familiar lines, his chin, a stubble, and his yellowed hair mussed, he looked like an emotionless stranger. Fear shook her from her head to her toes. What had happened to the soul of her daddy?

Torie shook off that memory now. She'd let him doze. She scanned the front page of the *San Antonio Express News* to get the real news. The Bremerhaven weekly newspaper that came out on Wednesdays was mostly ads and family events, though the editor occasionally featured some actual local news like Torie's push for courthouse security. She didn't often have the time to read any paper. She'd read the headlines on her cell phone and watch a television news station, time permitting. Mostly she lived an insulated life.

Her father stirred after a few minutes and opened his eyes. "Torie, when'd you get here?"

"Just now. Having a little sleep?"

"Ah, yes." He shifted around on the glider, which, being made of small wooden slats, couldn't have been comfortable. "I've gotten to where I like a little nap in the afternoons especially on balmy days like today. Your mother had me tilling the beds out back so she can put in some vegetables." He grunted. "Wore me out."

"I saw the front yard. Peuwee!"

"The smell will go away in a few days."

"Are you sure tilling's not too much for you? That old tiller is really heavy and hard to handle."

"Nah. Howie got me a new lightweight one. A baby could do it."

Howie again. Always Howie. Torie bit back the comment she was tempted to make.

"What're you doing here in the middle of the day?" He laid a warm hand on her arm and squeezed.

"I met with the governor today."

He slapped his knee. "That's wonderful. That must mean you're really in the running. He doesn't meet with everyone who wants the job, does he?"

"Don't know, but kinda doubt it. He's busy like you wouldn't believe, people coming in and out, the phones ringing, buzzing, chirping, e-mails beeping on his computer, bells and whistles on his cell phone.

"Wait, Torie. Let's go inside and let your mother hear all this."

Something was off. His face looked wan, his lines and wrinkles pronounced. Maybe it was the light, because he slid off the glider and stood with no more than a moment's hesitation and ushered her ahead of him. "I'm going to get a drink of water. Will you find your mother?"

The whirring of the sewing machine drew Torie down the hall. Her mother was stitching a large mound of flowered fabric and watching a 1940s black and white movie on a small flat screen TV mounted on the wall. She wore pink velour pants with a T-shirt and sweater over them. Her hair was pinned up in the back.

"Hi Mom," Torie said, leaning over to give her a kiss. Her mother's clothes bore a strong flowery scent and a fainter smell of manure. Wouldn't she have showered after working in the garden? Old people . . .

"I didn't hear you come in." Her mother switched off her machine and stood.

"What're you making? Pretty material."

"This?" She glanced at the pile of fabric. "A ruffled tablecloth with matching place mats and napkins."

"That's nice, Mom." Would Torie ever get to the point that she'd enjoy spending hours sewing something she could buy in a department store for a few dollars? She didn't think so, but to each her own.

"Something wrong, dear? We so rarely see you during the day on a weekday." She took Torie's arm, her eyes journeying up and down Torie's body.

"That's because I work outside the home, Mother." Why did her parents think it necessary to comment on her rare weekday appearances? Maybe they were both getting a little senile. She didn't like to think very far into the future—to a time when she'd be without parents. She patted her mother's shoulder. "I'm sorry. I didn't mean to sound so sharp."

"I think you've put on a few pounds. Filled out a little. It becomes you."

Torie glanced down at her belly. She couldn't be showing yet, could she? "It's that sit-down job. I'm going to have to get more exercise. Listen, let's go out to the living room with Dad, okay?"

"Something wrong?" Her mother's mouth tightened into a question.

"No, Mom." She clasped her hands in front of her face and grinned. "It's that I've just been to see the governor and wanted to tell you both about it. Come on."

"The governor! How exciting."

Torie led the way down the hall, pleased that both her parents were happy for her.

"How does he look in person? Does he wear makeup? I always thought he probably wore makeup to look so young. And hairspray. Do you think he uses hairspray?"

"I don't know about that, but he's a lot taller in person than he looks on TV in his ads." They found her dad in his recliner. She took the sofa to his left and her mother pulled up the ottoman near his feet. Almost ritualistic. No, territorial. Her dad had his space. Her mom had hers. And where Torie was sitting was where Howie usually sat, particularly when he came over and watched sports. Actually, she was surprised that, though he held the remote in his lap, her father hadn't turned on the television.

"I've never met the governor," her dad said.

"Of course I haven't either," her mother said. She sat with her legs together to one side and folded her hands in her lap, every bit the proper, church-going lady.

"He was really very nice. It's practically like a prison in there, though, you have to go through so many people and so much security." She cupped her hands and made like she was weaving through a crowd. "Good that he deems security important. That's something I would want to be sure we had plenty of if I was on the Texas Supreme Court."

"Sure. Absolutely," her father said. "Security is extremely important."

Torie glanced at him to see if he was going to make reference to the beating, but though his eyes flitted over her face, he stopped before alluding to it.

"So tell me," he glanced at her mother, "us, what did y'all talk about? Who all was there?"

"Judge Frothingham met me there. Since he knows the governor very well, and since he's the one sponsoring me, it was only right he be there. But that was it, only Adrian."

Torie looked from one to the other of them. She always wondered what they would think if they knew she'd had an affair with Adrian. It would kill them. Her father and Adrian had known each other in college but didn't run in the same circles now. She wished she could wave a magic wand and change that part of her history, but she couldn't.

"Not Sergio?" her mother asked.

"No, Mother." Torie straightened in her chair. "People don't take their spouses to meetings like that. It wouldn't be appropriate."

Her father cut his eyes at her mother.

Torie laid her hands on the armrest. "So, anyway, we were ushered up to his office, his outer office where we met with one of his aides. Eventually some people came out, and after a few minutes we were told we could go in."

"What was his handshake like?" her father asked. "I like a firm handshake."

"Very warm and yes, firm. He's one of those people who puts one hand over yours and looks you right in the eye like meeting you is the most important thing he's done all day."

"That's nice," her mother said. "Did you like him?"

"Not that it matters, but I did. I found him to be very personable. We sat across from him, his desk is absolutely huge and carved, ornate." She spread her arms wide. "Like from where you're sitting Mom to where I am, with a thick sheet of glass over it. The walls are covered with pictures of previous Governors and mounted animal heads and paintings of hunting scenes. Very masculine."

"So what did he ask you? What did he want to know?"

She gave a little shrug. "My judicial philosophy. Where I stood on individual rights. What I thought the role of the Supreme Court should be. I thought that was kind of odd, but with all the rhetoric about activist judges, I understood." She deliberately didn't mention the governor's question about abortion rights. It struck close to home, and though she gave the standard party-line answer, the conflict within her had made her hands shake then and caused her to clench them into fists now.

"How long did the meeting last?"

"Oh, goodness, maybe fifteen or so minutes. But I felt really good about it when we left. I think Adrian did as well."

Torie talked about the meeting for a few more minutes, and they adjourned to the kitchen. Her mother made some sandwiches. Tuna salad for Torie, her favorite, with sweet pickles and mustard as well as mayonnaise, and the three of them sat at the counter and ate while her mother discussed what was going on at her club. Torie had cleared her docket for the day, so it was nice for once not to have so many things scheduled that she had to race from one to the other. Nice that she could take the time to enjoy a visit alone with her parents.

Afterward, her father walked her to the door while her mother straightened up the kitchen. He took her arm as she started to leave. "Torie, I have to ask you. Are you sure this is what you want?"

Surprised by his question after their many discussions, she patted his cheek. "Don't you think it's a good thing, Dad?"

"Oh yes, sure. But in case you want to change your mind, I want you to know it's not too late. You'll always have our support no matter what." His eyes met hers, his eyebrows drawn together.

What was going through his mind? Did he know about Sergio?

Did he suspect about the baby? She searched his face but couldn't tell anything except that he was worried, though there was just a little movement at the corner of his mouth that could mean he was holding something back.

"That's exactly what you said both times I walked down the aisle, but I'm sure, Daddy. This is what I've wanted for a long time."

He kissed her cheek and she, his.

On the drive home she pondered his unsaid words and whether and when she would be able to pry them out of him.

Chapter 28

THE FOLLOWING DAY, ON A MIDMORNING break from the Campbell jury trial, when Torie opened the door from the courtroom, a foot, a leg, a long torso came into view, and her brain registered a presence where there shouldn't be one. Adrenaline spiraled through her. She paused in the doorway, in fight or flight mode, her heart skittering to a stop before she realized who it was. The back of her ears flamed at the presumption of anyone, anyone at all, thinking he could enter without permission and behave as casually as though he were on a picnic.

She let the door close behind her, and said, "*What* are you doing?" in an octave previously reserved only for her ex-husband.

Adrian Frothingham sprawled on her sofa, pen in hand, legal pad on his lap, one of her court files spread around him like the ingredients of a dismantled sandwich. His Lucchese-booted feet, crossed at the ankle, were propped on the coffee table. His look said *she* was the intruder. He arched an eyebrow as though asking *what-do-you-want*, but said nothing.

She bypassed her desk and snatched the file folder. "I don't care if you are the administrative judge for our region, you have no right to invade my chambers and read my files." The case was one she'd taken under advisement some time earlier, a complicated real estate case with difficult issues involving title to land and mineral rights. There had been cogent arguments on both sides. She'd spent far more time studying it, pondering her decision, than was the norm and still hadn't made up her mind which side was in the right.

Adrian's face looked like a plaster cast. The familiar brows, eyes, nose, mustache, and mouth were still there, but long, vertical wrinkles ran down his cheeks. Dark circles hung under his eyes like sand bags. Stress stripes painted his lips.

"What are you doing, Adrian? Answer me." She'd never seen him look so bad. The change in him from only the day before was frightening. "Are you ill? Should I call an ambulance?" Torie had felt drowsy, which was why she'd taken a break from the case she'd been hearing. Now she was on high alert.

Two legal pads of her notes lay next to him, out of her reach unless she crawled over him to get them, which she was unlikely to do. There had been enough crawling over each other in the past, in a different sense. Now it would be more of a fight. "This file may be a matter of public record, but those are my private notes." She waited for an explanation, one hand on her hip and the other held out for the legal pads.

He stroked his mustache and tugged on his lip. "Close the door to your outer chambers." He set aside his notepad.

Anger flared in her cheeks. "What I'm going to do is use the ladies' room, drink some milk, and go back on the bench so I can send the Campbell case to the jury today." She unzipped and threw her robe on the back of a chair and fled to her private restroom. She didn't know what Adrian was up to, but whatever it was, she didn't need it right now.

The ex-Campbells were driving her mad. Her stomach had been rumbling like the monster it had become since the nausea had passed, never satiated. Her head felt empty and light. She knew enough to know her blood sugar was low and probably her blood pressure had been as well, though it had risen since she'd entered her chambers.

When she emerged, Adrian stood staring at the bathroom door like a predator ready to attack, a glint of steel in his eyes. The door between her chambers and Nettie was closed. That didn't bode well.

Ignoring him, Torie pulled a one-quart carton of fat free milk from her little refrigerator and chugged a few swallows. The cold bland taste satisfied her yearning for something to fill her stomach. She could almost feel it splash as it landed, quieting the hunger pangs she'd suffered all morning. She wiped her lips with her fingers and put the carton back in the fridge.

Adrian held the clerk's docket sheet in his hand. "You need to rule on this case. It's been two months."

She strode to him and snatched the docket sheet out of his hand. "What business is it of yours?"

They faced off for a few moments, her head tilted up, her chin no higher than his breast pocket even though she wore her standard stilettos. "This is *my* court, *my* chambers, *my* case. What's up with you?"

"One of the lawyers asked me if I knew what the holdup was."

He stepped closer, as though he would reach for her waist like a dance partner. She stepped back. Everything between them was long over. Having him in her personal space felt uncomfortably invasive, almost threatening.

She held his gaze, not intimidated like she had been years earlier when she'd been the litigant and he, the judge, or when she'd been a new lawyer and he, the regional presiding judge, or even when they'd been lovers and his eyes held hers, entranced, as he caressed her body in ways her ex-husband never had. She no longer feared him or loved him.

Since their relationship had ended, she had continued to admire him. That admiration shattered the moment she entered her chambers and found him with her file. He had crossed over—to where she wasn't yet sure. "What right does any lawyer have to ask you about my case?"

A muscle flexed in his jaw. "You need to rule and soon."

"All of a sudden you're minding my business? Don't you have enough to do being administrative judge for this whole region?" She put the docket sheet into the file folder and laid it on her desk and began picking up the documents that still lay scattered on the sofa and coffee table.

He followed her, put his hand on her shoulder. "Victoria—"
She shook him off.

He grabbed her arm. "These people supported you in the election, and they're supporting you for Supreme Court. They're getting impatient. You need to rule on this case immediately." His tone sounded like a funeral knell.

"They can wait like everyone else. I'll get to it as soon as I can." She skirted around him, stacking the file contents on her desk. "I haven't had time to finish studying it. It's complicated, and there's only one of me. Besides, what if I rule against them? Are they prepared for that?"

"I spent the last half hour reading it. It looks to me like they should prevail."

Torie spun around. "*I said*, I haven't finished my study of it. It's my case, and when I'm ready I'll rule on it." She snatched her robe off the back of the chair and stuck her arms in, zipping it up to her throat.

"If you don't rule in their favor, they may pull their support."

A shockwave swept up her arms and across her shoulders. She halted in mid stride on her way back to the courtroom. "They can't do that. They've already recommended me to the governor."

"You don't get it, do you?" He gripped the chair like a crutch, his face pale, the skin stretched tight across his bones. "Everything in this world has a price. Did you think their endorsement would come without one? In fact, did you think their support in your re-election bid was something they did for their health? They were responsible for tens of thousands of dollars of campaign contributions."

Another jolt pierced her. Then cold. The hair on her scalp stood up. "I—I thought they liked me. I thought it was for good government. Because I did a good job."

He stroked his mustache. "Even you couldn't be that gullible."

Torie stared into his contempt-filled face and swallowed several times to force the milk back down her throat. "When Nolan's family started pouring money into his race, you said you'd help me get re-elected. You didn't say it would come with strings attached."

He let go of the chair and said, in a softer, more-humane tone, "I thought you knew. They *always* want something in return."

Torie clutched the doorknob, propping herself up as comprehension settled on her. No wonder that other firm had objected to her hearing their case. They knew more than she did.

"And what about you, Judge, have these same people been your supporters? Did they help you?" She looked him steadily in the eye.

Adrian looked past her, toward the window. His breath was so faint, he could have been the walking dead.

"I take it by your silence the answer is in the affirmative." Her chest burned. She swallowed several times again. Milk had never given her heartburn before, not even when she'd been pregnant with Cassie. She stared up at him. He didn't look like the man she'd known and admired. A veil had been lifted from her eyes. He looked like a skinny, repugnant, white rat.

"Victoria—"

Her chin jutted out. "That's Judge Van Fleet to you."

"*Judge Van Fleet . . .*" His lips flattened against his teeth. "I thought I'd get away from them when I became regional presiding judge, but it seems they're responsible, to a great extent, for my getting this appointment."

Her shoulders felt like creepy-crawly bugs forayed across them. She shook her head, her hair brushing across her neck as she tried to shake off the thought that she'd once slept with a man who might be guilty of bribery and racketeering. And conspiracy? She could puke the milk onto his expensive boots.

She pulled her hand from the doorknob. "And what have you done to pay for their kindness?"

"We're talking about you, not me. And I don't appreciate your sarcasm."

"What did you do? What could you do to help them? Recuse or not recuse judges who had motions filed against them?"

Adrian wouldn't look at her.

She stepped into his line of vision. "Your power of appointment? The assignment of certain judges to hear certain cases?"

He stepped back to her desk and picked up the file on the real estate case.

Before he had a chance to say anything, Torie said, "Is that it? And you use your influence with other judges, presiding judges, and even the governor—"

"Judge, listen to me. You need to grant the summary judgment on this case. And I mean today. This afternoon. As soon as you get out of trial. Do you understand?" He threw the file back onto her desk.

Torie took a long step toward him until she was only inches away. "*You* do not tell me what to do." She poked her manicured finger in his chest. "*They* do not tell me what to do. I work for the people of Germania County. The *people* elected me. I answer only to them."

He grabbed her by her shoulders and shook her. "You have to listen to me."

"No, I don't." She raised one foot and jammed her stiletto heel on the top of his boot, bearing down on it with all her might, then pivoted back toward the courtroom door.

Adrian sucked in his breath and grabbed his foot. "Goddammit!" He hopped on the other foot. "Christ! You little bitch! Umph!" He chuffed several times like a dog.

Torie spun back, hands on her hips, wishing there was something more she could do to him, but she was too short to hit him where it hurt unless she used her fist instead of her knee, and that didn't sit well with her.

"Goddamn that hurts!" He tested his weight on his injured foot and winced. "Victoria, listen. If you don't rule right away and in their favor, they'll pull their support. They'll tell the governor they made a mistake. That they didn't vet you properly." He grasped the back of a chair for support. "They'll say your fitness for the bench is questionable."

She pointed her forefinger at him as she approached him again, backing him to her chambers' exit door. "You apparently did not hear me very well, *Judge* Frothingham. Nobody tells me what to do. I'll resign before I'll let them do that." She flung open the door. "Now get out of my chambers."

"I'm going, Judge, but you'd better think about what I've said." He stumbled out the door and muttered under his breath, "I think you broke my Goddamned toe."

As he hobbled past Nettie toward the hall, Torie shook her head at Nettie's wide-eyed shocked expression. She'd deal with her court coordinator and the infraction of letting him inside her chambers later.

As soon as he rounded the corner, Torie slammed the door, her body tingling with electricity from standing up for herself. She'd made the right decision. Now she had to find the strength to handle what they'd throw at her.

Chapter 29

TORIE GRABBED THE WALL FOR SUPPORT. ALL her energy had gone into the confrontation. She felt like wilted spinach. After a few moments of wall-holding, she wobbled to the sofa and perched on its arm. She couldn't remember ever having clashed with another person like that—except for arguments with her ex. She despised how it made her feel—angry and frightened at the same time.

In her chambers' bathroom, she patted the back of her neck and her forehead with a cold, wet paper towel. Holding onto the sink, she peered into the mirror to see if her face looked as red as it felt. The slammed door would give the court participants enough to gossip about without Torie returning to the courtroom with her face looking like a vein was going to pop.

A few minutes later, she re-took the bench. She'd like to stomp on Adrian's other foot for making her violate her own rule that everyone return to the courtroom on time, including herself.

"Be seated. Sorry about the delay, folks." Torie made eye contact with the jurors. "Sometimes even the judge is forced to violate her own rules." She forced a chuckle and was gratified to see a couple of them laugh with her. "I would hold myself in contempt if I thought I could benefit from it." Again she was rewarded with a few smiles. Nodding at the attorneys and their clients, she looked at the teacher-witness who sat on the first row of benches. "Mrs. Schechter, you may retake the stand."

When the testimony resumed, Torie leaned back in her chair and tried to focus. Her knees felt weak. Her mind went back to the scene in her chambers and the things Adrian had said. How could she have been so stupid? She had known long ago there were corrupt people in the world, having represented some of them when she'd practiced law, and having sent many to prison as a judge. She had never, however, thought corruption would knock on her door, introduce itself, come inside, and try to make her its slave.

She'd thought herself immune from such goings-on. She'd done all the right things at the right time, held herself accountable for the decisions she'd made, and she would do so now, as well. But this situation, this predicament, this quandary was not something she was prepared for. Yes, it was of her own making. But not knowingly, not intentionally.

Where had she made her mistake? As clichéd as it sounded even to herself, how could she have been so blind? How could she have known her own regional presiding judge was a conspirator? It had never occurred to her in her wildest dreams. Never would have. What indications had she missed? Most importantly, what should she do now?

She couldn't comply with Adrian's request. She had threatened to resign. Not her first choice. Not even her last choice. Not a choice at all. She had a plan: ascend to the Texas Supreme Court, then Federal District Court, then Fifth Circuit Court of Appeals, and, finally, the United States Supreme Court. If she resigned, she'd be giving up everything she'd hoped and prayed and dreamed about for years. What would her father think of her then?

God, she needed someone she could talk to. Someone she could trust. But who? Not Beth. They were barely on speaking terms. Besides, what evidence did she have? Beth would think she was threatened by the complexities of the appointment process—that she'd gone off the deep end.

Not Sergio. Sergio would have supported her, protected her, even gone to bat for her, but Sergio was gone. Gone for good? No way of knowing that yet, though he never took her calls.

How devoid her life was of real friends, people in whom she could confide something like this. She and Howie never discussed their workaday worlds. She didn't know why except she'd always been in competition with him, whether he knew it or not. Mary and she weren't close. Mary wouldn't understand. Neither would her mother. That left her father.

Torie studied the witness's profile, tried to focus on the woman's answers, keep her mind where it belonged. The woman had one of those voices that sounded like she was on the verge of tears at all times. When she talked about one of the children's school records, she kept exhaling loudly into the mike. "Um," she said before each answer. "Um, um, um," and drew a long breath. She scratched her upper lip constantly. Brushed her bangs back several times. Her eyes danced from the paper to the attorney and back again.

Someone tapped Torie on her shoulder. She flinched. Nettie knelt on the floor next to Torie's chair in an effort to conceal herself from the jury. She handed Torie a note. "Call your mother. Emergency!"

Torie bolted up. Her father. It had to be her father. "We'll take a five minute recess." She followed Nettie into her chambers. "What did she say?"

Nettie shook her head. "She wouldn't. Just for you to call immediately. I hope it's not serious." She backed up until she was through the door and into her own office.

Torie punched in her parents' home number. It rang and rang until she lost count. She hung up and tried the cell phone her parents shared.

Her mother answered on the first ring, her voice sounding breathless. "Torie, come to the hospital. Your father's had another heart attack."

Torie threw off her robe and grabbed her purse and keys. As she ran through Nettie's office toward the door, she said, "Tell the jury court's in recess until tomorrow."

When she left the courthouse for the hospital, the world outside still looked normal, trees still putting out leaves, the sky still blue, clouds still floating by, people still driving their cars. Somehow she'd thought things would be different. Life would be different. Her whole world was falling apart. Her husband had left her. Her mentor had turned out to be a crook. Her father had suffered his second heart attack and could die before she arrived at the hospital.

When she entered the emergency room, antiseptic smells permeated the air, stirring her already nervous stomach. Staff directed her to the cardiac intensive care unit waiting room where she found her mother and Mary. They were the only people there. The three of them hugged.

"I'm so glad you could come," her mother said, her face bereft of all color.

"What's going on? What do the doctors say?" Torie took her mother's hands and sat next to her.

"They took him into surgery," Mary said. "Told us to come on up here and wait. I'm not clear what the procedure is they're doing, though."

"Maybe a stent? Mom, could they be putting in a stent?" Torie tried to find the answer in her mother's eyes.

Her mother shook her head. "I don't know. I never understand these things."

"They didn't tell y'all anything?" It was hard to wait for her responses. She knew her mother was most likely in shock, but Torie wanted to shake the answers out of her.

"I'd rather them be in there trying to help your father than out here talking to me."

"Tsk. They should have sent someone out here to tell you something." Torie went to the doorway. She would nab the first person who looked like a hospital employee and make them find out some information.

"Torie, I have to tell you something." Her mother pressed her fingers to her mouth. "I should have told you kids before, but your dad made me promise not to."

Torie's stomach knotted up. She sat back down next to her mother. "What, Mother?"

Her mother's smudged eyes brimmed with tears. Deep lines made her pale face look older than it had the day before. "I think you have a right to know now. Your father hasn't been well. His heart—the doctors—he's suffering from congestive heart failure."

"Mo—om, no!" Her father was dying, had been dying slowly for a long time. She'd seen he was deteriorating but hadn't wanted to recognize it for what it was.

Her mother's lips trembled as she stroked Torie's cheek and stared into her eyes. "He didn't want you hovering over him. He wanted you and Howie to live your lives as you always had."

Torie glanced at Mary. Mary's parents had passed away several years earlier, first her mother and six months later, her dad. Torie's were the only parents Mary had. Mary had her head bowed, one hand covering her eyes, the other clutching the edge of the chair.

The three of them sat together for several hours. A doctor came out and told them they'd keep her father overnight. When Torie questioned him, the doctor said even if her dad was really weak, once he was awake if he insisted on going home, they'd let him. They'd have an ambulance transfer him. Torie took that to mean go-home-to-die.

After Mary and Torie switched out peering at him through a little square window, confirming that he wasn't awake, that he couldn't talk to them, and after Torie and her mother argued over who would stay in the room with him overnight and her mother won, Torie left. She promised to return and drop off a few toiletries before going home for the night.

The following morning when she went back to the hospital, Torie peered inside her father's intensive care room. He lay with his eyes closed, the white sheet pulled up under his arms, a light blue hospital gown covering the rest of him up to his neck. He was as pale as the coverings. Tubes ran in and out of his body. His breathing was shallow, the slight rise and fall of his chest the only indication he was still alive. Her mother sat in a chair, head back against the headrest, eyes closed, newspaper folded to the crossword puzzle resting in her lap.

In that setting, Torie viewed them with fresh eyes, saw how very much they'd aged. Her parents had evolved into old people while she hadn't been looking.

She stood outside and thought about how to handle her visit. She didn't know how much longer he had. Would he be able to go home and die in his own bed? Obviously not right then, not with the tubes and machines still hooked up to him. Did he have any time left at all? She knew if he didn't, he'd insist on going home. He'd always said he didn't want to die in a hospital. She swallowed a sob. He was dying. She needed to be a big girl about it and not let him see how she was affected.

If he asked how things were going, she was going to lie to him for the first time in her adult life. He didn't need to be burdened with her problems. She backed against a wall and tried to muster the courage to keep her mouth shut, think only of his comfort. She was forty-five years old. Time to stand on her own two feet. She was sure, had he been asked, he would have said he'd raised both his children to be self-reliant, capable people, fully able to function in society with no interference from him. She would, of course, want to prove him right.

A murmur came from the room so she headed inside. Her mother met her at the door.

Torie kissed her cheek and held her, the apple scent of her mother's body wash comforting. "How's he doing today?"

"You can see for yourself. I was just going down to the cafeteria for a cup of coffee and a snack, honey. Go on in and have some private time with your dad. He's been asking for you."

"Where's Howie?" She knew why he wasn't there. Howie, like an immature youth, didn't have the stomach for illness and death.

"Oh, you know your brother." She shrugged. "He was here this morning for a few minutes. Mary came for a while after she got the kids off to school. She'll be back later."

Torie bit back the words she'd like to use to describe her brother's behavior. He needed to man up and spend some time with their father before it was too late. But Howie wasn't her problem. She squeezed her mother's arm. "You go ahead and take all the time you need, Mom. I'll be here when you get back."

Torie approached the bed. Her father's normally large, expressive eyes had sunk into his head, deep in the shadows of their sockets. His skin had lost its flushing pink. His little bit of hair had become a washed-out yellow instead of white. His body smelled musty. In addition to a fluid drip, he was hooked up to two machines, one on each side of the bed.

Torie held his warm, puffy hand to her cheek—the strong hand she'd known her whole life. The hand that had picked her up off the sidewalk when she'd crashed on her skateboard. The hand that had held her close when her boyfriend never showed for prom. The hand that had raised her own in victory when she won her first election.

He opened his eyes. Torie forced a smile. "Hi, Daddy." She leaned over and kissed his rough, unshaven cheek. "How are you feeling this morning?"

He grunted and cleared his throat. "I want to go home to my own bed." His voice was raspy, hoarse. "I don't want to die in the hospital."

"You're not going to die, Dad. As soon as they can, they'll ship you home." She brushed her fingers across his forehead. "Insurance companies don't want to pay for protracted hospital stays, you know." She smoothed the sheets around him. "Would you like me to puff up your pillow?"

"Nurses' aide did a while ago." He let out a labored breath. "How's everything going? Have you heard from Sergio?" He caught her hand again.

She shook her head. "I left him a message on his cell last night. He come by?" She didn't want to talk of Sergio. Didn't want to worry her father. The focus should be on her father's health.

"Not yet. He's a good man, Torie. Don't let him get away." He squeezed her fingers.

"I'm sure you've figured out by now that he's staying at the resort. It was his decision to leave. It has to be his decision to come back. Let's not worry about him right now, though, okay?" She put her cheek next to his and whispered, "I just want you to get well."

"You could help his decision along, little girl."

"Dad—I have worse things to worry about right now, and that's getting you better."

He pulled her closer to him. "I want things settled for you before I go. With Sergio. With the appointment."

Torie held his hands. It was all she could do to hold herself together. "You're not going anywhere so don't worry. We need to get you up and out of here. Your health is the most important thing right now."

"I got those letters taken care of." His eyes followed her every move.

"I know you did, Dad, shh—" She put her fingertips to his lips. They were warm and dry and as swollen as his hands. His silver whiskers glinted in the florescent light.

He pushed her fingers away. "I want to talk to you about it. I love to hear about my children's successes and even their failures. I'm afraid I've lived my life vicariously through you kids." His cloudy eyes searched her face.

"Well, maybe Howie with his football and baseball and—"

He uttered a tortured cry. "No, Torie. Not just Howie. Why would you say a thing like that?"

"Shhh, quiet, Daddy. This isn't good for your heart. Let's drop it. Can I get you anything? Are you thirsty?" She tried to pull away, but he held on.

"Is that what all this has been about? The judgeship? This appointment?" He rose a bit on his elbows. "Your ambitions to be on the high court?" Almost imperceptibly, he shook his head and fell back on the pillows. "Don't you know how proud you've made me? How proud I've always been?"

Torie covered her mouth and glanced away. She didn't know if there ever would be a time and a place for a discussion like this with her father, but she knew for certain this wasn't it. He didn't need any stress or anxiety. "Calm down, Dad. It's okay."

He pulled on her hand again, though his grip was not so firm. "Look at me. Don't you know how much I love you?"

Torie's eyes fixed on her father—the face of the man she'd admired and loved more than anyone in the world—the face of the man she mistakenly put before her husband. "Dad—"

"I love you, daughter, didn't you hear me? I know I haven't said it often enough. I love you." His smile was slight, but genuine, coming from his lips and his eyes, his crows' feet crinkling.

She couldn't remember ever having heard him say it at all, not even when she would speak those words as she was on her way out the door. He would say things like, "Bye, dear. Come again soon." Or, "You be careful out there in the cold, cruel world." His saying those three words now frightened her to the bone. He knew he was dying.

Torie spread her arms and laid her head on his chest. "Daddy, I love you so much. Please don't leave me."

"I want you to know something, honey child . . ."

She lifted her head and breathed the same air.

"It never mattered to me if you were elected dog catcher or the Queen of Sheba, I couldn't love you more than I already did. Don't you know that?"

"But Howie—"

"Howie is . . . Howie. My first-born. My only son. A man loves a son, but no more than a daughter." He drew a deep, shuddering breath. "Howie is good at sports. He's a good old boy. But he's not you. He doesn't have your intelligence," he coughed, "your courage and wit and strength. Don't tell anyone, Torie," his voice but a whisper, "I always loved you best."

Torie fought back tears even as she wondered whether her father had held a similar conversation with her brother that morning, telling Howie he loved him best. Always the skeptic, always suspicious, always demanding the evidence, that was she. But this time maybe she could trust the one who lay in the throes of death and revealed what was in his heart. And even if it were not true, her father had cared enough to make her think it was.

"Daddy, don't talk now. It's too hard on you."

"But I want you to know." He gasped for breath. "You're a brilliant, beautiful woman, strong and full of integrity. I have so much respect for you."

Torie shivered. "Thank you, Daddy." She held his hand to her cheek. "That means so much to me, but let's not talk about it now."

"Just one thing I want you to remember. I can tell something else is on your mind."

"Dad—"

He put his forefinger to her mouth "Just remember. Your integrity is everything. Without it, your life won't be worth living."

A little twinge tweaked her heart. "I know that, Dad. It's really hit home recently, but I've always known it." Their eyes met. His wore a hint of a smile.

He closed his eyes and drew his shoulders together. "Honey child, I'm so very tired now. Find your mother."

Nodding, Torie said, "I'll be right back." She stood.

His eyes flew open. They were clear now, vibrant, and full of anguish. He squeezed her hand like a vise and grunted, his face stricken with pain. "Call the nurse, Torie," he whispered. "Get your mother."

Her fingers pulsing as though electric shocks shot through them, Torie dug the call button from between the mattress and the bed frame and pushed it over and over and over.

'Uggggh!" Her father writhed, the skin on his pale face stretched taut, his eyes squeezed shut. "Oh God! Oh God! Oh God!"

"Help!" She ran into the hall and spotted her mother stepping off the elevator. Torie beckoned with both arms. "Mom, now!"

Her mother stumbled past Torie into the room. "Matthew!"

Scrub-covered people raced down the hall, yelling at Torie to make way. She flattened herself against the wall. The doctors and nurses squeezed through the doorway, pushing her mother to one side, everyone barking instructions and tearing at the bedclothes.

Her mother came out, and Torie wrapped an arm around her. They stared into the room. Stunned, she listened to the commotion, the efforts being made to save her father's life. Backs of doctors and nurses, working at a frenzied pace, blocked her view like in a scene from a television doctor show.

She held her mother and listened to the demands and exclamations that became background noise as everything became clear. Her father . . . such a wise man. Her real mentor. Her counselor. Her most trusted friend. They were losing him. What would she do without him? Another cry came from him. She gripped her mother tighter. Her breath caught. Her mother was taking deep gulps of air.

What had her father said? *Your integrity is everything.* She'd known that. Her parents had instilled values in her that had served her well, though it helped to be told one was doing the right thing, especially when making the most difficult decisions. She'd been right when she'd told Adrian off the day before. Her father had merely confirmed it. Anyone could make the easy decisions, the ones with no consequences to speak of. But character was truly revealed by how one handled the hard ones. How one responded had to do with integrity. The bad guys had raised the stakes until Adrian capitulated. But for her, the stakes would never be high enough.

Her mind floated in and out, evading reality. She and her mother clung to each other. Neither of them spoke. They barely breathed. She didn't know how long they stood there—how long the team worked on her father. She'd lost all sense of her surroundings. The world consisted of herself, her mother, and what was going on in her father's room.

Eventually a white-coated physician appeared in the doorway. His look—a deep frown—said everything.

Torie couldn't feel her mother, though her mother stood in her arms. She couldn't feel her hands or face. All sensation had drained out of her. The bottom had fallen out of her life.

"May we see him?" her mother asked.

"Take all the time you need," the doctor said. "I'm so sorry. His heart was very weak. He seemed ready to go."

"I know," her mother said. "I think he was."

The doctor walked down the hall, his head down. The rest of the team, who cast grim glances at Torie and her mom as they passed, followed him. One of the women reached out and squeezed Torie's mother's arm. "I'm so sorry."

They entered the room where Torie's father lay unhooked from everything, the sheet pulled up to his shoulders, his face blank yet peaceful. Torie walked to the left side of the bed, her mother to the right.

Torie took one hand in hers. Her mother took the other. His hand was still warm. She looked at his face to see if maybe they had been mistaken. Maybe he was still alive. Maybe he was in a coma or taking a little nap. "He's still warm, Mom." She hiked herself up on his bed and laid her head on his chest to listen for a heartbeat, fully expecting him to breathe out and tell her to get off.

His sheet-covered body still felt soft. She could smell his musty scent, feel the give of his flesh under her weight. He wasn't dead. She pushed her ear closer, mashing it against his heart, closing her eyes, her whole being focused on the hope of a heartbeat. "Daddy? Daddy can you hear me?"

Her mother touched her shoulder. "Torie what are you doing? He's gone."

"Maybe they made a mistake. Be quiet. I think I hear a heartbeat."

"No, Torie. He's gone."

She opened her eyes and spotted a stethoscope on the table behind her mother. "Hand me that, Mom. That stethoscope."

"Torie, no."

In her judge's voice, Torie said, "Give me that stethoscope, Mother. Right now."

Her mother did as she was bid. Torie, still on the bed, pressed the chest piece to his heart and put the headset on. "Now, shh."

But there was no heartbeat. There was nothing. No sound. She pushed it around on his chest, trying different places, but could hear no sound. She looked at her mother whose face was white and eyes were red, tears streaming. Was her mother thinking the same thing? *What would she do without him?*

Torie kissed her father and stroked his balding head. "Daddy, I love you so much." She lay next to him for a few moments, feeling the warmth of his body seep away, before climbing down. "Goodbye." Her mother still held her father's hand. Her eyes followed Torie as she laid the stethoscope over the foot of the bed.

"I'll give you some private time," Torie said and walked out into the hall.

Hugging her stomach, she leaned against the wall opposite the room and slid to the floor. She needed to be strong for her mother. She dug in her purse for some tissues and wiped her face, swallowing several times, breathing deeply. There were details to attend to. Defying hospital rules, she got out her cell phone and called Mary and told her to bring Howie to say goodbye. Then she called Sergio. When the call went to voice mail, she clicked off.

Some time later, after Mary and Howie showed up and after the arrangements were made for her father's body, Torie left Mary and

Howie to take their mother home. She desperately needed some time to herself. And then she had something very important to take care of.

One more conversation with Adrian.

Chapter 30

TORIE LOCKED HER CAR DOOR AND PUT HER head down on the steering wheel. Out-of-control sobs erupted from her body. She gripped the sides of the steering wheel and held on tight as if her car were racing around a track with the accelerator stuck to the floor. Her nose ran and saliva dripped from her mouth onto her lap. Her eyes burned. Her heart pounded like it would leap out of her chest. She remained that way for the better part of half an hour.

Finally, when she could think of her father without sobbing, she sat up and stared through the windshield at nothing in particular. Life without her father was unimaginable. He was too young to die. She was too young to be fatherless. In truth, she needed him. He'd always been there for her, guiding her, even if it had been in sports metaphors. In their last conversation, right at the end, he seemed to know what was in her mind, her heart. He had never been one to speak words of affection. They could relate to each other if she pinned him down, but usually his words were like, *have you seen the game today?* Or *what do you think of the Cowboys this year?*

He and her mother had known of his condition and not told them. As angry as she'd been when she'd learned that, there was nothing she could do. She was grateful for their time together, grateful for his last words. Her father had known how important her integrity was to her. He had raised her to be honest and fair and just, to treat people with dignity and value and worth, to speak honestly and keep her word and impress on others the importance of keeping theirs.

Having exhausted the supply of tissues from her purse, she found some more in the glove box and wiped her face. Her makeup was a mess, but it didn't matter now. She started the car. She knew what she had to do. She'd known it all along, but the difficulties she faced were hard and would have been easier if someone had her back.

No use wishing. Her father was dead. Sergio had left her. Adrian was—Adrian and his cronies were the problem. She had the solution.

She drove to Adrian's office, fighting to keep from breaking down again. She forced her mind away from her father and to her predicament with Adrian and his gang. She might be as naïve as Adrian had said, but he was the one who hadn't been honest with her. How dare he put her in that position. Anger engulfed her. Anger had replaced the good old-fashioned cry she'd been carrying around for weeks.

She'd wanted to cry from the moment she'd finally figured out what Adrian was trying to tell her. No, from before that. From the time she realized her father's health was failing. Wait, before that. From the day Sergio left. She wasn't sure which had come first. But crying hadn't been her way for—for years. Since Cassie's death.

Now she'd had that cry and, yes, she'd let herself do more of it later. At home. In private. But right now, she had something she had to tell Adrian. It couldn't wait. She owed it to her father—to her mother as well—and to herself. When tears started down her face again as she drove, Torie rooted around until she found some napkins from a fast food joint. They'd have to do. She blew her nose into the coarse, scratchy paper and cleared her throat and resolved to control her anger, to channel it where it would do the most good.

She reached Adrian's office and took purposeful steps on the flagstone walkway, her resolve strengthening as she grew closer, until she knew she was strong enough to withstand all argument she was likely to face. Inside, where the coffee aroma overwhelmed the small suite of offices, where the air conditioning was too cold, and where, in earlier years, she'd felt welcomed and at home and loved and safe, she now felt uneasy and insecure.

She stopped at the side of Viola's desk, a few feet from Adrian's door, and crossed her arms. "I want to see Judge Frothingham immediately, and I won't be put off."

Viola reared back in her chair, her mouth dropping open. "Good heavens, Judge, take a seat. I'm sure he'll be off the phone in a minute." She gave Torie a look that said *something's wrong with you, girl.* "Anything I can help you with?"

"My father just passed away." Her eyes met Viola's, and Viola shook her head.

Torie's father, her advisor, had just died. Adrian, who had stood in the stead of professional mentor, if not father, had recently been lost to her as well, as surely as if he'd died.

"I'm so sorry." Viola laid her glasses aside. "Is there anything I can do?"

Torie put her hand over her mouth and pinched her nose shut, shaking her head, breathing into her hand. She absolutely refused to lose control in Adrian's offices. She blinked away tears as she stared at Viola and took the offered tissues.

"Cup of coffee?"

She'd had nothing to eat since the night before, but coffee wouldn't sit well on an empty stomach. "Water?"

"Bottle?"

She nodded. "I didn't mean to snap at you."

When Viola went down a short hallway that Torie knew led to a closet-sized kitchen, Torie fanned her face and mopped at it. She was going to do this. She had to. Her shuddering breath evened out by the time Viola came back and twisted the cap off the bottle, handing it to her.

"How many months along are you?"

Torie was in the middle of swallowing and almost choked. "What?" A chill caressed the back of her arms. "How'd you know?"

"Oh, I apologize. You have that look. Were you keeping it a secret?"

"Yes, I was—well, except for Adrian. He didn't tell you, did he?" She took another sip, feeling the water trickle down her throat.

"No, Judge. But there's something—maybe you're not as skinny as you used to be?"

"Okay, if you're trying to insult me, you're doing a good job of it." She allowed herself a ghost of a smile.

"I didn't mean it that way. There's a beautiful roundedness about your—to your face and your body."

"My clothes are getting a bit tight." She wasn't feeling very beautiful just then and wondered whether the stress she was undergoing could be felt by the baby at this early stage.

Viola tapped her lips. "I still remember those first months of pregnancy."

"Hard to forget." Torie's first months with her current pregnancy had been torn with indecision, not celebratory like they should have been. But that was something she couldn't dwell on at the moment. She glanced at the closed door at the end of the long hallway. "Do you know how much longer he'll be?"

"Let me poke my head in." Viola walked down the hallway again and knocked. A few moments later, she returned. "He knows you're here."

Practically right behind Viola, Adrian came out, his giraffe legs bringing him within about a yard from Torie. No apparent limp. Torie was relieved she hadn't done any permanent damage to his foot, though he certainly deserved more.

"Judge, what brings you by?" His face, stony.

She stood, and he shook her hand, something he'd always done in public if other people were around.

"A few matters to discuss with you in private, if you don't mind." She kept her tone even so nothing would pique Viola's curiosity.

Viola rolled her chair back toward her computer as Adrian ushered Torie into his office and closed the door. "Have you calmed down? You look like hell, by the way." He walked away from the door toward his desk, giving Torie a wide berth.

Torie ignored the jab at her appearance. She wasn't there to win a beauty contest. "I have something to tell you, and it can't wait."

"This is not a good idea," he said in a low voice.

"Coming here, you mean? We can go out in public, for coffee, if you want. I don't care. I've just got to have my say."

"What do you mean? Sit down." He took the chair adjacent to the one on which she perched but turned it so he was squared off with her rather than shoulder-to-shoulder. "Just keep your voice down."

"I mean," she said, looking him dead in the eye, "I'm not going along with this."

"I think you made that clear the last time I saw you."

"I'm not sure I made my entire position clear. I've never intentionally favored one lawyer over another, one case over another. I don't care what *they* think. And I'm not about to start now." She clenched her teeth. The more she thought about it, the more insulted and furious she became. That they could even think she was approachable . . . "For any reason."

"You wanted this. You said you would do anything—"

"I never said I'd do something like that. *You* made that assumption. If you think about it, I never said anything. Adrian, I've been so flabbergasted by this whole thing—"

"You said you would *do anything to be on the Supreme Court. Anything.* They're not going to let you change your mind at this late date."

"About what, the Supreme Court? I have no intention of taking myself out of the running. I'll win that appointment on my own."

"It doesn't work that way." His eyes flared. "You've got to have support from many corners."

"I've got my father . . . " Her father's death struck her like a punch to the belly.

"What is it? Are you sick?"

"My father just passed away. I came straight here from the hospital."

"I'm so sorry." He reached toward her.

"Don't . . . don't, Adrian. I'm only here to tell you I'm not going along with the deal, and you can tell that bunch of thieves and extortioners. Not only that, but . . . " She stood and gripped the edge of his desk to support herself. Her knees wanted to give way.

"Those are harsh words, Judge. Sit down and let's discuss this before you go off and do anything half-cocked."

She sat back down and took a long drink from the bottle of water, hating the taste of plastic, as well as the thought that more than likely the bottle would take its place in a landfill soon. *What the heck was she thinking about landfills for when she was in the middle of such a dire situation?* She was losing her mind.

"You want to share with me how you propose to secure that appointment without any help?"

She closed her eyes and recited the list she'd made on the drive over. "First of all, I've had help, thank you very much. I've already had my introduction to the governor, thanks to you, so my name is on the short list, and he knows who I am.

"Secondly, you know my father mounted a letter-writing campaign as soon as I told him my plans. Those letters are in the governor's hands.

"Thirdly, there are still some *honest* lawyers and judges out there who have made recommendations for me.

"Fourth, on my own merit. I was active in the state bar for many years, and I've presented at several judicial conferences.

"Fifth—"

Adrian stopped her with a hand on her arm. Her eyes flew open. She picked up his hand with two fingers and moved it away.

"Okay, Victoria. I understand where you're coming from, but it's not going to be enough. When Hawkins's law firm withdraws their support and the others withdraw theirs . . . "

"They would do that wouldn't they? And give some lame excuse?"

"Yes." He nodded. "They wouldn't hesitate for a moment. And then there's my support, as well."

"You would do that?" She clenched her teeth.

"I have no choice."

A storm raged inside her, yet outside the spring day was clear, trees green and lush. Flowers had pushed up from the edging around the parking lot. She had a new life inside her she had to think about. She knew she'd been a good mother to Cassie, at least until she and Bert had divorced and both of them became nuts. She'd be a good mother to the baby she carried, too. Part of being a good parent was doing the right thing. "You'll have to withdraw your support then, because I'm not going along with it. I can't. It's just not in me."

"They'll do more than withdraw their support. They'll ruin you. You have no idea of the things they can do. They'll take you down one way or the other."

She shook her head. "I'm not going to do it. Don't you hear me? No."

"Not only will you not get the appointment to the Supreme Court, but they'll find someone to run against you in the next election. They'll do everything they can to stop others from contributing to your campaign while raising and donating vast sums of money to your opponent. You'll be defeated, Victoria. Out of a job. Then what will you do?"

Nausea rose in the back of her throat. "I can always go back to practicing law."

"Think of Sergio and the baby."

The baby and Sergio were exactly who she was thinking about. She stood again, shaking her head. "I am. I'll withdraw my name from the running, but I'll never fix a case. Never. You may live your life that way if you want, Adrian, but I just couldn't. I feel sick just thinking about it." She headed for the door.

"Victoria," Adrian hissed her name as he followed her. "Victoria, they're going to tell the world about our affair."

Heat consumed her face. Her body went rigid with fury. She reversed her direction, her eyes cutting into him, backing him up several steps. "First of all, I don't even want to know how they know about us. Secondly, they wouldn't dare."

"They've been keeping tabs on me—"

"I said I don't want to know. I think I really would vomit all over your floor if I thought those sleaze bags knew every time we met at the hotel."

Adrian kept his distance. "Don't underestimate them, Victoria." His eyebrows were like a bushy thundercloud. "Letting that out would ruin both of us personally as well as professionally."

"They're underestimating *me*. Do they really think a little public humiliation like that, the embarrassment of having had an affair with the judge who presided over my child custody case about a child who is now dead will stop me from doing the right thing? If that's what they think, they have no idea who I am. *"*

She glared up at him, making herself as tall as she could. "Oh, and I'm forgetting the main reason I came here. I wanted to tell you my next call is to the Texas Rangers. We'll see what's what after I talk to Ranger Perez and the Rangers get through investigating *Lawyers for Lawsuit Equity.*

"And the next time you talk to *him, they,* or *them,* you tell 'em I said, *fuck you.*"

Chapter 31

ADRIAN SLUMPED AGAINST THE EDGE OF HIS desk after Victoria slammed out of his office. The scent of her gardenia perfume still hung in the air. She'd always worn that fragrance. He'd recognize it anywhere, which brought back memories of their afternoons together, satin teddies, and vodka martinis, stolen moments he would give almost anything to get back.

She'd looked as sexy as ever. No. Even more so. Roses in her cheeks in spite of the stress in her jaw when she spoke. Eyes, though teary and smeared with makeup, a purple-blue as they pierced his in anger. Thin and fit with just the tiniest hint of a life growing inside her, a thickening of her waist that someone who didn't know her as well as he would never have noticed. A life that hadn't come from him, but from Sergio. Lucky fellow. He tried not to think about the two of them together, not to feel companion twinges of desire and jealousy. Was Sergio pleased about the child? Did he even know about it?

He wasn't surprised at Victoria's angry reaction—except for the still-painful assault on his foot, which had certainly caught him off guard. The real surprise had come years earlier when she became his lover.

She'd demonstrated the highest principles in the courtroom, in her cases when she practiced law, truly demonstrating her word was her bond. As the judge who presided over her divorce, he saw her take the high road. Since her husband came from a wealthy banking family with money to burn, there'd been a protracted jury trial. But even before that, during pretrial hearings, he'd seen her rein in her attorney, not permit certain tactics, giving the other side leeway when they didn't strictly abide by the rules.

Why would a young woman like her have a relationship with someone like him, a married man old enough to be her father? Though he'd been curious since the beginning of the affair, he'd never questioned her about it. He was just grateful for the time they'd had together.

A car door slammed. Adrian strode to the window and raised the shade. Victoria drove away, tires spinning on the gravel driveway. If there was a way to make her understand, to make her see the gravity of the situation, to make her grasp the danger in which she was placing herself, he didn't know what it was. He'd tried subtle hints in the beginning, but she hadn't taken them. He'd tried coaxing. Then ordering. Nothing got through to her.

He should have told her no in the first place, when she came to him wanting the appointment. Told her she was too young. Not experienced enough. That she didn't have enough support in the legal community. What was her hurry anyway? At one time, forty-five would have been considered young for a judge. These days, young attorneys who met only the minimum number of years experience required by law, youngsters still damp behind the ears, were throwing their hat in the ring before they had the maturity and experience and wisdom to make a good judge. Not that Victoria was as young as all that, but still, judges used to be twenty years older.

Still, he should have stopped her. When she told him she was pregnant, instead of encouraging her to get rid of the baby, he should have counseled her to withdraw her name and try for an appointment later. He should have squelched her ambitions any way he could—for her own protection—but he didn't. He never could come up with a good reason. He couldn't have given her the actual reason, couldn't very well have told her LLE planned to corrupt whoever got the appointment just as he now knew they had Justice McWillams—the justice she sought to replace.

"You see, Victoria, my dear, I've been taking graft for well over ten years and if you accept my help and that of the Lawyers for Lawsuit Equity and their ilk, you will have to do the same. You'll have to fix cases. Let their people win their appeals most of the time, especially when a lot of money is involved."

No, he couldn't have done that.

While he stood at the window, the sky grew dark in the distance. He hoped she'd slow down on the highway, ease off the gas and drive safely. He wouldn't want her to have a wreck, as incongruous as that was in light of the situation with LLE.

He stroked his abdomen, as though the burning in his midsection could be abated with such a simple act. When her Mercedes was out of sight, he strode back to his desk, regretting what he was going to have to do for self-preservation. He picked up his cell phone and called one of the men who wore a gray silk suit.

"We have a problem," he said when the man answered. "Judge Van Fleet has just left my office, and she refuses to cooperate."

"That's unacceptable," the suit said. "Did you tell her it was too late to change her mind?"

"She says she never agreed in the first place." Inky blackness, like a shroud, descended in the sky, enveloping the landscape all the way to the horizon. He hoped Torie would be all right.

"Did you tell her she was jeopardizing her entire career if she made a wrong choice?"

"She doesn't care. She's ready to throw it all away rather than go along with us. As long as I've known her, I've never seen her so angry." Not that he was surprised. He would have been more surprised if she'd agreed to go along.

"And we know what a long time that's been. Right, Judge?"

Adrian held his ire in check. "That was unnecessary." The man on the other end of the line might be sitting in the catbird seat, but there was a limit to the abuse Adrian would take. As that thought crossed his mind, he realized how ridiculous he was being. He had no dignity left; no use pretending he had.

And the suits had no respect for him; no reason they should.

"Well, look," the suit said. "I'll make a few calls and figure out what we need to do about her. Sit tight. I'll call you right back."

Adrian clicked off his cell phone and set it on his desk, his hands shaking. *Do about her?* He walked back to the window. What had begun as a clear day became night. *Ping.* A tiny bit of hail hit the window. *Ping. Ping.* Hail rained from the sky, at first looking like heavy snow, though it was too late in the year for snow. Then pea-sized hail. Then marble-sized, bombing the building's tin roof like rocks. A hunk of ice rattled the window, and Adrian jumped back.

Minutes later, as quickly as the hailstorm began, it ceased. The blackness faded like it was sucked up into the sky. Hail blanketed the ground like a heavy layer of fertilizer.

Ah-roo-guh. Ah-roo-guh. Adrian snatched his cell phone off his desk, dreading what he would hear. Clicking on, he heard a different suit's voice, but one he was all too familiar with, Karl. "That you, Judge?"

"Yes." He wished it wasn't, wished he had the option of being anywhere else, talking to anyone but a suit.

"We're going to give her one last chance. Talk to her again. Tonight or tomorrow at the latest."

One last chance? Or what? "If she'll see me. She was outraged when she left—when I told her y'all would reveal our past relationship."

"And she still wouldn't give in?"

"Outraged, I said. She was *outraged.* The last thing she said was she was going to the Texas Rangers." Well, not the *last* thing. But he wasn't going to tell the suit Victoria said *fuck you.*

"We can't allow that to happen," Karl said.

Adrian winced and dropped into his chair. He didn't like Karl's tone. "I have to tell you something in the strictest confidence. She's pregnant." Maybe they wouldn't hurt her if they knew she was carrying a child.

"Then tell her if she knows what's good for her, she'll do what she needs to do to protect her baby."

Adrian's hair prickled. The message couldn't get much clearer. "But there's another thing—besides the fact that she's not just anybody—she's a district judge—she has no evidence to show them. Nothing. Nada."

"Then how does she expect to get the Rangers to help her? No. She's gotta have something, or she'd be making a fool of herself."

"Even if she tells the Rangers her suspicions, there's nothing they can do about it with no evidence. They'll think she has some other motive." Adrian knuckled his mustache. He shouldn't have said anything about the Rangers.

"You call her right back and tell her you have to meet her for lunch tomorrow. Tell her Ralph's. Tell her not to do anything until she talks with you again."

Adrian pulled the phone away from his ear and stared at it, wishing he could see through it, see what Karl was thinking, planning. "All right," he whispered. "I'll give it my best shot."

"Make sure you do. And make sure when you speak with her she understands if she doesn't get her act together she could end up like Justice McWilliams.

Chapter 32

TORIE HEADED STRAIGHT FOR RANGER PEREZ'S office in Kerrville, several towns away from both Adrian's office and her own in Bremerhaven. Ordinarily she would have enjoyed the drive, admired the bluebonnets, the red paintbrushes, the orange and yellow fire wheels, even the lavender bull nettle, but rage blurred her vision. Instead of driving a few miles over the speed limit as was her habit, she reduced her speed, knowing her focus wasn't on the road, realizing her mind was still engaged in argument with Adrian, still searching for a reasonable way out of the mess she'd gotten herself into.

Within minutes of seeing the little town in her rearview mirror, the sky grew dark, thunder crashed, and huge raindrops splattered her car. Seconds later, tiny bits of ice bounced off her windshield. There was no overpass to hide under, no shelter of any kind. All there was on both sides of the road were open fields. To the right, a barbed-wire fence. To the left, an empty, rocky field with trees in the distance.

As the hail came down in heavier and larger chunks—from pea size to marble size to golf ball size—she jerked the steering wheel to the left and bounced her way across the landscape pulling into a stand of trees, parking under a gigantic spreading oak. She flinched every time a chunk of ice or a piece of tree hit the windshield. She might not be safe under the tree but couldn't think what else to do. Baseball-size hail struck the ground like meteorites. If she'd had something to cover up with, she'd have felt better. Intellectually she knew it was unlikely the glass in the car would break, but the blanket in the trunk would have made her feel more secure.

When the storm had passed, when calm settled over her, she phoned the Ranger's office on her cell, which her Blue Tooth picked up and blasted into the car. He was not in. The secretary asked if she'd like the call to go to voicemail, so she left a message. "Ranger Perez, this is Judge Victoria Van Fleet. I know you remember testifying in my court last year in that divorce case where the wife alleged her husband stole three pieces of heavy equipment from her family's construction site? You stopped by for coffee a while back? Anyway, I need your help—" *Beep.*

Of course he remembered her. How dumb to mention that. It was just so awkward to call a ranger—to call anyone from the perspective of a person-in-need as opposed to a judge making an order.

She redialed and asked the secretary to put her through again. "This is the judge again. Sorry I was so long-winded." She thought about how to make her message succinct "Anyway, I need to speak to you about a serious matter involving our court sys—" *Beep.*

The third time, she asked the secretary for his cell number. It was probably best not to put everything in a message anyway. She punched in that number.

"Perez," he said in a deep voice.

"Ranger Perez, this is Judge Van Fleet—"

"Hey, how are you, Judge? I still need to get back over to your court so we can have coffee."

She cleared her throat. "I was on my way to see you when the hailstorm began. I have a very confidential, uh, delicate matter I'd like to discuss with you." Her hands tingled. She didn't know why she was nervous.

"I'm on my way back there now. I can meet you in about fifteen minutes if that works for you."

She glanced at the balls of ice on her car's hood. "I don't know if I can make it by then. I'm kind of stuck—well, I don't know if I'm stuck or not. I'm afraid of being stuck." She shook her head. "I'm not making any sense, I know." She huffed out a breath. "Actually, I'm in a field under a tree, which is where I went when the hailstorm began. I thought I probably ought to wait a while until it melts a little, and then see if I can make it back to the road without sinking into any mud the rain and melting ice might have caused."

"Whoa. That's a predicament. Where exactly are you?"

"On the road from Judge Frothingham's office. I had just left there when the hail started."

"Okay, well, hang tight, I'll come to you, and we'll see if we can get you back on the road."

Torie's shoulders relaxed. "Great. I drive a Mercedes."

"I've seen that sweet little car you drive. Don't worry. I'll find you. It'll be a few minutes, but don't try to leave until I get there." The phone went dead.

Torie returned the phone to its holder and leaned back, closing her eyes. Now she had to remain there until the ice began to melt. She only hoped the ranger wouldn't be very long.

Even though she figured Sergio wouldn't answer, she punched in his cell number. When her call went to voice mail, she said, "Sergio, we really need to talk. Please call me." Her stomach growled. Digging around in the glove box, she found a package of saltines. She tore them open and watched the road as she munched on them and chased them with bottled water. She called Nettie next.

"Judge Van Fleet's office," Nettie said in a singsong voice.

"It's me," Torie said. "Anything exciting going on there?" She fervently hoped not. She couldn't take one more blessed thing.

"Nada, how's your father?"

In the last hour, between being threatened by both Adrian and the weather, Torie had put her father out of her mind. Now his death came rushing back. Tears tumbled down her cheeks. She pounded the steering wheel. She didn't want to think about her grief right then. She couldn't handle so many things at once. She needed help. She needed Sergio, but Sergio wasn't there and might not ever be again. She had to hold herself together at least until she got the matter with the LLE people settled, until she talked to the ranger, whatever it took. She wet her lips, thirsty again, and reached for the water. The way things were going, if it had been Adrian who had handed her the bottle instead of Viola, she wouldn't have drunk it. God, could she be any more distrustful and paranoid?

"Judge? You still there? I said, 'How's your father?'" Nettie's voice had become flat and serious.

"M-my father died a couple of hours ago." Torie swallowed the urge to sob, but her eyes welled up with tears.

"Oh, I'm so sorry, Judge. Are you all right? What can I do?"

Torie wiped her face with a paper napkin and blew her nose. "Well, for one thing, clear the calendar until next week. I need to help my mother with the arrangements." She hadn't given any real thought to the funeral. Mary would help. She was always right there, but Torie wanted to make sure it was the kind of sendoff her father would have liked. The kind her mother would be comfortable with.

Her mind raced. She needed to talk to the ranger—needed to help with her father's arrangements—needed to decide about the baby. She'd have to focus. First the ranger. He should be there any moment. Surely, he'd have the time to hear her out.

She'd stumbled out of the hospital and driven to Adrian's, leaving her brother to take their mother home, to comfort her. She needed to call her mother and find out what she wanted to do about the funeral.

Nettie said, "The jury trial settled, believe it or not. While they waited for you yesterday, they worked it out. I can reschedule everything else, no problem."

"That's good news." There was a case on her docket for the following day that really needed to be heard. The woman had appeared before her for an emergency protective order and temporary restraining order. The facts that led the woman to leave her husband and file for divorce and for protection were horribly frightening. "Wait, Nettie, leave the Mitchell case on the calendar for tomorrow morning. That poor woman—"

Beep. Another call was coming in. She had never been very good at picking up one call while in the middle of another, so she ignored it, hoping it wasn't the ranger.

"You want to get that?"

"They can leave voicemail." Weariness seeped into her. What she wouldn't give to lie down for a few minutes with her feet up. "Mrs. Mitchell needs a final protective order and an order to stop the foreclosure sale on her house next Monday and temporary orders for child support. So leave that on the calendar." She stared at the field of ice. Her chest felt heavy. Her breath didn't come easily. "See if Judge McGruter will hear any emergency matters that come up in the next few days."

"You want me to call Judge Frothingham's office and see if I can get a visiting judge?"

"No!" Torie almost choked. No telling who Adrian would send over, who would have access to every one of her files, or how that visiting judge might rule on her pending cases. "Definitely not. Just go talk to Charlotte or Judge McGruter. Please."

"Hold on, the phone's ringing."

While on hold, Torie tried to figure out how to look at who called her without disconnecting the call with Nettie. Nettie clicked back on the line. "It's Judge Frothingham. He said he tried to reach you on your cell—"

"Guess that's who I didn't pick up. What'd you tell him?"

"To try you again in a few minutes. He said it's really important."

What now? What else could he have to say? "Anything else I need to know, Nettie?"

"Judge, I'm really very sorry about your father."

"Thank you, but let's not talk about it. I can't handle any sympathy right now. So you'll tell Judge McGruter and Charlotte and everyone about my father?" A bright reflection struck her eyes, the sun on someone's windshield. Alarm rang through her body as a huge, black, dually truck drove off the road and headed toward her. She prayed the truck contained the ranger.

"Look, I've got to go. I'll see you tomorrow." Blinded by the glistening light, Torie couldn't see who it was. Putting on her sunglasses made no difference. Either someone was coming to help or she was in big trouble, trapped unless she got going before the truck reached her.

"Where are you anyway?" Nettie asked.

"Parked off the road. Gotta go. Tell you tomorrow." She thumbed the phone button on the dashboard and started her car.

The truck drew close, and Torie shifted into drive, bumping toward the road. She came parallel to an unmarked Ford. The driver laid on his horn, and Torie, swallowing her fear and anxiety, put down her window. Ranger Perez. The tension drained out of her. She cut her engine and unlocked her car so he could come around and get in the front seat.

"How'd you find me?" she asked after he climbed inside, and they'd shaken hands. There was nothing like a big hunk of police authority to make one feel secure. His musky, sweaty man smell filled the air.

"Not that many Mercedes Benzes sitting under trees in a field." He laughed. "Glad you're all right."

"I headed for the trees when the hail started."

"Lucky you've only got a couple of dings in your windshield. I won't leave until we see if you can make it through the slush and back on the highway."

"I'm really glad you're here."

"I'd been a couple of counties over and was headed back to the office."

Her phone rang. Adrian's name popped up on the screen. "Please don't leave, Ranger. I have to take this."

He started to get out, but she grabbed his sleeve and put a finger to her lips.

"Yes, Judge," she said in a monotone. "What can I do for you?"

His voice blared through her hands-free system. She couldn't have had a better set-up for the situation, for the ranger to hear the conversation.

"Victoria, I tried you a few minutes ago, but your line was tied up. You weren't talking to the ranger, were you?"

Ranger Perez's face lit up, eyes wide, eyebrows raised.

"No—you called my office. You know I was on the line with Nettie. Don't play games with me, Adrian. If you want to know something, ask me. I've always been upfront with you."

"Where are you now? Have you gone to the ranger's office in Kerrville?"

"I haven't had time yet. I was on my way there when the hailstorm hit. I've been sitting under a tree in a field somewhere out in someone's north forty."

"So there's still time."

She didn't like the sound of that and glanced at the ranger. "For what?"

"For you to change your mind."

Ranger Perez ran his hand through his hair and leaned closer to the dashboard even though the system's speakers were so loud they could practically hear Adrian swallow. Perez's aftershave made her think of Sergio again and how much she missed him. The ranger looked like he was in his late thirties, close in age to Sergio. She pushed all thought of her husband from her mind. She needed to focus on the problem at hand.

"Adrian, I'm not about to change my mind. I don't know how many ways there are to tell you I won't be a part of it." Torie glanced at Perez and wished she'd had time to brief him before he heard the conversation so he could understand what was going on.

"Look, Victoria, I talked to—to one of my . . . uh . . . associates. They want us to discuss it further, want me to convince you to listen to reason. Could you give me one more chance to make you understand their viewpoint?"

"I'm confused. They threaten to air my dirty laundry in the press, and now they want me to come to the table again? For what? So you or they can abuse me even more? I don't get it. What are you saying?" Torie's eyes met Perez's. He circled the air with his forefinger. Draw Adrian out.

"Let's not discuss it over the phone. Suffice it to say it's an offer you can't refuse. Why don't you meet me tomorrow for lunch at Ralph's on the River?"

"I'm getting kind of sick of that place."

"This is no time to be flippant."

Torie smiled at the ranger and shrugged. "I apologize, but I see no reason to discuss this whole matter further and, in fact Adrian, I need to help my mother with my father's funeral arrangements. I drove to your office and haven't even talked to her for more than a few minutes since my father died."

He sighed into the phone. "Jesus Christ, Victoria, I'm sorry about your father, really, he was a fine man, but it's imperative I talk to you."

Torie glanced at the ranger. He nodded. "Do it," he mouthed.

"I guess I can postpone going to the ranger's office until tomorrow afternoon. I need to see my mom this evening anyway."

"Thank you, Victoria. What time can we meet?"

"I'm actually doing a hearing on temporary orders in a divorce case at ten, so after that. Probably straight-up noon. I'll come to the restaurant. And Adrian, I want you to consider going to the ranger's office with me afterward. I know you think you're going to change my mind, but please know I intend to change yours."

"We'll talk about it. Look for me on the balcony." He clicked off.

Torie punched the disconnect button on her Blue Tooth to be sure she had cut off Adrian before she spoke to the ranger.

"This sounds serious, Judge."

"It's starting to get scary." She explained what had been going on for the past several months since she'd put her hat in the ring for the Supreme Court, starting with the first time Adrian had questioned her about a ruling.

The ranger studied her as she spoke, only stopping her momentarily to ask questions, to clarify a point. When she was through, she breathed a long sigh and folded her hands in her lap, exhausted, wanting to crawl into bed for a nice long sleep.

"I don't like it that Frothingham wants you to meet him at a specific time and place." His frown was as pronounced as any she'd ever seen.

"I'm uneasy about that, too. Are you thinking what I'm thinking?" Chills ran up her arms.

He scratched the shadowy whiskers on his chin. "I'm thinking it's a setup."

"I've been scared for several days." She clasped the steering wheel to steady herself. "I've been worried for a while, ever since I started refusing Adrian—Judge Frothingham's—requests. I should have come to you sooner." She caught herself fingering her hair like she had when she was a little girl and pulled her hand away. "So much has been going on in my life that I'm afraid my judgment has been impaired."

"That's to be expected in your current situation, ma'am. You've been handling a lot of responsibility by yourself, dealing with that crew. Tell you what I think. I trust your sheriff, do you?"

"Jim Bob? A hundred percent."

He pulled out a cell phone and tapped some notes into it. "Okay, here's what I'm going to do. I'll give him a call and ask him to have one of his men from the Organized Crime Control Unit come wire you after you get through hearing your case but before you go to Ralph's."

"I can deal with that." She already felt better. Now if she could just make it through the night.

"In the meantime, I'll be at Ralph's well before the appointed time. And I'll have a couple of men with me."

"Okay. He likes the table that's on the overhang, you know which one I mean? The one overlooking the river."

"I know which one it is. We'll have you covered at the restaurant, and I'll have a man in the parking lot. You'll be safe, believe me."

Torie released a deep breath. "Thank you, Ranger. I'm glad you took my call."

He grinned and saluted her with two fingers. "Glad to be of service, ma'am. Now why don't you see if you can maneuver this little jewel out of this field and back onto the road and get on over to your mother's. I'm sure she needs you. May I suggest you spend the night at her house?"

"I'll do that." They shook hands again. He had a nice, firm, warm grip, the kind of handshake her father had been talking about a few days earlier. "Thank you so much."

He climbed out of the car and, leaning his head back down, he said, "If you get stuck, I'll call a wrecker and wait with you. And oh, by the way, I'm very sorry about your father. I knew him and would love to share a story about him with you sometime."

Torie waited until the ranger got into his truck and made a U-turn on the ice-covered ground before she put her Mercedes in drive and let it creep and crunch over chunks of ice, working through the field to the two-lane farm-to-market road. She concerned herself for a moment with the possibility that Adrian might come searching for her. But only a few cars had begun to venture out, and none looked like Adrian's. A part of her was glad. Another part of her thought that after all they'd been to each other, he should have shown some concern for her welfare, which he didn't do over the phone either. But then if he had come, would it have been to help her or harm her? She was glad she didn't have to find out.

When she eased onto the road, relief flooded her. Most of the hail on the pavement had already melted. She settled into her seat and punched in the number for her mother in the hands-free device.

The Ranger saluted as he sped by her, heading in the direction of his office.

When her mother answered, she sighed as if the effort was almost too much for her.

"It's me. How're you doing? Are Howie and Mary still there? Have you eaten anything today? Tried to rest?"

"I'm fine, honey."

Her mother's soft voice plucked at Torie's heart. To be alone after all those years—there was no way to even imagine what she must be feeling. That day was the beginning of a long journey of grief for her mother, for all of them, but Torie would have the baby, if not Sergio—and she wasn't ready to give up on Sergio yet. Before she said another word, Torie realized she'd made her decision. She'd keep the child. In fact, she was looking forward to having it. "I knew you'd say you're fine. Did you eat? You need to eat."

"Your brother picked up a sandwich for me."

"I'm going to spend the night with you. I'll bring some things, some food." Just following through on the Ranger's suggestion made her feel better but also reminded her the Ranger thought she was in danger. Fear for her personal safety had been in the back of her mind for a while. Not just the threat of Carr coming after her again when he was released from his incarceration, but the LLE people. Would they really do something to her if she didn't do what they wanted? She could only hope they stuck with their Plan A and didn't come after her at her mother's house. She'd hate to endanger her mother.

She glanced into her rearview mirror to see if anyone was following her and realized she probably should have been more vigilant ever since she and Adrian had their confrontation. The highway was mostly empty. People were probably hesitant to venture out with hail still on the ground.

"Having you here would be a comfort to me, dear."

Her mother's voice brought Torie back to the situation at hand. "I need to go to my house to pack a bag, but I'll be over this evening. I have to hold court in the morning, a case that really needs to be heard, but after that I'll be off for several days, Mom. I'll be there for whatever you need."

"I'm sure you'll take care of everything. You're so capable. Should I start dinner—no, you said you'd bring food. You did say you'd bring food?"

"Yes, Mom." The confusion in her mother's voice was no more than Torie expected. "I'll pick up something. But without sounding crass, I guess you'd better be thinking about the funeral arrangements and what you want the obituary to say."

"Mary called the paper and got the requirements. And you know how the Chamber of Commerce puts out those little sheets with death notices all over town? She contacted the chamber for that, too."

"Good. We can discuss whether we need to put an obit in any of the papers of the towns around this area and maybe in one or two of the big city ones. A lot of people knew Dad."

Her mother sighed again. "A lot of people knew your father, yes."

Torie could easily break down again, but if ever she needed to be strong . . . "Don't worry, Mom. I'll do it. I don't want you to feel overwhelmed."

"Thank you." She could almost see her mother nodding.

"Did Mary call the church?"

"Yes. I hope you don't mind her doing all this. Howie said he wasn't up to it."

"Women seem to be able to handle these things better. I don't mean that unkindly, really I don't, Mom. But . . ." She approached the bypass for one of the small towns in her district and slowed almost to a stop. A fender-bender. The cars had pulled to the side of the road, but not far enough for traffic to get around them easily.

"Hold on a moment, Mom. There's a traffic snarl." Torie waited until the oncoming traffic cleared and then circled around the wreck.

"Most women do handle family matters better." Her mother's voice sounded a bit stronger with that assertion. "They always have. And Mary picks up the slack for Howie."

"She does, and I don't mind a bit if she wants to help. I've had a lot on my plate today. Some things I needed to take care of."

"I understand, honey." Her mother sighed again, her breath coming heavily into the phone.

"Um—have you heard from Sergio? I know he probably doesn't know about Dad, but I just thought . . ."

"Yes, I did, honey. I don't know how he knew, but he called to give his condolences."

"That's good." His call gave her hope. "Well, uh—I guess I'll hang up. It'll probably be after dark by the time I get there so don't worry. And I'll definitely bring us dinner so don't think you have to take care of me. I'll take care of both of us."

Chapter 33

A BIT AFTER NOON THE FOLLOWING DAY, TORIE stepped down from the bench and swung open her chambers' door. Adrian stood in the center of the room, his cell pressed to his ear.

The same chilled-blood feeling she'd had a few days earlier filled her. The scary full-chest feeling caused the feathery hairs on her neck to rise.

"What are you doing here?" She slammed the court file onto her desk. The man had the balls of Zeus.

He pressed a button on his cell and stepped toward her.

She took a long backward step toward the courtroom door. "Don't make me repeat myself." Oh for a bailiff. She'd have Adrian thrown out so fast he'd think he never arrived.

Adrian's face drained of color. "I thought we could talk safer here than at Ralph's. I'm not going to hurt you." He took another step toward her, his hand out as though he intended touching her arm and kissing her on the cheek like he used to do in private.

The door to the courtroom behind her stopped her retreat. She put out her own hand. "Back off, Adrian." The idea that he thought he could greet her, touch her, even as a friend, disgusted her. Didn't he realize what a slimeball he was?

She couldn't be sure he wasn't there to do her harm, though she saw no sign of a weapon, no telltale indications from his facial expression that he intended to be aggressive. He stood still, his eyes on her face. After a moment, he backed to the other doorway—to the entrance to Nettie's office.

Nettie's lights were off, the coordinator obviously having gone to lunch. She and Adrian were alone. He knew it. She knew it. If he did want to hurt her, no one would stop him.

Her temple throbbed like a migraine was coming on. She tried to conceal her anxiety as best she could. "Do you want to answer me or should I call the S.O.?"

She edged around him to her closet and hung up her robe, slipping her cell out of the pocket. If he threatened her, she could lock herself in the bathroom and call for help.

"Goddammit, Victoria. Quit acting like a cornered animal." He remained in the doorway, his hands at his sides, facing her. His three-piece suit looked like a wadded up washrag. "I just want to talk to you. If you'll go to your desk I promise to stay on the other side. I know you need to sit down in your condition. *Jesus*."

Torie glanced at her desk to see if anything was amiss. Not knowing how long he'd been there, she didn't know what to expect. Could he have been looking at her case notes again? She had one case in several cardboard boxes on her credenza, a stack of files on another case next to the boxes, one she'd started mapping out the ruling on in the center of her desk, and several others on the table under the window. Glancing at them now, they all looked in order.

"Victoria, please. I have something important to tell you. You don't have anything to fear from me."

His tone was reassuring. His face wore a plea. His body language looked nonthreatening. She breathed out in guarded relief and walked to her desk as far from him as she could. When she was seated, he closed the door to Nettie's office and took one of the chairs across from her.

"The Sheriff called on your chambers' phone, but I told him you were on the bench. He said he'd call back."

"You answered my phone?" Anger licked at her again.

He shrugged. "Nettie was gone. It was your chambers' line, and I thought someone needed to answer it."

"You're worse than impossible." The call was probably about the wire she was supposed to wear to lunch, to record Adrian. They'd have to forget that now. At least Jim Bob knew Adrian was there. Maybe he'd send someone over to make sure she was safe. She kept her cell phone in her hand, just in case, and waited for Adrian to say what he'd come to tell her.

Stress lines ran down his face. He was pale and his silver white hair looked like a cotton mop fresh from the grocery store, stringy and gray. She'd never seen him look so bad, but he deserved it. How had he sunk so low? What had been so important all those years ago to make him take money? Fancy dresses and jewelry for his wife? A larger house? A more expensive car?

When he didn't speak she said, "I guess you saw we're finally getting a metal detector."

He nodded and stroked his mustache with the knuckle of his

forefinger. "Looks like the installation will be complete in the next couple of days. What about the other entrances to the upper floors?"

"Commissioners finally authorized them at all three upstairs entrances. I think they're going to put up a gate or a wall that will include the elevator and the stairs. I tried to get them to do the entrances to the courthouse, to protect all the people who work here, not just those of us who work upstairs, but they wouldn't hear of it. Said they didn't want to inconvenience anyone more than necessary." She didn't want to talk about the metal detectors. She wanted to hear that he'd come around to her way of thinking, but she bit her tongue and waited for the conversation to play out.

Adrian cleared his throat and shifted in his chair. "You've got to give it to your commissioners. You dragged them kicking and screaming all the way, and they're not giving in any more than they have to. You've made them wrong, and they don't like that, especially your county judge."

Why was he talking about security when what she wanted to hear was that he was going with her to the Texas Rangers? There was no other reason for him to be there. But she'd let him get to that topic when he was ready—provided it didn't take much longer. She rubbed at her temples. "The commissioners are so incredibly stupid. I don't get it. If something happens, don't they realize they've been put on notice and will be held responsible?" She tapped her cell phone. She wished she knew how to use the *record* app.

"I guess I'd better get right to the point." His eyes flickered. He crossed one leg over the other and rested a hand on his knee.

Her phone rang. She grabbed it, her eyes on Adrian. "Judge Van Fleet."

"Jim Bob, Judge. Couple of things, and I won't keep you."

"It's the sheriff," she mouthed to Adrian. "Yes, Jim Bob, what can I do for you?"

"First, I wanted to give you my condolences on the passing of your father."

Torie blinked burning eyes, and her throat closed. She'd been making herself focus on other things, trying to compartmentalize her problems, not think of her father.

"Judge, should I have not said anything?"

She stroked the twisted muscle in her neck and forced a deep breath into her lungs. "No, that's all right. Thank you."

"You okay?"

"No—but I don't want to talk about it."

"Okay, new subject. Judge Frothingham answered your phone a while ago. Is he still there and if so, threatening you in any way?"

Torie and Adrian watched each other. "Yes and no, I don't think so, Sheriff."

"Okay, good. Sorry we didn't get you wired. When I hang up I'll call Perez and inform him. Maybe we can do this another way, another time." He cleared his throat. "Regretfully I have another piece of bad news. Carr got out of jail a couple of days ago."

Fear clutched her chest. "*You're kidding me.*" She was glad she'd stayed at her mother's the night before. Carr could have been at her house. Even with the alarm system, she wasn't safe, and she knew it. He could have gotten to her. She had to get control of her imagination. "I thought you were going to let me know when he got out."

"I just heard a few minutes ago. The man I had on it was on vacation."

"I don't suppose anyone could be following Carr."

"Um. Sorry again, Judge. I have people out searching for him now. But look, you'll be all right, you have a husband and an alarm system at home—"

"Yes, but . . ." Torie shook her head. She didn't want to tell him Sergio and she were separated. She didn't want to tell him she wasn't staying at the house right now because Adrian would overhear. Jim Bob might be right; she might be fine; the security system might protect her. But everything was getting out of hand. No wire. Adrian sitting across from her. Carr out running around somewhere. Where was she supposed to go? What was she supposed to do?

Jim Bob swore loudly on the other end of the phone. "You've got to let me in on what's going on. What were you about to say?"

"Can we discuss it later? This afternoon maybe?"

"There's something you don't want to say in front of Frothingham."

"Right." She watched Adrian's face as she spoke, wariness dancing in her stomach.

"Okay, well, the metal detectors are going in—lots of workers around. I'm sure you'll be safe in the courthouse." He cleared his throat. "I'll send a deputy to escort you to and from your car. Call me later. I'll come over there."

"Thanks, Jim Bob." She stared at Adrian and he, at her. "I'll alert my alarm company that Carr is on the loose—that if they get a call from me, don't call to check on me, just send help."

Torie said goodbye and clicked off and whacked her palm on her desk. "When I go home, I'm loading my gun."

Adrian's nostrils flared. He licked his lips and stroked his mustache. "I've made a decision, Victoria."

That got her attention. She pulled her shaking hands into her lap and arched an eyebrow at Adrian. "What?"

"Victoria, they could very easily kill you if you don't do what they want." He glanced down. "And me, too."

Her breath whooshed out of her as if she'd been punched in the stomach. After a moment, after she calmed her herself, her trembling legs, her shaking hands, her twisting gut, she said, "If I do what they want, I might as well be dead." They stared at each other in silence for a few moments. "Have you taken a look at yourself, Adrian? You look like a zombie. I know you. These years have taken their toll on you . . ."

His face screwed up, and he hung his head down between his knees as though sick to his stomach. He raised his eyes. "Would you shut up for five minutes?"

"I can hardly stand to look at you. You've lost all respect for yourself, and now you want me to do the same?" Her father's voice echoed in her ears. "If I don't have my integrity, I don't have anything."

"All right, goddammit!" He drew himself up to his full height and walked over to the window like he wanted to jump. "I said I've made a decision. You won't think of yourself or your unborn child. If they come after you—kill you—your baby will be every bit as dead as you are."

Torie pushed away from her desk and faced off with him. She didn't need to be reminded of her responsibilities to her child. She had thought it all out. She wouldn't be any kind of mother if she sold her self-respect to the highest bidder. She wouldn't give in over a threat of exposure, and she wouldn't give in over a threat to her life. Her life wouldn't be worth living if she couldn't sleep with herself at night.

"Let me tell you something, Adrian Frothingham—"

"No. Just shut up. Shut up!"

The look on his face finally silenced her. She crossed her arms over her chest and waited.

He started toward her with his palms out, extended as though pleading with her. "I called my family together last night." His voice dropped to a whisper. He stumbled.

"What?" A shiver ran through her body.

"I told them everything."

"Everything?" She didn't want to stop to think what that meant.

His knees buckled. He reached out for support.

Torie hurried to his side and put her arm around him, leading him to the sofa where they both sat down. He smelled of sweat and fear, acrid like sulfur. "So you *are* going with me to the Rangers." She didn't quite know what else to say, so she let go of him, putting some distance between them on the sofa and waited for him to tell her anything else he wanted her to know.

He nodded and wiped his face with a handkerchief. He spoke for a good ten minutes, staring at the coffee table like he was reading from a script. Finally he said, "I won't have much of a life after this . . . I don't even know if my wife and children will ever speak to me again . . . or wait for me assuming I ever get out of jail . . . "

She felt sorry for him, but he did it to himself. "I know how hard this must be for you, but you're doing the right thing."

His eyes, bloodshot, the whites yellowed, followed her. "If only—"

"Don't," she said. She touched his arm. "I admire you for taking a stand."

He got to his feet, wobbled a bit for a moment, and brushed at his jacket and pants. "Let's go before I lose my courage." He held out a hand and helped Torie up.

She retrieved her purse and slung it over her shoulder. In a few hours, their lives would be irrevocably changed. Relief filled her as she walked toward the door. "I guess we're not going to lunch."

"Not funny, Victoria. But I sure could use a drink."

"Yeah, me too. But it's probably not appropriate to go to Ranger Rick's office with liquor on your breath." She squeezed his arm and whispered, "You'll feel better after the meeting."

"I doubt that."

Linking her arm through his, she walked with him to the stairs. She glanced at the elevator. In only a matter of months, she'd be so big she'd have to be careful taking the stairs so as not to fall, as her body grew round and her balance off-kilter. No more stilettos. For now, the stairs were a bit of additional exercise each day. She could certainly use that.

The workmen had already framed-in the counters that would surround the metal detector and the big open stairwell. The machines, the one people would walk through and the one with the belt people would place their belongings on like at the airport, stood at the ready, but weren't yet plugged in. Torie would breath a sigh of relief once they were.

She and Adrian walked down the first flight and rounded the landing. It being noontime, not much activity was going on below. One workman sat across from the new counter, his metal lunch pail in his lap, a sandwich in hand. Another man came out of the men's room and stared up at them as she and Adrian started down.

There was something familiar about the second man's face. His eyes. She would never forget the eyes of the man who had jumped up on her bench and—and there was an object in his hand now. A sleek, silver pistol. "Carr!"

He aimed the gun at Adrian. Torie shoved Adrian, knocking him down. Someone shouted. Something tore into her shoulder. She fell, her head crashing onto the stairs, her body beginning to tumble down as Carr shot Adrian almost point-blank in the chest. Carr turned the pistol on her, and as she turned her head away, another shot rang out.

Chapter 34

WHEN TORIE AWOKE, SEVERAL PEOPLE IN scrubs stood whispering at the foot of the bed in which she found herself. A beeping noise came from behind her. Her head pounded. A sheet and blanket were tucked tightly around her. She could hardly move her feet. The cold room reminded her of when she had delivered Cassie. The hammering in her head intensified when she rose up on her elbows to ask a question. "My baby?"

Someone whispered, "Everything's going to be all right."

Pain pierced her head so she lay back down. Why was she there? Had she been shot? What about Adrian? She drifted off.

When she came to again, an antiseptic smell made her nose twitch. Her shoulder throbbed. The people were gone. The beeping noise was still there. Tape held a number of wires to her skin. Her mother sat in a chair to the right of the bed, hands twisting in her lap, eyes fixed on Torie's face. She came to the bedside when they made eye contact.

"Hello, honey, how are you feeling?" Her mother took one of Torie's hands in her own cold one and squeezed. "I've been so worried." She bent down and put her warm cheek to Torie's.

Torie wiggled her feet, loosening the coverings. She flexed the fingers of her other hand. Everything worked, though her shoulder felt like someone was squeezing it with all his might. A bandage pulled on her skin under the hospital gown. The back of her head felt like it was being beaten with a drumstick. Her mouth was dry. "Water?"

Her mother poured some water and held the cup for her. Torie sipped and nodded her thanks.

Memories flooded her brain. Carr's eyes. Adrian. Loud noises. The huge gun.

"Mom. Adrian—"

Her mother's mouth quivered. She stared at Torie for a long moment and shook her head. "I'm sorry, sweetie. He didn't make it."

Torie's body jerked involuntarily, and she drew a sharp breath. Pain, like hands gripping her lungs, filled her chest. Tears overflowed. "Oh my God. And Carr—"

Her mother grasped Torie's right hand in both of hers. "They shot him. The deputies shot Wesley Carr, but he's going to live."

"Adrian—he was a good man after all." She wiped her eyes with the edge of the sheet.

"After all? I don't understand."

"It's not important." She took another deep breath, the memories flooding her mind. "We had come halfway down the stairs from the landing when Carr came out of the men's room. He was waiting for me—to ambush me, I thought, but he aimed his gun at Adrian."

Her mother stroked Torie's arm. "Shh. It's okay. You don't have to talk about it."

"I can still see what happened." She wiped at the flowing tears.

Her mother pulled some tissues from the box on the table next to the bed and pushed them at Torie.

"When Carr pointed his gun at Adrian, all I could do was push Adrian as hard as I could. I saw where the gun was pointed, but it should have been me he was after." She glanced at her mother. "I know now he wanted to shoot both of us."

Her mother's face blanched. "Oh my God, Torie."

Torie heaved a huge sigh. "Poor Adrian . . ." She could only imagine what had been going through his mind from the time she insisted on going to the Texas Rangers. He never got a chance to tell his side of things or to make amends.

A nurse stuck her head in the room. "Awake? Feeling all right? Ready for breakfast? Coffee with that?"

"Yes to all of the above. Would you help me to the restroom?"

"Yes, Your Honor." The woman's smile looked like it held a secret. She came inside the room, bringing the drip on wheels around so Torie could roll it inside the restroom with her.

"Do I know you?" Torie stared hard at the nurse. She looked vaguely familiar.

The woman winked. "You heard my divorce, Judge. The first year you were in office." Her mouth tightened. "I know the circumstances that brought you here. Sorry about the other judge."

"Thank you." Torie closed the door behind herself. She leaned on the sink, letting herself feel the pain of Adrian's death like a knife in her ribs. When she pulled herself together, she glanced in the mirror. Someone had washed her face, but her hair badly needed brushing. When she came out, a food tray and a cup of coffee waited for her. The nurse assisted her back into bed and left the room. Torie scarfed down the scrambled eggs, still warm, and a bite of the biscuit with grape jelly, cold but not yet rock hard. The coffee left a lot to be desired, but at least it was hot. Her growling stomach was assuaged.

The food helped clear her head. She pushed the tray away and reached for her mother's hand. "Mom—Mother . . . has the doctor been in?" She weighed her next words. Now that she had decided to keep her baby, she prayed nothing had happened to it. She was pragmatic enough to know she could have miscarried when she fell and so tried not to let her fear of its loss make her emotional. Her mother's face was like an impassive mask as she waited for Torie to finish her thought. "Did the doctor say anything about the baby?"

Her mother hesitated, her eyes searching Torie's. "Oh—oh Torie, I overheard him say you could have lost it with a fall down the stairs like that, but you didn't." She covered her mouth with her hand, tears welling up in her eyes. In a quivering voice, she said, "I hope you don't mind my overhearing. I wasn't prying, sweetie. But—should I be happy for you?"

"Then the baby's going to be okay?"

"The baby's fine."

"Have you told anyone?"

"I haven't told a soul—it's not my news to share."

Torie put her hand to her lips to stop the sob that wanted to come out. Her eyes overflowed. She pressed the tissues against them. "I ache. I must have a lot of bruising, and my left arm is stiff." She pressed on her arm. She pulled the gown off her shoulder. A heavy bandage covered the top of her shoulder down almost to her elbow.

"You were shot—grazed, really, the upper part of your left

arm—at the shoulder, they said, really more than grazed, but the bullet didn't lodge inside." Her mother cleared her throat. "Listen to me making no sense. The doctor said the bullet went through and through. Is that what they call it? They're keeping you for another day."

"What day is it? Is it still Friday?"

"Saturday. You've been here since yesterday afternoon."

"I was really out of it. Has Sergio come?"

Her mother shook her head. "I haven't seen him if he has."

"You didn't call him?" Torie bit back her disappointment.

"Well, yes, but I left a message. I hope you don't mind. I talked to him after your father—well, you're not angry, are you?"

Torie shook her head. Her chest felt tight. Even if he was going to divorce her, wouldn't he at least care enough to want to know she was all right? "What about Dad's funeral? Did y'all have it already?"

"No, honey, it's only been a few days, but we wouldn't have it without you."

Torie stroked her mother's hand. "I guess I know that. Everything's so foggy."

Several baskets and vases filled all the available counter space in the room. "Nice flowers," Torie said. "Do you know who they're from?" Sergio might have sent some flowers, though there were no yellow roses in the bunch.

Her mother went to the windowsill, to a smallish ivy with a few spring flowers mixed in. "Nettie." She picked up the card for the next one, large and garish. "County commissioners and county judge."

"That's a surprise. Guess they're hoping I won't figure out a way to sue them."

A tall vase of irises stood in a corner. Her mother read the card.

"This is from Beth and Charlotte. The one next to it is from the Family Law Association."

Torie held her breath. There were three left. He could have sent something, anything.

"This large plant is from the District Clerk's Office," her mother said. "Isn't that nice? You told me they don't get paid very well."

"They don't, believe me. That's really sweet. And the other two?"

Her mother opened the cards. "Are you expecting something from Sergio? Because these are from law firms."

"Oh, well, that's nice of the lawyers." She didn't want her mother to see her disappointment.

"Maybe he doesn't know—didn't get my message."

"Maybe so." She bit the inside of her cheek.

The door opened after a short knock. Torie hoped it was Sergio, but Beth peeked in. She was dressed in a skirt and jacket. Awfully formal for a Saturday. She hugged Torie's mother and hurried to the bed. "Glad you're finally awake. I want to hug you, but I know you were shot."

"Hug my neck and my right side. My left side is off limits."

Beth complied and kissed her cheek. "Do you have enough energy for a couple of visitors? Besides me, that is?"

Torie glanced from Beth to her mother. Sergio, maybe? Who else could it be, unless someone from the courthouse? She really wouldn't mind waiting a day or two before seeing them. "I guess it depends on who it is."

"Mrs. Van Fleet, would you mind if I had a moment alone with Torie? We have a bit of business."

Torie's mother picked up her sweater and purse. "Of course, I'll be down in the cafeteria."

"You don't mind, do you, Mom? And when you come back, bring me another cup of coffee, will you, or some tea? Something with fun stuff in it? I'll be changing my diet for a while." She and her mother exchanged glances.

"Okay. I'll have a snack and read my book. Call my mobile phone when you want me." She left with a backward glance at the two women and a smile that held the secret of the baby.

"Okay, Beth, this better be good to kick my mom out." She pulled Beth down to sit beside her on the bed. "By the way, I'm really glad to see you."

"Me, too. I was so scared when it happened. We all were. I didn't want anything to happen to you but especially when we weren't on good terms with each other.

"Thanks, girlfriend. I feel the same way. So what's going on? Who's outside wanting to see me? If it's courthouse regulars, I wouldn't mind not seeing them until another time. Monday maybe. I don't even have any makeup on, and my hair's a mess."

"Oh, no one expects you to look any way other than how you do look, which is just fine."

A wave of disappointment that it wasn't Sergio outside washed over her, but then she would have been surprised if he'd stood on ceremony and waited behind Beth to see her.

"Remember our agreement about the Supremes?"

So, their agreement. If one didn't get it, they each hoped the other would. Goosebumps rose on her arms even though with all that had happened, the appointment was not important to her any more. "You got it? The governor's appointing you?"

Beth nodded and bit her lip. "You don't mind too much, do you?"

"Congratulations, girlfriend! You deserve it. Come here and give me another hug."

Beth hugged her again. "You're okay with it?"

"Honey child, as my father used to say, I couldn't be happier if it were me. I'm fine, really. Today I'm just so glad to be alive. When did you find out?"

"Bless your heart. I was so afraid you'd hate me after we had words." She breathed a sigh. "Believe it or not, about an hour ago, the governor came himself and told me."

"What? So that's why you're so dressed up. Someone must have told you he was coming."

"Yeah. About thirty minutes' warning. He said he had other business in this area. He's really a hands-on kind of guy sometimes. I think I like him, even though I haven't agreed with him on some issues."

"Good. Since he's appointing you, you'd better like him. Can I just ask one favor? When you get to Austin, would you kindly do what you can for our families?"

"That goes without saying," Beth said. "And I'll see you often. I'm not giving up my home here."

"Good. Now, can I be nosy and ask why the governor came to our little town?"

The door to Torie's room flew open, and a young clean-cut man in a slick-looking dark blue suit and a Bluetooth earpiece in his ear hurried inside. He looked behind the door, peeked into the bathroom, scanned the remainder of the room, and said, "Judge McGruter, I'm going to have to ask you to step outside."

Beth got up and kissed Torie's cheek again. "The governor came to see you, girlfriend. Gotta go." She squeezed Torie's uninjured shoulder and left.

Adrenaline spurted throughout Torie's body. "What?" But Beth was gone. Had she seen unshed tears in Beth's eyes? Beth had moved so quickly, she couldn't be sure. And now she had no time to wonder. What was the governor doing coming to see her?

A few moments later, the governor, wearing a black suit over a white shirt and red tie, pearl gray Stetson in hand, trod through the doorway. A trail of more young, clean-cut men in suits waited in the hall. "Good morning, Judge Van Fleet."

The first guy backed out and closed the door behind him.

Having seen herself in the mirror, Torie knew what she looked like. Couldn't someone have given *her* thirty minutes' warning? She wished like mad she had at least a hairbrush and a lipstick. It was one thing for her mother and her best friend to see her looking like yesterday's unwashed laundry, but another altogether for the chief executive of the state. She ran her fingers through her hair. "Good morning, Governor. May I say what a surprise this is?"

He indicated the chair next to the bed. "May I sit, Your Honor?"

Torie laughed. He'd been a trial lawyer—not allowed to sit until the judge said so. "Certainly, Governor, we're not in court."

He flashed his famous smile at her and pulled up the chair adjacent to the bed. "Thank you, ma'am. I'm sure you're wondering why I'm here so I'll get right to the point."

Torie straightened the covers around her chest and legs. "I wish you would."

"We have a dilemma on our hands, Your Honor."

"That somehow involves me?" She hadn't a clue what he was talking about.

"Yes, you see, you're a hero, Judge Van Fleet. A true Texas heroine."

Torie cocked her head. Now she really didn't know what he was talking about.

"Yes, you. The trouble is, if the story of your heroism gets out, it will be bad for the State. Especially the judiciary. Do you understand?"

"Not a clue."

"Let me explain. You probably don't know what's happened since you were shot yesterday—since you've been out of commission—but plenty, believe me. I don't know if you know the full extent of Judge Frothingham's involvement with the Lawyers for Lawsuit Equity."

"I'm sure I don't. It wasn't until the last few days I really understood what they were trying to do."

The governor nodded. "Judge Frothingham didn't know this, and obviously neither did Karl Hawkins and his cronies, but we've had an investigation into their activities going on for a long time."

"Then you know way more than I do, Governor."

"I have to tell you it was gratifying when Ranger Perez advised us you had come to him for help. Before that, of course, I thought they had you in their pocket."

Her insides flip-flopped. "So when I met with you at your office, you thought I was on the take?"

"They were sponsoring you, so yes. Exactly."

She straightened her shoulders, the left one complaining. "That's galling."

He glanced at his watch. "Here's the deal. I'm asking you not to make public all the things you're privy to about Judge Frothingham and the LLE group."

How could he ask that of her? "I don't understand."

"Well, for one thing, the rangers aren't through with their investigation. When they are, they expect to make a considerable number of arrests for bribery, extortion, and even murder."

Her breath caught. "Murder?"

"We have reason to believe LLE hired Mr. Carr to murder you and Judge Frothingham."

"Holy Cow, that's fast."

"What do you mean?"

"One of the last things I understood from Adrian was he suspected they killed Justice McWilliams. The implication was that if I didn't go along with them, they'd kill me, too."

"He apparently told them you were going to the rangers."

She covered her mouth. Adrian must have decided he'd had enough after he told them about the rangers. He really had cared about her. "Adrian was so torn. I know he—he had a lot of affection for me." She pressed her lips together. She didn't want to blubber in front of the governor.

"That's okay. We've known your history for a long time. We know LLE threatened to blackmail him and you with that information and when you still wouldn't back down, they met Carr practically at the door to the jail and hired him to take you out. We surmise that yesterday was Adrian's last chance to get you to do what they wanted and that Carr had orders to do the both of you if you departed your office together."

"You surmise?"

"Carr's in the hospital, but when he can be transferred to the county jail, he'll be charged with capital murder. The district attorney and our office are willing to make a deal for life without parole if he'll dish what he knows about LLE, who hired him, the details of the hit, and how he was paid."

"So what am I supposed to do, go on, business as usual and avoid the press? Can you guarantee my safety? If Hawkins and his crew made a try for my life once, what's to stop them from doing it again?"

"As far as they know, your only link to them was Judge Frothingham. You'd look foolish saying anything to the newspapers or the D.A. with no evidence. They know there's no case against them without Adrian."

"You know, Governor, it's odd. I didn't have any more than that the day before yesterday either and yet in the end, Adrian had agreed to go with me to see Ranger Perez. You think he, perhaps, was tired of all their games?"

"I suspect he'd reached his limit."

Nodding, Torie said, "I feel sorry for him, for his family. The humiliation."

"Here's the thing, Judge. Right now the press will be reporting the killing of Judge Frothingham as a mistake, as having been done by a man irate with your having given custody of his children to his ex-wife, a man aiming for you, and who missed and got Judge F. We'll do everything we can to keep things quiet, to keep the judge's family out of the news."

"I appreciate that."

"Well, and you may not have been aware of this, we also had an ongoing investigation into the judges Frothingham had been assigning throughout the region."

"I don't understand."

"We suspect the lawyers connected to LLE had been requesting certain judges be assigned when their regular judge was on vacation or otherwise out of the office."

"You mean you think some of the judges sitting by assignment were corrupt, too? Ruling in favor of certain lawyers?"

"At least that, ma'am."

"I suspected that, but I don't think I want to know any more, Governor. Thank you for coming by."

The governor chuckled. "I'm sure this has been a trying time for you the past few days, Judge Van Fleet, but I thought it necessary to ask you in person for your help. It's confusing, at best, but we hope it'll be wrapped up before the year's out."

"Yes, sir. I'll help any way I can, now that I know what's going on."

"Thank you." He glanced as his watch again. "One more thing, though. I'm sure you heard that I'm not going to appoint you to the Supreme Court."

Somewhat disconcerted by the change in the conversation and surprised at his directness, Torie's neck and shoulders flushed. "I certainly wasn't going to mention it."

"I let your friend, Judge McGruter, come tell you because I thought it would be easier on you. She's a fine woman and judge."

"Yes, she is. She'll be a fine Texas Supreme Court Justice. You'll be proud you appointed her."

"I feel confident of that. And, Judge, I think you're a fine judge as well and, as I said earlier, a true heroine, and I want you to accept the appointment as Administrative Judge of the Tenth Judicial Region of Texas."

A jolt of electricity shot down her body. "You want me to replace Adrian?"

"Yes, ma'am, that is if you want the job. It'll be a full-time job, no district court duties, just recusals, administrative meetings and the like."

"And I would answer to no one but you?"

"Absolutely. No one."

The law would only allow her to serve at the pleasure of the governor. She could easily be out of a job when the next governor took office, whenever that would be. But she was young and healthy, and she wasn't going to worry about that. She had but one hesitation, which she had to mention to the governor. "Of course I'd love to take the job. And thank you for choosing me, but I have to tell you, Governor, I'm pregnant. My baby is due in late September, early October, and I'll need some time off. Is that going to interfere with things?"

Grinning, he said, "That'll be just fine and congratulations. In fact, since you'll rarely have to be in a courtroom, you could take the little Texan to work with you, how about that?"

"That would be a first for an administrative judge in Texas."

"Yes, ma'am." He stood. "You need to think about it? Talk to your husband or anything or may I take that as a yes?"

Torie thought of Sergio. She wished he were there to discuss it with, but he wasn't and might not be again. "You may take that as a yes."

"Good. I'll expect you to start work immediately. My office will be in touch with you about the paperwork and the press release. Congratulations, again."

"Thank you, Governor. And thank you for your faith in me."

He reached over and shook her hand. "Thank you, Judge, for your service to the great State of Texas." When he reached the door, he put his hand on the knob, and said, "And as your first act and deed, I'll be expecting some recommendations pretty quickly for people to appoint as replacements for you and Judge McGruter." He nodded and swung out the door.

Chapter 35

TORIE SMOOTHED THE WRINKLES OUT OF THE sheets and gulped some water. The medication must have dried her out in spite of the drip in her arm. She felt drowsy, weak, and shut her eyes for a little nap. The visitors had worn her out though there was one visitor she still hoped would appear.

She drew in a deep breath and let it out, another and let it out, and her monkey mind engaged.

She didn't want to think about Sergio and possible impending divorce proceedings.

Who would mind her court? With Adrian dead, no one would assign a judge to hear her cases. There would be a backlog a mile high by the time—wait, she wasn't going back.

She would be the one making the assignment until the governor appointed someone in her stead.

Still, she had been in the middle of several important cases that needed finishing.

She'd call Nettie to have the clerk pull all the files for her to review.

Was it too late to ask the governor to give her time to wrap things up? She could dispose of them pretty quickly if the attorneys would cooperate, but on the other hand, when had that ever happened?

She must have dozed, because when she awoke, she thought she smelled Sergio's aftershave, and it made her smile. Opening her eyes, she peered at a huge bouquet of long-stemmed yellow roses. She moved them aside and met Sergio's hazel eyes only a few inches away, but there was no sparkle. She drew back. His face was bleak and drawn and wan. Dark whiskers covered his cheeks and chin like he hadn't shaved in several days. His hair was uncombed. He looked almost alien, his eyebrows drawn together, his lips in a frown.

Why was he there? Was it because he still loved her? Or did he want to make sure she was still alive so he could have her served with the divorce petition? It had been two days. Three days since her father had died. If he really loved her, wouldn't he have been by her side immediately, like her mother? He must have waited, deciding to come once the furor had died down, to break the news when no one was around. He was like that, considerate, not wanting to share their personal business.

And yet he held yellow roses in his arms.

She had so much she wanted to tell him.

What a dimwit she'd been.

And how much she loved him.

And about the baby.

They looked at each other in silence for an endless length of time.

She wanted to reach for him, to pull him to her, but would he come?

She spoke first. "The governor was here."

He nodded. "I saw him leave. There were so many men around him."

"Bodyguards and aides," she said. "Constantly updating him. While we talked, their cell phones droned like wasps. The nurses didn't have the nerve to tell them to switch them off. Well, except one. I heard her out in the hall chastising a young man who was in the middle of a call, chasing him off the floor, telling him to take it outside. And then she went after another . . ." She was babbling, putting off the serious stuff. She didn't want to talk about the governor.

He laughed. His face relaxed. His eyes shined. "So you got the appointment?" Sergio held the roses in one arm and gripped the chair's arm with the other hand, his knuckles blanched and white. "No, let me say that differently. I want to say, it's okay if you get on the Supreme Court. Whatever you want to do is fine with me. I want you to know that."

A warm feeling seeped into her chest. How sweet was he? "I didn't get it. Beth did."

"Oh, I'm so sorry." His eyes glimmered.

"Don't be. I'm not." She bit her lower lip to keep from bursting into tears.

"You're not?" His eyes grew wide and watery.

"Sergio, I'm not dead. If I want to go for it another time, I still can."

"I see." He shuffled the roses around as though their thorns pricked his arms.

"No, you don't, but if you want to know, I'd love to tell you all about it."

"I'd love to hear it." His face filled with a child's hope.

She reached her good arm out to him. "You're my husband. I want to share my life, my hopes, my dreams, my joys with you." She blinked several times so her tears wouldn't overflow.

Sergio clambered out of the chair so fast it fell over and clattered on the floor. "Darling *esposa*," he said, wrapping her in his arms, the roses crushed between them.

Torie yelped. "My shoulder—"

"*Aiichiwawa!*" Sergio jumped, releasing her onto the bed. "You're hurt? I didn't know you were injured, just that you fell."

"Carr shot me." She pulled back her hospital gown to show him her bandaged left shoulder. "A bit more than a graze." She winced.

"*Hijo de puta!* Wait 'til I get my hands on him." He picked up her right hand and kissed her fingers. "He could have killed you."

"That was definitely his intention. But don't worry, he's in jail and probably won't ever get out."

He cupped her hand and kissed her fingers again. "I could have lost you forever."

"Maybe, but don't think you're going to get rid of me so easily."

"How can you joke after all this?"

Torie gasped out a sob. "I'm afraid the dam will burst, Sergio." She pulled her hand away and covered her face.

"Oh, my darling girl," he said. "It's all over. Everything's going to be all right." He sat on the side of the bed and gently gathered her into his arms again.

"I thought you didn't care. When I came to and you weren't here and Mother told me she'd called you, I thought you didn't want me anymore."`

"That's never going to happen. I'm here. I'm never leaving you again."

"I've been so scared the last few weeks," she said between sobs and gasps.

"I should have been with you."

"And Daddy died."

"I know. I'm so sorry."

"And now Adrian. Carr killed Adrian," she said and sniffed, wiping her nose on the sheet.

"I know. I'm very sorry. I know Adrian was your friend."

The tears came full force as she recited what happened. "I saw Carr and recognized him right away. Adrian didn't know who he was, but Carr was aiming at Adrian, not me. I knocked Adrian back, and the bullet hit me." She wiped the tears away and blew her nose. "I fell and Carr shot again, hitting Adrian in the chest." His face contorted as she described the incident. "When Carr aimed at me, a deputy took him out."

Sergio blotted her tears with the edge of the sheet. He pulled some more tissues out of the box and pushed a few into her hands. She blew her nose before continuing.

"All I heard before I lost consciousness were gunshots and commotion and more gunshots."

"My poor girl," Sergio murmured. "My poor little *jueza*. I almost lost you."

His arms were warm around her, the texture of his short-sleeved polo shirt soft against her face, the smell fresh and normal, somehow, mingled with his musky body odor. She'd like to remain like that for hours, held in Sergio's arms.

He spoke into her hair. "I called that *estúpido* county *juez* this morning when I got back to town and told him he should have listened to you sooner about putting in security."

When he got to town? Called the county judge? Where had he been? Torie didn't know which question she wanted him to answer first. "What did he say, the county judge?"

"He apologized over and over. He was sorry they took so long. He hoped you would be all right." Sergio shook his head. "What a *estúpido hombre*."

"What he really meant was he hoped I wouldn't figure out some way to sue." She pointed in the direction of one of the many vases crowding the room. "Do you see the huge bouquet of flowers the commissioners' court sent?"

"Are you going to sue? I think you should. He was such a *pinchazo* about security."

"Yes, he was a prick, but I don't know. I don't have to decide right now, though I guarantee you Adrian's family will be challenging any laws that would bar them from suing." She wiped her eyes and blew her nose. "I bet I look terrible."

"No, *mi amante*, you look beautiful. Don't worry though. I hope you don't mind I went through your things and brought a bag for you."

Something stirred inside her. She didn't know if it was happiness or the baby. "Ever the thoughtful husband. Thank you so much."

"*De nada*. I was happy to do it. I know how you like to have your face on, as my *abuela* used to say, when you see people. I only wish I could have brought it yesterday."

"So were you away? I thought—"

He put a finger to her lips. "You thought I didn't care enough to come to you. But no, I didn't know. I was at the International Hotel

Conference. I had to drive home." He squeezed her hand. "I should have been here."

"Oh, Sergio, I've missed you so much. I've been an idiot."

He shook his head. "I've been so stubborn. You told me how you felt before we married, but I thought after we married I could change your mind."

"But Sergio--"

"No. You are the most important thing in the world."

"Yes, I understand, truly I do, but—"

"*Mi amante*, all I want is you. We have a nice life together, don't we? We have a beautiful house, fine cars, plenty of money."

"But—"

He put a finger to her lips. "We can get a dog. A nice little dog to keep you company and bark if anyone comes near the house so you can get your gun."

"I'm not going to need that gun anymore. Not only will Carr be locked up for life, but the governor's got another job for me."

His eyebrows danced. "Another job? Not *jueza*?" He cocked his head. "Will it take you away from home?"

"I'm going to take Adrian's place. Be administrative judge of Region Ten, but I won't have to hold court, except for the occasional hearing around the region on recusals and such. My office will be here in Bremerhaven.

"But that's wonderful. We can spend more time together." He kissed her and then reared back, laughing.

Sergio's loud laugh brought the nurse into the room. When her eyes met Torie's, Torie winked.

The nurse winked back as she pulled the door closed behind her.

Feeling another little twinge, Torie took his hand and put it on her abdomen. "Now about that baby, Sergio . . ."

Thank you for reading!

If you enjoyed *Texas Style Justice*, I would appreciate it if you would help others to enjoy this book, too.

Recommend it. Please help others find this book by recommending it to friends, readers' groups, and discussion boards.

Review it. Please tell other readers why you liked this book by leaving a review wherever your got your copy of this book. If you do write a review, please send me an email at susan@susanpbaker.com so I can thank you with a personal email.

If you would like to be on my mailing list so you can receive news of upcoming events and publications, go to www.susanpbaker.com.

About the Author

Susan P. Baker, a retired Texas judge, is the award-winning author of seven novels and two nonfiction books, all related to the law. As a judge, she dealt with a wide range of cases from murder to divorce regarding adults and children. Prior thereto, she practiced law for nine years and, while in law school, worked as a probation officer. Her experience in the justice system is apparent in her writings. Currently, she has three novels in progress.

Susan is a member of Texas Authors, Inc., Authors Guild, Sisters in Crime, Writers League of Texas, and Galveston Novel and Short Story Writers.

She has two children and eight grandchildren. She loves dark chocolate, raspberries, and traveling on and in every mode of transportation. An anglophile, she likes to visit cousins in England and Australia. On her bucket list are a trip to New Zealand, a long trip back to Australia, living in England for several months, visiting all the presidential libraries and authors' homes in the U.S., and driving Route 66.

Read more about Susan and sign up for her mailing list for newsletters and other offers at http://www.susanpbaker.com.
Like her at http://www.facebook.com/legalwriter.
Follow her on Twitter@Susanpbaker.

9 780996 620219